Transformational Journaling for Coaches, Therapists, and Clients

In *Transformational Journaling for Coaches, Therapists, and Clients: A Complete Guide to the Benefits of Personal Writing*, more than 50 coaches, therapists, and journaling experts from around the world share their best practices and explain in detail how they use journaling to improve their work with clients.

This edited collection brings together the leading voices of the journaling world into one ground-breaking volume, providing practical techniques and tools to use with clients. Applicable and accessible, over 50 journaling luminaries share their experiences and insights across eight sections, including the logic of journaling, techniques and applications, using journaling with clients, journaling in groups, journaling for mental health and wellness, growth and healing, spirituality, creativity, and more. Through theoretical and practical applications, it illustrates the transformational process of journaling in helping clients grow, heal, and achieve their goals.

This book is essential reading for coaches, therapists, and other mental health professionals, as well as those interested in using personal writing for growth and self-awareness.

Lynda Monk is the Director of the International Association for Journal Writing. She is the co-author of *Writing Alone Together: Journalling in a Circle of Women for Creativity, Compassion and Connection*. She created *Life Source Writing: A 5 Step Reflective Journaling Method*.

Eric Maisel is the author of 50+ books, among them *The Power of Daily Practice, Lighting the Way, Coaching the Artist Within, Mastering Creative Anxiety*, and *The Van Gogh Blues*.

"This compendium of wisdom on journal writing offers sage advice on the promises, pitfalls, perils, and pleasures of journaling as a path of self-knowledge, insight, and healing. Eric Maisel, Joyce Chapman, Sheila Bender, Kathleen Adams and a host of other experts join voices in this book that holds everything you will ever need to know about what it means to love your journal as companion, mirror, and guide."

Mark Matousek, Writing to Awaken: A Journey of Truth, Transformation, and Self-Discovery

"I know the amazing benefits and transformational power of journaling firsthand, both in my personal life and in my work as a coach. Now I have this great resource to use, one that gathers together field-tested journaling exercises from all over the world. What an excellent addition to the coaching and therapy literature! Highly recommended."

Jacob Nordby, *life coach, author,* The Creative Cure *and* Blessed are the Weird: A Manifesto for Creatives

"Journaling can be as straightforward as taking pen in hand, opening to a blank page, and simply beginning. But imagine having access to a compendium of fifty journaling techniques and methods compiled by leading professionals from around the world. *Transformational Journaling for Coaches, Therapists, and Clients* is just such a resource. A rich and practical contribution to this ever-growing field."

Judy Reeves, *writing teacher and author,* A Writer's Book of Days

"I've been a therapist for more than fifty years and have been journaling since I was in college. This new book edited by Monk and Maisel is a powerful and practical resource for those who want to help themselves and help their clients survive and thrive in today's topsy-turvy world. You could spend thousands of dollars at conferences developing new skills and not get the value you will receive from this wonderful book. I highly recommend it."

Jed Diamond, *PhD, author,* The Enlightened Marriage *and* 12 Rules for Good Men

Transformational Journaling for Coaches, Therapists, and Clients

A Complete Guide to the Benefits of Personal Writing

EDITED BY LYNDA MONK AND ERIC MAISEL

Routledge
Taylor & Francis Group

NEW YORK AND LONDON

First published 2021
by Routledge
605 Third Avenue, New York, NY 10158

and by Routledge
2 Park Square, Milton Park, Abingdon, Oxon, OX14 4RN

Routledge is an imprint of the Taylor & Francis Group, an informa business

Library of Congress Cataloging-in-Publication Data
A catalog record for this book has been requested

ISBN: 978-0-367-62139-1 (hbk)
ISBN: 978-0-367-62574-0 (pbk)
ISBN: 978-1-003-10976-1 (ebk)

Typeset in Avenir and Dante
by Apex CoVantage, LLC

For Peter, my true love
and our sons, Jackson and Jesse,
my two greatest teachers.
And for journal writers everywhere.

For Ann, forty-three years into this adventure
and for the grandkids,
Ethan, Abigail, Elise, Kamila, and Katya

Contents

Editor's Introduction

There are many valuable tools that we, as helping professionals, can have in our toolkits to support the growth, well-being, and transformation of both ourselves and the clients we serve. In this book, we focus on one of the most powerful tools for cultivating self-awareness and personal growth, and that is journaling.

Personal Story

I have been a journal writer since I was a young girl. I wrote in a small pink personal diary with lock and key, and it was all very top secret. I hid it away and hoped that no one would ever find, or more importantly, ever read, what I wrote.

As I grew to adolescence, journaling emerged as something that I did to solve problems, express my feelings, and capture my special memories of daily life. I did not write every day, but often enough that I considered it a hobby of mine. Parallel to this, I was also an avid pen pal and had nearly 20 pen pals from all over the world. This letter writing felt more like a journaling exchange, especially with one pen pal in particular who, when I was about 14, became a best friend. She lives in Switzerland and to this day, we are still connected and our letter writing has been replaced with frequent text messages.

I have engaged in a wide variety of journaling practices and have kept many different kinds of journals over the years, including dream journals, gratitude journals, life vision and planning journals, travel journals, and more. At times, I am a daily journal writer, even if only for a few minutes a day, and at other times long stretches of time can pass where I get away from journaling. One of these dry journaling patches happened in my twenties when I was working as a frontline social worker in often high stress and high trauma situations. The days were long, filled with emotion and exposure to difficult stories and painful life events for many clients who I supported and served. Eventually, life got in the way. I was too busy to journal as I was working full time, tending to the early years of my first marriage, and studying for my master's degree part-time.

However, I began to notice that there were certain times I would journal, particularly after a difficult day at work. I would instinctively go to my journal to process my emotions from the day. I noticed it served to help me feel calm and balanced. Journaling acted as a way of clearing the emotional debris and impact of the work, in a profession known to be high risk for burnout—as is true of many helping professions.

In the chapter titled *Journaling for Coach and Therapist Self-Care*, I speak more about this and offer you insights into how journaling can be a very important self-care strategy, particularly when engaged in the types of work that are often focused on caring for and serving the growth and well-being needs of others, our clients.

Transformational Journaling

Not all journaling is transformational. That is not to say that journaling isn't generally helpful or useful as a cathartic form of self-expression, a place to vent, daydream, say thanks and more. However, I have grown to discover, both from my own first-hand experience with journaling, as well as my work in guiding thousands of other people to the page to know, grow, and care for themselves through journaling, that certain things make personal writing transformational. These include writing first to *raise awareness* about the self, others, and the world we live in and second, to *take action* on the awareness that is cultivated through this type of personal writing and exploration on the page.

I often say to my clients, so what, now what? Taking a moment to pause and reflect on one's journaling is often where the nuggets of insight, ideas for inspired actions and seeds of growth are planted.

About This book

This book presents many different perspectives and applications for journaling for coaches, therapists, clients, and journal keepers. We hope that you will find affirmation of the transformational power of journaling as well as very specific activities, prompts and exercises that you yourself can benefit from and that you can introduce within the transformational work you do with your clients.

The book is organized into various categories, including the following:

- The Logic of Journaling
- Using Journaling With Clients
- Journaling for Mental Health and Wellness
- Journaling for Growth and Healing
- Spiritual and Nature Journaling
- Journaling and Creativity
- Journaling With Groups and Leaders
- Techniques and Applications

We have done our best to organize these varied chapter contributions into a cohesive whole for you, our readers.

The authors who have generously contributed to this book are experts in their respective fields. Some are counselors, coaches, and researchers, while all contributors are writers and journal keepers. Some journal daily, some write sporadically when trying to solve a problem. Some are poets and memoirists, others are artists. We hope this rich array of perspectives, tools, and offerings will inspire you to keep exploring how journaling can enrich your own life as well as your clients' lives.

You might want to journal or at least take notes as you read this book. You might engage in reflective learning while you read by asking yourself the following questions:

What is standing out to you?
What has value for you?
What do you want to remember?
What do you want to try?
What surprises you?
What inspires you?

From the Pages of My Journal

Before embarking on co-editing this book with Eric Maisel, I decided to journal about my decision. Here is what I wrote:

> What do I know? I know that I would love to work with Eric. I have admired his books and writing for many years now, and in more recent years, through our connection as a result of the IAJW, I have grown

to really admire him as a person. I would learn so much from working with him. I like working with people who take action, who move along fairly quickly, who can work with the details but also stay in the macro lens on a project and get things done. I don't want this project to take years, but rather months, and one-year tops. I believe working with someone like Eric, this would be doable and possible.

Why would I say "yes" to doing this book? I am absolutely passionate about the transformational power of journaling. I have been teaching others how to use journaling as a self-care and wellness tool for over twenty years in some form or another. I love teaching on this topic and I love learning about it too! What better way to learn than to invite experts in the field of coaching and therapy, to write about how they use journaling in their specific work, and then have the chance to read, edit and engage with what they write. I also love helping other people get their messages and wisdom out in the world. Books are a great way to share thought leadership, my own and others too. An edited book like this one, allows for many voices to be shared and read. It is a win-win for authors and readers alike!

If we do proceed with this book, what do I hope for? I hope that it can be published by a great publisher. I hope that it will help a lot of people to really see the breadth and depth and possibilities and benefits of transformational journaling in their own lives and how it can be a great asset in their work with clients too. When I think of all my clients who I have supported to journal, and the ways we have used their journaling insights to inform the coaching work we are doing together, and more importantly to inform the lives they are living, I really want as many coaches and therapists and other helping professionals to bring journaling into their life-enriching work with clients.

I can think of so many examples of insights and actions that have flowed from my clients' journaling, combined with our coaching work together. Inner truth and wisdom really can rise up from within through journaling. How amazing is that? To be able to simply sit down and write—with only pen and paper as our tools, we can truly tap into and respond to the truth and desires in our lives.

So, what's my decision about this book? Yes! Yes, yes, yes. I want to give some time, care, energy and resources to make this book happen. I think it can have value for a lot of people. Writing, teaching and making a difference are among my life purposes. Bringing this book into being supports me to do all of these things. It also helps me support others to do the things that are important to them.

Once again, a win-win.

Why Did I Share This Excerpt From My Journal?

First, the obvious, because this is a book about journaling. The best way to teach the power of journaling is to engage with it. Go to the page and write. Notice what you see when you are there. Reflect upon your own reflecting. What do you notice? How do you feel? What's different? What do you want to do now?

As you can see in my own journaling excerpt, I wrote about my thoughts, my feelings, my questions, my experiences and then I came to a conclusion about what I wanted to do, in this case, proceed with creating this book.

Journaling is not magic. But it can be transformative!

Lynda Monk

Editor's Introduction

Every helping professional develops his or her own style of helping. Some of these are rooted in the mental disorder paradigm, where the helper diagnoses and treats. Other helpers are very Rogerian and nondirective and steadfastly return the work to the client. Many coaches focus on the art and practice of helping clients set goals and then monitoring their progress toward achieving those goals. Each helper arrives at his or her own style—usually flowing from and even dictated by that helper's personality.

I am a directive coach who makes suggestions, helps clients set goals, makes sure that clients leave the session with "the right" homework, and holds clients accountable by inviting them to check in with me daily via email. I am also a coach with many "tools" in his "toolkit": ideas that I regularly share, say, about the difference between life purpose and life purposes; invitations that I regularly make, for instance, the invitation that clients create and maintain one or more daily practices; exercises that I suggest, for instance, a three-step cognitive exercise designed to help clients think thoughts that serve them; and so on.

As a coach who believes in "tools" and as a helper who is convinced that when a client works on increased self-awareness, that helps the client with all aspects of his or her life, I am an advocate of client journaling. Because I specialize in working with creative and performing artists, including many writers, I regularly need to underline a certain distinction: that journaling is not the same thing as working on their book. If they have journaled on a given day, that doesn't mean that they have "gotten to their writing." That important proviso aside (and it's an important one if you're working with creatives), there's no better way to gain and maintain self-awareness than through journaling.

In this book, I present clients with a certain sort of journaling "method" that I call the focused journal method. It helps a client move step by step from the identification of a problem or a challenge all the way through to announcing solutions and intentions to ultimately aligning one's thoughts and behaviors with those intentions. That's a lot for a simple method to accomplish! I recommend that you take a look at my chapter on the focused journal method and, as a corollary activity, maybe dream up your own "method." There's no better way to add a "tool" to your "toolkit" than by creating the tool yourself!

This book is chockful of such tools. We've brought together an excellent group of practitioners who have a longtime, firsthand experience of journaling and who also regularly invite their clients to keep journals and who provide their clients with unique and innovative journaling exercises and experiences. Our contributors come from all over the world and work with clients in all sorts of settings. We think that their breadth and depth of experience will impress you and that their offerings will help you in your work with your clients.

We are eager to hear from you. We'd love to hear your thoughts about this book and also any stories you might like to share about how you've benefited from introducing journal keeping into your own life or into your helping practice. All thoughts and comments welcome! We hope you enjoy this compilation and benefit from it.

Eric Maisel

Acknowledgments

Thank you to all of our coaching and counseling clients over the years who have taught us so much about compassion, resilience and what it takes to grow.

A heartfelt thanks to our families and our beloved spouses, Peter and Ann—who love us and hold up so much of the backdrop of daily life to make the space possible for our respective creative work and writing.

Deep gratitude to all of the incredible contributing authors to this book, this offering would not exist without you. We created the container, you each filled it up with your heart and stories and teachings and brilliance. Thanks to one and all.

A huge thanks to our editor Heather Evans and others, including Ellie Duncan, Katherine Tsamparlis, Ramachandran Vijayaragavan, and others at Routledge, who helped edit, design, and make this book a reality. We were in the first weeks of the COVID-19 global pandemic when we forwarded our proposal for this book to Heather and a short time thereafter she said yes. "Yes" makes everything possible!

Thank you to Eric Maisel for turning a seed of an idea into a full growth experience. It has been a true joy and learning experience to have you as a mentor and co-editor on this project, our first project together, but not the last.

And finally, our appreciation and acknowledgment to journal writers everywhere and to those individuals who have not journaled yet, but will soon, as a result of this book.

The Logic of Journaling

PART
I

A Therapist's Guide to Using Journaling With Clients

1

Susan Borkin

This chapter highlights three organizing principles for therapists who want to use journaling with their clients. First, I describe therapeutic journaling and how my own origin story weaves into this narrative. Next, I look at therapeutic journaling as an adjunct to clinical practice. Finally, I address how therapeutic journaling actually works and I provide a broad overview of best practices for integrating therapeutic journaling into your work with clients.

Therapeutic Journaling

Therapeutic journaling is any type of writing or expressive process intended for personal growth or psychological healing. It is an evolving, creative, organic process with few actual rules.

The intermingling of words and feelings has been a theme in my life. As a child in middle school, I remember my class sitting on the gym floor for some kind of real or imagined misbehavior and writing on the floor with my finger to express my anger at what I felt was an unfair punishment. This early form of writing out my feelings helped me feel better. In college in the late '60s, I jotted down the phrase, "Writing as therapy. . .??" in my personal journal.

A few years later, I had moved from the Midwest to San Francisco and joined a women's group. I loved it so much that for months I had no idea that it was actually a gestalt therapy group. Among other things, I experimented with using a method from gestalt therapy. I took dialogues, a conversation between two conflicted parts of the self, and wrote out dialogues between them in my journal.

When I had the opportunity to start graduate school in psychology in 1977, my committee accepted my thesis, *Journal Writing as Self-Therapy*. At that time, so little was known about the topic that my thesis was considered radical. Next, I took what I had been exploring and learning on my own and began teaching workshops called "Journal Writing for Personal Growth."

As I taught, I watched workshop participants writing in Free Form, a manner of rule-less writing without stopping. I watched participants scribbling "I Want" lists and dialoguing with themselves and with troubled relationships in their lives. I saw faces change, little bursts of understanding, moments of insight and awareness that minutes earlier had been unconscious. I watched participants return from a Walk and Write exercise outdoors, beaming with new understanding. I witnessed personal growth and psychological healing.

Therapeutic Journaling as Adjunct to Clinical Practice

As I continued teaching workshops and working with clients in private practice, I learned that as powerful as journaling is, it is best used as an adjunct in clinical practice. Journaling is an enhancement to and not a replacement for sound clinical work and judgment. Therapists must always rely first on their experience, their skill as a clinician, their relationship to a particular client, their attention to the presenting therapeutic issue and, of course, their care for the safety of the client.

Interestingly, at times, a client's response to a suggested journaling exercise can also provide clinical data. For example, a client's excessive difficulty selecting a physical journal may speak of perfectionist standards or obsessive-compulsive disorder. Or, extreme reluctance to write may indicate an underlying trauma or perhaps performance anxiety if the trauma was related to shame or humiliation.

How Journaling Works

Journaling has much to contribute to therapeutic work. Suppressing emotions takes energy. Journaling can release stuck energy and provide a safe place to explore feelings. Traumatic memories are frequently stored in bits and pieces as disorganized pieces of a puzzle. Creating a written narrative makes a story whole, bringing these disparate pieces together. Journaling can also lead to self-reflection, which in turn may self-empower clients.

As much as you can, begin with a clear clinical picture before introducing journaling to a new client. As you create a working diagnosis, selectively choose how and when to best integrate journaling. Bringing therapeutic journaling together with solid clinical work provides a richly enhanced experience for your clients.

Even though I have stated the flexible nature of therapeutic journaling, there are nonetheless numerous guidelines, suggested methods, and best practices for integrating therapeutic journaling into your work with clients. These are available from additional sources, including from my own book on the subject, but I will provide a sampling here.

If, for example, your client's diagnosis falls into the category of an adjustment disorder, it can be useful to begin with a *QuickList*, a rapidly written unedited list to identify underlying issues. A *What's Bugging Me List* is an example of this. Depression might be eased by *Giving Depression a Voice*. In issues of grief and mourning, one of the most important tasks is letting go without forgetting. *I Wish I Could Tell You* in either the form of a list or a letter can be repeated over time to remember one's loved one.

While most clients are unlikely to identify low self-esteem as the presenting issue, it is almost always present in some way. Positive psychology offers both a *Strengths Introduction* and *Three Good Things*. In a *Strengths Introduction*, a client is asked to write a story, introducing herself via her strengths. In *Three Good Things*, a client is asked to write down three good things that happened each day for at least a week. In what I think of as *Three Good Things Plus*, a client is additionally asked to identify her part in creating these positive experiences. The addition of the causative piece makes this exercise additionally powerful.

How journaling is introduced to a client can significantly affect the results. I have found it best to emphasize the positive benefits to the client. For example, I frequently ask a new client to write a brief autobiographical statement at the beginning of our work together. There are several advantages to this approach. Writing about your history stimulates memories and events. As I review a client's autobiography, I look for patterns, the structure of the family system and coping mechanisms my client has used. I also explain to a client that this written information is cost-effective in that it will save hours of interview time. Indirectly, too, this written assignment can help a client become engaged with the therapeutic work and feel responsible for his or her own progress.

Similarly, giving a client between-session assignments is a useful way to keep the therapy coherent and moving forward. One such tool I created is

ATTENDD, a mnemonic device for tracking thoughts, feelings, and distractions. Another is W.R.I.T.E., for becoming aware of and shifting belief systems (for details on both tools, see Tips for Helping Professionals next).

There will be occasions when a client is reluctant or resistant to journaling. This may be a clinical issue to explore or it may be something more basic. For example, dyslexic clients may find writing too challenging. Clients with a known or unknown learning or processing disability may also be reluctant to write. Journaling is simply not for everyone. Work with your client and yourself to find creative alternatives.

---

5 Tips for Helping Professionals

1. **ATTENDD**—Try this mnemonic to help clients organize responses to their experience, particularly between sessions. Ask them to pay attention to:

   Awareness (Have you noticed any changes in yourself?)
   Tension/Physical sensations (Are you feeling any tension in your body? Where?)
   Thoughts (Has your thinking changed in any way?)
   Emotions (Are you feeling happy, sad, angry, relieved? Do you feel elated, joyous, fearful, depressed?)
   i**N**tuition (Do you feel differently about your inner sense of "knowing?")
   Dreams (What are you noticing in your dreams?)
   Distractions (What has been distracting you lately?)

2. **W.R.I.T.E.** can be useful when working with clients on their beliefs.

   W—What are your current beliefs?
   R—Which beliefs are no longer working for you and need to be released?
   I—Identify memories, search for beliefs from family, friends, and teachers
   T—Transform into new beliefs (note: especially useful with EMDR)
   E—Empowering new beliefs; how would you like to live with new beliefs

3. If the client wants to share what they have written, that's absolutely fine. However, therapeutic journaling does not require the therapist

---

to see, read, or know what the client has written. The therapeutic value for the client is in the writing itself. This is an excellent point to use when explaining the method to clients.

4. I can practically guarantee you that if you do your own journaling work, you will feel much more at ease when presenting journaling to your clients. Therapist, heal thyself.

5. Lighten up. There is very little about journaling that is right or wrong. Explore, experiment, and enjoy!

5 Tips for Clients and Journal Keepers

1. QuickLists. To answer a question or brainstorm ideas, quickly make a list without editing. This rapid-fire list-making may be in the form of kernel sentences, short phrases, or even a question. For example, "What are five things I can do right now to improve my health?" Or, "If I found myself with a completely open day, I would . . .".

2. PenVisioning combines both positive and negative visualizations. Move back and forth between a positive visualization and a visualization in which something goes wrong, taking notes after each picture. Move back and forth between these two pictures until you feel relief or clarity on how to proceed with your positive visualization.

3. Feeling sluggish with your daily journaling? Get outside, walk and breathe some fresh air. Sit down and try writing again.

4. There will be times when no matter what you do, your journaling will feel stuck. Try shaking things up a bit. Write with your nondominant hand.

5. Write four or five nouns in different colors on a large sheet of paper. Write a short, short story that includes all of the words you have written down.

3 Journaling Prompts

1. This is a three-part prompt, but it can be highly effective in drilling down on an issue. One after another, respond to these three questions

and repeat until some clarity is reached: what am I doing? What am I feeling? What do I want?
2. If I could be or do anything I wanted right now, what would it be?
3. Close your eyes and feel, see, and hear a favorite memory. When you are ready, write down what you remember. What did you notice?

 ## About the Author

Susan Borkin, PhD, is a psychotherapist and speaker. Since 1978 she has pioneered the field of journal writing. Borkin is the author of three books on the transformative power of journaling, *Writing from the Inside Out*; *When Your Heart Speaks, Take Good Notes*; and, most recently, the award-winning *The Healing Power of Writing: A Therapist's Guide to Using Journaling with Clients*.

Journal Therapy

2

Foundations of Practice

Kathleen Adams

Expressive and therapeutic writing is hailed by therapists, facilitators, and writers worldwide as a holistic practice that is accessible to nearly everyone, requires very little skill or training beyond basic literacy, and can be a powerful agent of transformation.

Yet relatively few people are aware that there is evidence-based theory and standards-based practice that guide the writing process toward best outcomes in a reliable and sustainable way.

In this chapter we'll look at four foundations of practice that are central to maximizing the potential of writing as a tool for healing, growth and change.

Five Qualities of Therapeutic Writing

The Journal Ladder is a theoretical construct I developed to help writers match their cognitive and emotional processing styles, preferences, and desired outcomes with writing techniques that would help them get there. Built into the Ladder are five qualities:

- **Structure.** Every journal technique has a structure, from sentence stems ("finish this sentence") to freewriting ("write whatever comes"). More structure helps when time is limited or the client wants quick answers or information.
- **Pacing.** Writing can go to deep internal places. Pacing is about diving deep and surfacing, taking a breath, having a stretch, relaxing the mind, and then returning.

- **Containment.** If a client is spinning or spiking out of control, encourage good journal containment skills. Draw a shape on the page and write within it, or write for one paragraph and stop, or write for three minutes and stop.
- **Balance.** Everyone has areas of overfocus and underdevelopment. Balance in the journal offers fresh and even startling perspectives. Find an area of imbalance (e.g., self-criticism) and counter with its yin or yang ("3 Things I Did Well Today").
- **Permission.** There is no wrong, just write. Encourage clients to rethink limitations they may be putting on their own process. It's their journal, which is to say, it's their life. Permission granted!

The Reflection Write

Journal coach Joyce Chapman taught me the reflection write about 30 years ago, and it's been a mainstay in my practice since. The reflection write comes after a journal entry is written and read back. It focuses on the process of writing and observes details such as physical and emotional responses, surprises, insights, or notations of areas for further exploration.

The reflection write is often only one or two sentences and begins with, *As I read this, I notice*—or *I'm surprised by*—or *I want to*—or whatever organically arises.

This simple starter, *As I read this, I*—, often leads to immediate insight, clarity, or even an "aha" moment. The reflection offers a predictable capacity to synthesize and codify insight and awareness of cognitive or emotional shifts within the write itself.

The following guidelines aren't a linear checklist but rather a way of thinking about the writing process. The reflection write might center in any of these areas:

- Where did this write or the read-back "land" in your body?
- What did you notice immediately upon reading back?
- What was your emotional or cognitive experience during the write? During the read-back?
- Any surprises, "aha" moments or flashes of insight?
- What else happened during the write or read-back?

In my own journal, I make my reflections stand out by writing them at a 45-degree angle across the page, then drawing a thick box around them. When I'm keyboarding, I boldface them and put them in a bright color.

The Journal and the Self

The relationship with the journal is often a reliable predictor of the relationship with Self.

Some writers struggle with self-concept. They might have problems with self-doubt, have a strong internal voice of criticism, or have another disempowering state of mind and being. Their journals often reflect this disempowerment with entries filled with tension, self-recrimination, or self-judgment. When asked to give three words or phrases that describe their relationship with their journals, these writers often respond with words like *conflicted, unproductive, downer.*

But when they're encouraged to shift into more positive writes that affirm better outcomes, convey more gentle messages, and take other steps to shift toward an empowering state of mind and being—their self-concept and relationship with Self begin to change for the better.

On the other hand, some writers who struggle with self-concept have journals filled with hopes, desires, and goals for a more balanced life, even if they don't know how to get there. These writers often use words such as *friend in need, supportive, anchor, safe place* to describe their journals.

Encourage them to explore the "self" that writes nurturing and supportive messages. Teach them how to support that "self" in taking small action steps toward goals or other empowering action. These clients are thus primed to grow into the healthier, happier selves that they've been predicting in the journal.

As with any healthy relationship, the client and the journal will grow together. Choices may change as the relationship evolves. This is not only normal but something to be celebrated. The self is catching up with the Self, and the journal is scribe for the journey.

Silence

"As it is in poetry, silence is part of the form," said Tristine Rainer in *The New Diary.* Journal silence is not only normal, but it can be a valuable messenger. Here are three types of silence and what each might signal.

- **When life gets in the way.** Time and energy don't always leave space for writing. If there's nothing left in the tank or on the clock, give permission for the client to let it go without self-recrimination. Suggest a list of three, which takes under a minute, or an action plan in a Five-Minute Sprint.

- **When one is rendered mute by trauma, fear, or rage.** Some stories are bigger than can be emotionally managed or sometimes even named. The client might feel sickened by the idea of writing. Trust that instinct; respect that boundary. Instead, focus on strength-based writing. What's the client's superpower? What's a ray of light from today that can be captured in prose? How is the client experiencing beauty in everyday life?
- **When it isn't yet word-ripe.** This is the silence that falls on the 19th day of really wanting to write and not writing. This is the silence of the not-yet word-ripe, a write-in-process that hasn't yet surfaced. Encourage the client to stay with the silence, think of it as an incubator, and imagine this journal entry growing strong roots. Creative arts, bodywork, meditation, and other integrative practices are viable languages for this silence.

---

5 Tips for Helping Professionals

1. **Predictors of client success.** If even one of these predictors is in place, the capacity for a client to effectively use a journal in treatment is enhanced.

    - Prior experience with journal writing, even if it didn't turn out well in the past
    - Motivation (e.g., if writing offers a pathway to something they deeply desire)
    - Positive experience in general with writing or literature
    - Strong alliance with therapist

2. **The power of writing in community.** "There is nothing so wise as a circle," wrote the poet Rainer Maria Rilke. The many powerful aspects of writing groups include the capacity to bear witness and be compassionately witnessed; the role-modeling of courage, resilience, or creative adaptation that is shared among peers; and the opportunity to feel accepted and valued for being "real." These benefits can be equally effective in person or on a video platform.

3. **The journal as agent of neuroplasticity.** Washington, D.C.-based psychotherapist Deborah Ross has codified intentional and purposeful writing as a form of self-directed neuroplasticity, much like mindfulness meditation, in her signature work *Your Brain on Ink*.

---

4. **Three feeling words, top and bottom.** Feelings change with time and process. To demonstrate this, I ask clients to write three words describing how they feel before they start a write, and again after they have completed the reflection. This gives real-time data on how writing helps feelings shift (usually, but not always, for the better) in very little time, using the process of writing.

5. **Budget an in-session Five-Minute Sprint.** When a client is on the edge of insight, discovery, or integration, we "stop, drop, and write." Slide a pad of paper over and ask the client to write what's going on, then read the entry or a reflection to you. It's often the most powerful five minutes of the session.

5 Tips for Clients and Journal Keepers

1. **Protect your privacy.** Find a way to keep your journal safe and secure. Paper journals can be discreetly stowed in bookbags, briefcases, or backpacks. Digital journals can be password-protected or stored in folders with neutral names.

2. **Date every entry.** This one habit practiced in the present allows your future self a historical lens through which to note how this present moment unfolded across time.

3. **Be authentic.** Practice being you, with no expectations or obligations. Who would you be, what would you do, how would you express yourself if it were emotionally safe to do so?

4. **Write from your own lived experience.** Bring in details—the fuzzballs on the cardigan sweater, the moon shining crimson through the smoke of the forest fire, the smell of autumn decay.

5. **Forget the "rules."** Write what you want, how you want, when you want. Write in a notebook or on a keyboard or in a phone app. No wrong, just write!

3 Journaling Prompts

The following journaling prompts are adapted from *Journal Therapy for Calming Anxiety* © 2020 Kathleen Adams, Sterling Publishing:

1. **Rays of light.** No matter how challenging things may be, there's always at least one thing that's going well. It might be a stable relationship, a cause that fills you with purpose, a pastime that sparks your imagination. Write about a ray of light that is shining on you right now.
2. **Your superpower.** We might not be able to cast Spider-Man webs from our palms, but everybody's got superpowers. Often, they hide in plain sight. Maybe you're a good listener, or you're great at organizing, or you create lovely spaces. Make a list of things you're naturally good at. Choose one and write about it. How might it help you manage stressful situations?
3. **Can you change this?** Some things you can't control (the weather) and some things you can control (your choices). A great journal question is, "Can I change this [experience, feeling, circumstance]?" If no, then passively disregard it, say "oh well," and move on. If yes, write about what can be changed and list a few action steps to start.

 About the Author

Kathleen Adams, LPC, is a psychotherapist and registered poetry/journal therapist in Denver, Colorado. She is the founder/director of the Center for Journal Therapy, the Therapeutic Writing Institute, and Journalversity. Kathleen is the author of 13 books on journal therapy, including the best-selling classic, *Journal to the Self* (1990), *Expressive Writing: Foundations of Practice* (2013), and *Journal Therapy for Calming Anxiety* (2020).

How Journaling Benefits Your Coaching and Your Clients

3

A M Carley

When I began writing to myself in a green spiral notebook, I was a confused 13-year-old, desperate to make sense of life, whose only jobs at the time involved babysitting and housecleaning. I'd never considered becoming a coach. Over the decades, my journal has become a portal to my wisest, best self. I'm happy to report that my journal's value to me increases every day, for both my life and my work. Its form has changed, from smaller to larger blank books, and its contents now cover many more topics and kinds of expression.

A written journaling practice (there are other kinds) works for many people, including those who don't consider themselves writers. Because journals are personal and private, writers and nonwriters alike can explore and enjoy a singular freedom of expression. All you need to do is put pen to page and see what happens. You can also use digital devices, although perhaps there are some additional benefits to writing by hand.

In the context of coaching, I see journaling as a key tool for myself as a coach, and also for my clients. Many times when I welcome a client, I notice that, as she settles in, she pulls out a bound book and a pen before she feels ready to begin.

Self-Coaching for Coaches

In effect, my journal is an important self-coaching tool for me. Each day before work, I consider the interactions I'll be having with clients, and see if I notice anything calling for attention. By taking the time to write in my journal, and to feel out any inspirations and concerns, I prepare myself for the day. I also use my journal to reflect on the previous day's work, to celebrate successes, and to make notes and reminders for future use. My coaching improves with journaling because the process clears space, refines ideas, and anchors intentions so that I can be present with and for the client.

On a larger scale, journaling is hugely valuable to me for charting my course forward in my career. My journal is where I think through the big-picture questions: where I'm going with my coaching practice, where I want to be with all the other areas of my life, what course corrections I can sense will be necessary, and so on.

Free Expression

I use my journal not only to think about clients but as an all-encompassing space for free expression. When I flip through a typical volume, I'll see recollected dreams, notes from conversations with friends and advisers, ideas for my creative projects, lists, gratitudes, rants, doodles, citations from books I'm reading, quick summaries of movies, books, songs, and articles I've enjoyed, insights, descriptions of beauty, and more. And the margins! They contain my private symbology of arrows, squiggly lines, asterisks, abbreviations, and other indicators that help me find what I want later on.

To expand a journaling practice, you need to allow time. It can take years to relax and trust your particular slow, gentle process. It also takes minutes from your days, committing your material to written words. Slowing down enough to describe places, people, feelings, dreams, and experiences can take a while. When you make time for journaling, you find that you're honing your ability to perceive, in a virtuous cycle that nurtures itself.

When I sit with my trusty blank notebook and write down the sometimes random words that come to mind, I give permission to some wise voices to make themselves known. The written words will still be there in a week, or a month, or years later. The spirit of the moment in which they were first written will have passed long since. And the words remain on the page, ready to be seen with new eyes.

Rereading

Reviewing old pages is tremendously valuable. I can identify patterns much easier in hindsight than in the day-to-day tumble of a working life. Good choices come from the reflection that picking out those patterns makes possible. I'll often bring a few back journals with me when I go away on vacation with time for a mini-retrospective. I have gleaned so much from this habit.

Journaling helps me to cultivate new habits and to break old ones. When a new resolve is fresh and not yet a habit, journaling about it regularly helps reinforce a new intention and turn it from an idea into a practice. Also, rereading recent pages helps me to notice when an old unwanted habit may be trying to kick in again, so I can halt its recurrence.

Becoming Unstuck

You can use your journaling practice to deal with blocks and stuck spots. I have seen that a few days of journaling about a stuck spot can enable a client to see his or her way through and find a way to continue his or her creative progress. Here are two examples from my coaching clients:

- For a client who struggled with marketing her published books, journaling was the method she used to dig into the pros, cons, and compromises entailed in taking responsibility for continuing to build her audience of readers.
- For a client whose life was too chaotic for a steady creative routine, journaling about the quandary was a means toward seeing a picture of a future that worked. Significant changes in daily and weekly schedules resulted, and a much more productive creative period commenced.

When you need fresh ideas, an ongoing journaling practice is a wonderful tool for uncovering one or many ideas, either through reviewing old pages or committing to freewriting new pages each day. Use the pages as a filter for expressing material that may not belong in a given project, but which you want to keep for later. Journaling can be a warm-up tool, a method of extracting meaning, and a creative lab for experimenting with ideas and forms.

The Story Continues

Each of us has a story that we tell ourselves to understand the entire range of our life and our work. That story is subject to revision, especially if we're exploring it with a coach and/or through a journaling practice. My journal is my primary tool for developing and revising a coherent narrative of my life and work. I'm a good deal more patient with the process now than I was when I began with that green spiral notebook. And I'm grateful each day for the next blank page.

5 Tips for Helping Professionals

1. Deposit Brain Dumps

    Use your journal as a safe place for "brain dumps" where you can freely deposit all the random detritus that picks at your attention and distracts you from your purpose. Committing the flotsam and jetsam of your mind to the journal creates space and reduces anxiety. Just lay it all out on the pages or the screen. The release of worry, anxiety, random to-dos, what-ifs, and other bits of clutter will be refreshing. And you won't need to carry those details around in your head.

2. Add An Ally

    Your journal can be your ally—a trusted colleague, in effect—who listens unconditionally, keeps track of your various trains of thought, and never tells a soul what you've been up to.

3. Overcome Negativity Bias

    By adopting a daily Recap Routine[1] in your journal, you encourage your brain to outweigh any problems or hurts with the many accomplishments, moments of connection and gratitude, and acts of generosity that you experienced.

4. Correct Your Course

    Check in with yourself and your intentions. Have you gotten off course?

5. Do the First Draft

    When you're struggling with a difficult message you need to deliver, do a first draft in your journal. You can mark it up, cross things out, and be wildly imperfect while you sort out what it is you really intend to say. Typing that up into the final email, letter, or script will be simple and swift.

5 Tips for Clients and Journal Keepers

1. Protect your Journal's Privacy

    Your journal is your place for private expression. You can write your ideas, thoughts, dreams, feelings, insecurities, anxieties, frustrations, and more, secure in the knowledge that no one else will see your words. Develop habits to store your journals sensibly—past volumes as well as the current one—whether in physical or electronic storage.

2. Create a Routine

    Many people like to journal at the same time of day, habitually. If that appeals to you, set up a routine. It could be in the morning just before exercising, with your afternoon tea, at the end of the work-day, before bed, or at another regular time that works for you.

3. Find a Portable Journaling Tool

    Even if you prefer to write longhand in a special kind of bound journal, or on a desktop computer, devise another quick way to add to your journal. A tiny notebook, a clip full of index cards, a cloud-based tool like Evernote, an email to yourself, a voice memo to yourself—these are all examples of useful methods for on-the-go journal entries. Note: follow up later and incorporate them into the main journal where appropriate.

4. Log Your Entries

    Include the date, time, and your location for each entry. When you revisit previous entries, the date and time will ground you in the historical moment, so that you can view the entry in the larger sequence. Your location may jog your memory further so that you can picture the place where you wrote those words, and thus recapture more useful details.

5. Honor Your Practice

    Appreciate your journaling practice and its value to you. Establish and protect your boundaries so that those around you respect its importance as well.

3 Journaling Prompts

1. When faced with a question you don't know the answer to: *if I did know the answer, what would I do next?*
2. *What specific things do I notice at this moment?* Describe the small details: sounds, smells, noises, sights, textures, emotions, ideas, inspirations, thoughts, memories, etc.
3. *What happened in the last 24 hours that I'm grateful for? What do I appreciate about those events, and what do they mean to me?*

About the Author

A M Carley is a creative coach, author, teacher, and editor based in central Virginia, USA. Anne has been journaling since childhood, and considers the practice a rich resource for coaches and for creative people. Two of her non-fiction books, *FLOAT: Becoming Unstuck for Writers* and the forthcoming *CALM: Bold Creative Confidence*, encourage writers and other creative people to trust their own inner guidance. Unsurprisingly, her books, her online and in-person courses and workbooks encourage a journaling practice. You can learn more about her work at annecarley.com.

Note

1. A tool in A M Carley's *FLOAT: Becoming Unstuck for Writers* (Be Well Here 2016).

Journaling Your Way to a More Authentic Life

4

Eric Teplitz

Imagine the quality of a relationship with a partner, spouse, or significant other in which you rarely check in to see how the other person is doing. Or one in which you rarely let the other person know, honestly, how you are doing. Would you expect such a relationship to work in the long run? Bring out the best in each of you? Be fulfilling?

Now consider that the only partner you will have for the entirety of your life is yourself. Regular checking in is essential. Journaling, I have found, is a great avenue for doing this.

Five Key Benefits of Making Journaling a Practice

1. Honoring Your Inner Experience

In a world with endless distractions, and sometimes endless demands, it is all too easy to lose sight of our own thoughts, feelings, preferences, deeper needs, and priorities. Journaling provides an avenue for checking in to assess these things, for taking your psychic pulse on a regular basis.

When the day gets going, most of us—most of the time—are just responding unconsciously to the task at hand calling for our attention. Journaling creates an opening for our authentic selves to have their say. It gives us the space to tune in to what actually matters to us, important things worthy of our consideration that might otherwise slip through the cracks.

2. Increasing Self-Knowledge

By checking in with ourselves regularly, we get to know ourselves a lot better. We become more aware of our own patterns, habits, tendencies, strengths, and weaknesses.

Self-knowledge alone will not create a desired change, but it is the necessary first step, and it can help tremendously with making smarter decisions. For instance, if you know from observed experience that you won't exercise without a partner to whom you are accountable, then you can be proactive in finding such a partner as a means of motivating yourself to keep on track with a fitness goal. If you want to lose weight but know yourself well enough to know you are unlikely to resist the temptation of ice cream in the freezer, you can make the conscious decision to not bring it in the house. If you know that you need solitude in order to get some writing done, you can plan accordingly rather than just hope that the time and space will come your way.

You may feel that you already know yourself well enough to know these kinds of things *without* journaling. But I find, personally, that self-discovery and self-understanding are ongoing journeys, and reminders of "things I already know" are helpful!

3. Creating a Tipping Point for Change

There are a number of ways in which journaling can help facilitate change and decision-making. As noted previously, self-knowledge is key. But also, if you find yourself complaining about (or yearning for) the same thing over and over again in your journal, you might actually be moved to finally *do something* about it as a result. I have found that the simple act of writing down goals—in list form, or otherwise—is usually the first step in realizing them. It might require writing the thing down more than once—many times, even—but writing things down is *powerful.*

A journal provides a safe space to brainstorm, to dare to dream about things, and to explore possibilities for yourself. It can literally be the tipping point for making those decisions, small and large, that shape your life. By making such decisions more consciously, with deeper reflection and consideration, and from a space where you are more in tune with what's important to you, you increase the odds of your life being more to your liking and less filled with regret.

4. Developing Your Intuition

A journal is a place to record your thoughts and feelings about anything and everything. It heightens your powers of observation. By recording an impression on paper, you are more likely to pay attention to it and keep it in mind.

Do you like or dislike the way someone is treating you? Do you notice a pattern with this person's reliability or lack thereof? You might get a better sense of what you can expect from him/her and can decide more consciously to what extent you want to include this person in your life. You can also reflect back on your own behavior and see the ways in which you can act with greater integrity to improve relationships with others.

One of the cool things about a journal is that you can refer back to previous entries to remind yourself of what/where/when events in your life occurred. By looking back at previously recorded thoughts and impressions, you can gauge, in hindsight, how astute you were or were not about a given person or situation, and perhaps hone your skills of perception as a result.

5. Validating Your Own Existence

I write, therefore I am!

A journal is a place to record the happenings of your life. It can be a private container for your struggles and victories, both internal and external. It is a way to document those little details you would likely never otherwise remember when reflecting back years later. It can allow you, over time, to bear witness to your life, and note the ways in which you have made big changes as well as the ways in which you have remained essentially the same.

By flipping through old journals, you can revisit the past in (perhaps) extraordinary detail, and marvel at how rich life is in the variety and quantity of your experiences. You can see with the benefit of hindsight how limited (or perhaps visionary!) your perspective may have been. Old journals or journal entries can serve as a reminder that you never know what unpredictable bit of kismet is lurking just around the corner, and how much your world can open up with the introduction of a single new idea, book, blog post, experience, or person into your life story.

A journal is a way to prove that you were here. You have lived. You have endured trials. You have made efforts and accomplished things. In your journals lies proof of it all.

My Experience of Journaling

I have journaled in one form or another, on and off, for decades. It has been, and continues to be, an essential tool for me in:

- Following the promptings of my heart
- Being a student/explorer of my life and of Life
- Giving myself needed pep talks
- Living more creatively, daringly, passionately, and compassionately
- Crystallizing and clarifying what is and is not important to me, and there-fore what is and is not worth my time and energy
- Processing my feelings
- Generating ideas

It's impossible to say, of course, what my life would have been like without this practice, but I suspect that it has been *far* richer for it. How many curiosi-ties of mine would have remained unexplored, how many adventures left on the table, how many dreams shrugged off or delayed indefinitely, were it not for journaling?

From my perspective and experience, capturing your thoughts, desires, ideas, hunches, insights, and inspirations on paper where your eyes can see them—rather than have them just be groundless imaginings floating around in your head—greatly increases the likelihood of actually taking action on at least *some* of them!

Without my journaling practice, would I have climbed out of debt and depression? Moved to Los Angeles? Discovered a love of camping and back-packing at the age of 27 (when I had never previously spent a night in the great outdoors)? Hiked over 500 miles of the Appalachian Trail? Completed a triathlon, then a marathon, and eventually an Ironman triathlon? Married a wonderfully compatible partner? Become a regular blood donor (when I had long feared needles)? Tried and failed at any number of things, but at least *tried* them? Started blogging? Gone over a year without eating sweets? Become a vegetarian? Studied classical piano? It's possible I'd have done some of these things anyway, but it's doubtful to me I'd have acted as boldly and deliberately, that I'd have reflected as deeply, that I'd lived as full a life without having incorporated journaling into it.

Concluding Thoughts

As with any practice, you can significantly alter the trajectory of your life by journaling regularly.

Experiment with times of day, and time or page allotments, until you find your "sweet spot." Generally speaking, earlier in the day is better for developing consistency with a practice (as the day unfolds, duties and distractions take over and energy and willpower are depleted). That said, you need to honor your own schedule, rhythm, and life circumstances. Whatever works for you is the right approach.

Remember that the sheer act of journaling means you are taking yourself—your thoughts, your feelings, and your *life*—seriously, and is therefore a gesture of self-respect. It is a unique gift that only you can give yourself, and it only costs as much as the materials (say, pens and notebooks) you use and the time you devote to it. It is a way to greatly improve your relationship with yourself and, by extension, your relationships with others and even with Life itself.

---

 5 Tips for Helping Professionals

1. Recommend journaling as a tool for your clients to help them gain clarity and insights.
2. Develop a journaling practice of your own to avail yourself of the same gifts.
3. Consider keeping a "professional" journal in which you journal after client sessions to enhance your memory of details they have shared, record your impressions, and process your own reactions. This can deepen client trust and strengthen the relationship, effectively helping both parties.
4. Keeping a personal and/or "professional" journal can help you access inspired ideas for helping a client that may not otherwise have occurred to you. It's a great tool for accessing "below the surface" ideas in general.
5. If you do dreamwork you might encourage your client to keep a dream-specific journal by their bed for recording dreams that would otherwise go forgotten and have them present these to you in their sessions.

---

 5 Tips for Clients and Journal Keepers

1. Consistency is key and reaps the greatest benefits, but perfection is not necessary. Strengthen the muscle of "getting back on the horse" whenever you have drifted away from the practice for too long.

2. Especially when first starting out, choose a specific time of day reserved just for journaling, at a time when you can do so without distraction. *Schedule* it. *Prioritize* it. *Insist* on it. And *protect that time*, or it is far less likely to happen and stick. Remember: you can't do it wrong, as long as you show up.

3. It's helpful to record the date (and perhaps time) of each journal entry.

4. Keep in mind that your journal is meant for your eyes only, so there is no need to worry about grammar, spelling, or even lucidity. You can write in whatever manner you feel like on any given day. Stream of consciousness is fine, maybe even preferred. Messy, unorganized, all over the place? Great!

5. View this as a practice. Be patient with yourself and with the process. Give it a fair try, and see if you find it helpful. Think of it as time set aside for your own well-being. Give yourself credit for doing it.

 3 Journaling Prompts

- If I could choose exactly how I spend my time, I would. . .
- My ideal life would have to consist of. . .
- Before I die, I want to. . .

 About the Author

Eric Teplitz is a writer who blogs at Eric's Inspired Living Blog (www. inspiredlivingblog.wordpress.com), and also a singer/songwriter whose recordings can be found on Spotify, iTunes, and YouTube. His personal website is: www.ericteplitz.com.

The Focused Journal Method   **5**

Eric Maisel

The Focused Journal Method is a method of self-inquiry made up of the following eight elements or steps:

1. You identify an issue
2. You examine its significance
3. You identify core questions
4. You tease out intentions
5. You notice what shadows get activated
6. You identify the strengths you bring
7. You align your thoughts with your intentions
8. You align your behaviors with your intentions

This method makes simple, straightforward, but nevertheless sophisticated use of the best ideas from existential, cognitive, and behavioral therapy. Let's see how this works in practice. One of my clients, Mark, used the list of eight steps as a kind of checklist and proceeded down them one by one.

Mark:

1. You identify an issue

   The next step in my teaching career.

2. You examine its significance

   I simply can't afford not to offer my skills and abilities as a teacher.
   I feel this overwhelming sense of creative energy flowing through me during the most casual/informal encounters.
   I know I have to do something with this energy (I need to serve/contribute somehow).

3.   You identify core questions

Is there a demand for my services?
Do I know what my time, energy, and "expertise" are worth?
Am I willing and able to dedicate myself to my teaching?
Is what motivates me right now sustainable over time?
What will help keep the fire lit?
Should I specialize in one topic area? If so, what?

4.   You tease out intentions

My intention is to take my life more seriously and myself less so.
My intention is to make my life count by doing what matters most—first.
I intend to study the habits of people who share the same personal/professional interests as I do.
I intend to stretch myself professionally by engaging in activities that keep me on the edge of my comfort zone.
I intend to take more of my intuitive hits seriously and follow up on them by journaling.

5.   You notice what shadows get activated

My insecurities.
Fear of failing (failing at what, exactly?)
My lack of willingness to own the behaviors directly associated with my life purposes.
Maybe there is some shame attached also?

6.   You identify the strengths you bring

I am a great "student of the game."
I am creative.
I thrive when making something out of nothing.
I embody "the best teachers are often some of the best students."

7.   You align your thoughts with your intentions

I can be open to the many different opportunities to serve that are available to me.
I am open to change and the change process.
I am committed to listening to my inner voice.
I am my own dearest and closest friend and self-guidance is always available.

8. You align your behaviors with your intentions

    I will make a 3-item action list every day.
    Each action item will directly support my Life Purpose Statement (which
        I will create).
    I will journal my progress at least four times a week.
    I will ask someone "unattached" to my efforts to review my progress via
        email or in person.
    This reads like a self-coaching session. Well, maybe now I know how to
        self-coach!

Let's call Mark's way the checklist method. Using the checklist method, you
identify an issue and then go down the steps in order, addressing each in turn.
However, a narrative approach is also possible. With a narrative approach, you
start with an issue and have a journaled conversation with yourself, referring
back to the steps as you consider the issue. If you want to go an extra (valuable) mile, you might number your thoughts (see the following journal entry).

Here is how one journal keeper whom we'll call Mary used the Focused
Journal Method. This is a very abridged version of her fuller, more elaborated
effort.

Mary:

> So, the issue that's bothering me is that I've been training for the past
> two years as a personal development coach and journal facilitator, and
> I still have trouble stepping into this as a professional identity. I'm happy
> to coach and facilitate for free, but it's so hard for me to charge money
> for what I do [1]. All kinds of thoughts come up for me when I think
> about charging money for coaching: Who am I to do this kind of work?
> How can I coach other people when my own life isn't perfect? Why
> would anyone want to pay for coaching? What value is there in this
> work [5]?
>
> Being able to charge money for coaching and facilitation is important
> to me because I want to own my professional identity and expertise
> in these areas [2]. So, what would help me to begin charging for my
> expertise [3]? I think it helps if I remember that my professional exper-
> tise has been valued in the past. I have every reason to feel confident in
> my abilities as a coach and to actually charge for my time and expertise.
> I have a strong academic background and over ten years of teaching and
> facilitation experience [6].

What else could I do to become more comfortable with being paid for my time and expertise [3]? I could network with other coaches so that I feel part of a community of professionals [4]. As I write this, I realize that I really want to put together my website and launch myself more fully into the networks of professional coaches that I know [4]. One colleague (a fellow coach) actually told me that I was the best coach she knew [6]! Why is it so hard for me to take compliments like that seriously [5]? I have such a difficult time valuing my own gifts.

I will purchase my domain name and web host this week [8]. I know that my perfectionism is going to rear its ugly head once I get started with this [5]! I'll remind myself that my intention is simply to get my website up and running so that I can have my prices out there in the world and begin to own my professional identity as a coach and journal facilitator. I'll let whatever I create be good enough for now. My intention is to make a start at this, not to be perfect at it [7]!

Let's call Mary's way the narrative way. You write in a natural way, following your lines of thought, while at the same time keeping one eye on the eight steps. Once you're done (meaning that you've arrived at the place of articulating what actions you intend to take), you can then go back and insert bracketed numbers that correspond to the steps. Going back and inserting the bracketed numbers is an important part of the process and helps you really learn what it means to create an intention and to align your thoughts and your actions with that intention.

A third client, Joan, a painter, desperately wanted her painting career to take off. Here is a very abridged version of the place she arrived in her journaling, eventually arriving at step 7 (aligning thoughts) and step 8 (aligning behaviors):

Joan wrote:

I'm not sure exactly how to proceed but I do feel that I have an intention: to figure out how to make a name for myself as a painter [4]. And I think that I have the basic smarts, ambition, energy and backbone to pull that off [6]. So, in order to keep my thoughts aligned with that intention, I am going to begin to say the following things to myself [7]. I am going to say, "I can prove the exception" [7]. I am going to say, "I can figure out how to make a name for myself" [7]. When I hear myself saying things like "You have no chance" and "Who do you think you are?," I am going to counter those thoughts with, "You don't serve me, thought!" [7].

As to aligning my behaviors with my intention, first of all I'm going to do some basic research on strategies for "making a name for yourself" [8]. A lot of those strategies I want to rule out quickly if they sound too run-of-the-mill. But if I find one or two that have a feeling of rightness to them, I will start on them immediately [8]. After I've done that basic research, I'll check back in with myself through journaling to make sure that I am holding the right intention, and if I feel that I am, then I'll get cracking and put into practice whatever I've learned [8].

In my experience, clients intuitively understand the logic of this eight-step method and likewise intuitively understand how to make personal use of it. Some will opt for the list method, some will opt for the narrative method (with or without concerning themselves about bracketing steps), some will use it very loosely and impressionistically. All will benefit.

5 Tips for Helping Professionals

1. Try the method yourself on some issue that's up for you, whether it is a professional issue (like how to grow your practice), a practical issue (like how to better organize your day so as to get everything important done), or a personal issue (like losing weight, quitting smoking, etc.).
2. See if a particular step or steps strike you as harder than the others. This will be good to know when you instruct clients on the use of the Focused Journal Method.
3. You might work on a given problem in both the list way and the narrative way, to get a sense of how those two approaches differ.
4. Sometimes the way you frame an issue makes all the difference. If you frame an issue one way and have trouble making progress, try an alternative framing approach.
5. Don't be afraid to suggest to clients that they make use of this tool. They're likely to find it really valuable!

5 Tips for Clients and Journal Keepers

1. Read through the list of steps several times. You'll begin to get a better understanding of their logic the more times you go over them.

2. Try it out! Apply this Focused Journal Method with a variety of issues. Some may be more amenable to this method than others. Give several different issues a try.
3. Try to stay focused. The idea is that you are trying to get to solutions. Remember that you have goals and objectives here.
4. Once you've identified thoughts that align with your intentions, make sure to think them!
5. Once you've identified actions to take, make sure to take them!

 3 Journaling Prompts

1. If I were to make a list of the problems that are currently troubling me, my list would look like:
2. Looking at my list, the one problem or issue that wants to be addressed right now is:
3. I think the hardest step of the Focused Journal Method will be:

 About the Author

Eric Maisel, PhD is the author of 50+ books, among them *Lighting the Way*, *The Power of Daily Practice*, *Coaching the Artist Within*, *The Van Gogh Blues*, and *Life Purpose Boot Camp*. You can learn more about his work at www.ericmaisel.com and contact him at ericmaisel@hotmail.com.

Using Journaling With Clients

PART II

Journaling for Busy   **6**
Coaches and Clients

Hannah Braime

What does "busy" look like in your life? Perhaps it's juggling kids and work, perhaps it's long hours at your job, perhaps it's caring for others, or additional commitments outside these categories. When life is busy, the idea of adding something else onto your plate in the form of a regular journaling practice might feel impossible—even if you know it will benefit you. The good news, however, is that you can make reflective writing an enriching, rewarding, and supportive part of your day, whatever else is going on. In this chapter, I will talk about how you, as a professional, can make space for journaling in your life and encourage and guide your clients as they do the same.

The Many Disguises of Resistance

First, let's talk about a common obstacle that often hides under the guise of "busy": resistance. Resistance hits even the most seasoned and committed journal writers at some point or another. Whether it's because our practice feels a little stale or we're touching on topics that are uncomfortable to explore, resistance wears many disguises. It can look like "I'm too busy," or "I have more important things to be doing right now," or (my favorite) "Next week, when things are quieter, I'll start journaling again . . .". Of course, things are rarely quieter next week, or the weeks following, and when we notice months have gone by and we're still waiting for "next week," that's a sign it's time to address resistance.

Sometimes being busy becomes a cover for avoiding discomfort. If there are certain topics you find challenging to write about, or your current approach to journaling isn't working for you, this is an excellent opportunity to explore that further. How do you feel when you think about journaling? What physical sensations do you notice? Is it something that provokes excitement or joy? Or something that feels more like a chore you should do? If the latter, what would make journaling feel lighter and more enjoyable? If you ask yourself these questions, notice you have a fixed idea of what you think journaling *should* be like, and this fixed idea doesn't feel all that appealing, let's start by letting that go.

The idea journaling has to be long-winded and serious is a common misperception. It can be these things, if that's what serves you, but it doesn't have to be. The act of journaling is deeply personal and the most important thing about your practice is that it is yours—something that suits you, your personality, and your lifestyle—whatever that might look like.

At other times, being busy isn't a manifestation of resistance or avoidance, but a reality you need to work with. You want to journal; you see the benefits of having a regular practice; but creating the time to sit and write is proving to be a challenge. Here are a few suggestions that might help.

Finding Time Versus Creating Time

I used the phrase "creating time" in the last paragraph for a reason, because that's what we need to do. Can you remember the last time you found yourself with an afternoon stretching ahead of you, nowhere else to go and nothing else on your to-do list? Me neither. If we wait for this situation to magically present itself, we will be waiting a long time. However busy you are, you are far more likely to build and maintain a regular journaling practice if you carve out dedicated time for it and make it part of your daily schedule. As a professional reading this book, you're already aware of the many mental and physical health benefits of journaling. So, treat it like you would anything else you do for your health: brushing your teeth, exercising, self-care. It's not something you do after everything else important is done, it *is* one of the important things.

What Will You Stop Doing?

With that being said, trying to pile more and more onto your plate without making room first will only lead to an enormous mess. If life already feels packed to the brim, you will be more likely to create a solid journaling practice if you can clear a little space.

The first place to look is at what is not serving you. These are often the usual suspects: social media, mindless internet scrolling, TV, the go-to thing you reach for when you find yourself unoccupied for a moment. How much of your life do these activities take up? Is the reward worth it? What if you were to spend those moments jotting down a few thoughts in your journal instead, or using the time to check in with yourself?

Over the next week, notice where the micro-spaces show up in your daily life. Notice when you're waiting in queues, between appointments, when you have a few moments to yourself. Notice when you feel the urge to reach for your phone, to do whatever you do when you feel bored, aimless, or craving occupation. How can you use this time for journaling? It might not seem like these moments are enough time, but, as I'll share next, there are a few short and sweet journaling techniques that are perfect for the "what you can, when you can" approach; a few minutes here, a few minutes there.

Short and Sweet Journaling Ideas for Busy Writers

1.   Lists

Lists can be long or short, light-hearted or serious, entertaining or meaningful. You can complete them all in one go, or work on them over time, adding ideas as they come to you. Examples of lists you could make as part of your journaling practice include:

- 10 new things I want to try this year
- 5 places I want to see during my lifetime
- 20 enjoyable things I can do with my family/friends
- 10 things to do the next time I feel bored
- 10 new things I'd like to learn
- 5 old friends I'd like to reconnect with

2.   A photo diary

With two young kids at home, I rarely have the energy to sit down and write in the evenings. Instead, I use photos I've taken during the day as a springboard for reflection. I also make a note of at least three good things that happened that day. This practice is an easy but effective way of remembering those tiny moments that become meaningful later on, and it's a lovely way to end the day—smooth or challenging—with a dose of gratitude.

3.   Stream-of-consciousness journaling

Stream-of-consciousness journaling involves writing whatever comes into your head, whether that's thoughts about your purpose in life, or thoughts about what you are planning to have for dinner. Anything goes. The beauty of this journaling technique is there is very little thinking required. In fact, the point is *not* to overthink what you're writing, but to see where your mind takes you. Set a timer for two minutes, five minutes, or ten minutes and get ready for an interesting journey.

4.   Daily/Weekly/Monthly Check-ins

In my journaling practice, I've found it helpful to create a series of questions I can use to touch base with myself on those days when I'm not sure what to write about or want an "easy" journaling session. My daily check-in template contains questions like "How am I feeling today? What was the high? And the low? What did I create today?" I don't answer each question every single day, but having this template removes any inertia that comes with not knowing where to start and provides a prompt that will open the gateway and let the words flow.

 5 Tips for Helping Professionals

1. Open yourself up to explore your own resistance and obstacles to journaling. These are not a problem, they are a gift! Use your own experience of encountering and resolving these obstacles to inform your work with clients.
2. Empower clients to reclaim agency over their time. Help them unpack their reasons and resistance and encourage them to envisage their ideal approach to journaling. What needs to happen to make that a reality?
3. Incorporate journaling into your professional life. If it isn't already something that features in your work, try using journaling to reflect on how your work with clients is going, your professional goals, and anything else that would be useful to explore through writing.
4. Keep expanding your practice and looking for new techniques to try. For example, if you haven't done art journaling before, try it. Keep expanding your repertoire to keep your practice fresh and build your toolbox for clients too.
5. Start a journaling group for your clients or with other professionals. Groups add accountability and give participants a fixed time on

their schedule reserved for journaling. You can do this in-person or online, with other professionals who use journaling in their work or for a group of clients. Whatever the setting, there is no reason not to take part yourself.

5 Tips for Clients and Journal Keepers

1. Throw out the rulebook. Remember, there is no one right way to journal and whatever works for you and your journaling practice is fine. If you feel you're not journaling "properly," use this as a springboard: what would journaling properly look like? Where does this vision of proper journaling come from? How would your practice change if you let go of these rules?
2. Look for the cracks in your day. It might be hard to find 30 minutes of uninterrupted time when you can write, but you probably have several in-between times when you can do two minutes here or five minutes there. These are times like waiting in line, coffee or lunch breaks, between appointments, or during your commute.
3. Embrace different types of journaling. Journaling traditionally involves writing, but it doesn't have to. You can also journal using audio recordings, photos, and videos.
4. Make it fun! You are more likely to maintain a regular journaling practice during your busiest times when your practice is fun. Start compiling a list of your favorite techniques and prompts.
5. Use a template. If thinking of what to write about is creating resistance and/or you have little time to write, try creating a set of questions to answer at the end of each day or week.

3 Journaling Prompts

1. What would change in your life if you could dedicate regular time to journaling?
2. What is the number one thing you can start doing that would help you create a regular journaling practice?

3.   What is the number one thing you can stop doing that would help you create a regular journaling practice?

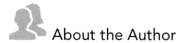 ## About the Author

Hannah Braime is a creative coach and author who writes about personal growth and creativity. She is the author of five books on journaling and self-care and you can read more of her writing at www.becomingwhoyouare.net.

"Best Outcome" Journaling

7

Steevie Jane Parks

Let me begin with a real-life example of how "Best Outcome" Journaling works. One of my therapy clients was coping with a difficult family situation involving a meeting with her siblings to discuss her mother's end-of-life care. There was a lot of longstanding conflict between the four siblings and my client often felt that she was "ganged up on" by her two older siblings.

In the past, she had become so overwhelmed with anger, shame, and fear, after being reprimanded for her views, that she would leave the scene before anything could get resolved. Her main goal was to get through the visit in one piece. I asked her to write down the "Best Possible Outcome" for her visit.

She wrote down that she would be able to remain calm and nonjudgmental and would be relaxed as she stated what she wanted for her mother and why. We then reinforced what she wrote by having her imagine the scene in her mind and by having her practice her "speech" while feeling relaxed and confident. A week later she flew down for the meeting, made her points confidently, and was able to feel heard and appreciated by her siblings, even though they vehemently disagreed with almost all of her ideas. She came home from her trip with an increased sense of pride in herself and with much less anger towards her two older siblings.

Another example of this technique, used with a creativity coaching client, involved preparing for an art show. After many years of not showing his work, due to a long and difficult illness, my client submitted several paintings to an outdoor art festival. He was anxious about traveling and worried that his work might no longer be appreciated.

Once his submissions were accepted, he became increasingly anxious about attending the event. I asked him to write down the "Best Possible Outcome" of his trip. He wrote down that he would see artists that he had not seen for many years and would have such a good time interacting with them and the people who came to see his work, that he would not focus on how well, or how poorly, his work was selling. He was able to attend the event, had a wonderful time, and even sold a couple of large paintings.

A final example involves a creativity coaching client who felt that difficulties with her vision that were related to aging were preventing her from putting enough time into her painting practice. She could not spend more than 20 minutes at a time painting without getting a severe headache due to eye strain.

I asked why she did not consider corrective surgery, and she admitted that she was simply afraid to have the surgery, even though she thought that it could solve her painting problem. I asked her to write a list of all of the possible positive things that might happen as a result of getting the surgery. Her list was huge. They included being able to paint every day, being able to fully see what she was painting the way her clients would see it, having no more headaches, feeling free to make contacts with some of her old galleries, having the energy to effectively market her art online, experiencing improved self-esteem, having energy to go to more parties where she could make contact with other artists, and being able to quit her day job if she started selling again like she had sold in the past.

Suddenly the list of positive outcomes that she had written down seemed more compelling than her fear of the surgery. She ended up getting the surgery and painting full time as well as finding a consistent stream of buyers for her work online.

These are just three examples where writing down positive expectations helped people to overcome their negative thinking. Much research has been done to show that physically writing things down on paper makes them seem more real and doable. It is generally preferable to handwrite this kind of journal exercise, but not mandatory. The simple act of focusing on a positive outcome is the main key to success.

It's also important to remember that the purpose of this exercise is not to force good things to happen, but to prime the mind to be open to the possibility that good things "can" happen. If our minds are primed for success, we will be focused on behaving in a manner that makes success possible. If we do not anticipate success, our minds will be primed for failure and we will not behave in a manner that is conducive to achieving our goals.

5 Tips for Helping Professionals

It is important to try to encourage your clients to think about constructing "Best Outcome Scenarios" that follow a basic "SMART" Protocol. This means that to be most effective, "Best Outcome Scenarios" should be S (simple), M (measurable), A (Attainable), R (realistic), and T (timely). Allow me to break this down a bit further.

1. An example of a "Simple" Best Outcome Statement would be "I will edit one chapter in my book today" versus "I will complete the editing of my entire book today."

People are more likely to accomplish a series of simple goals than they are to accomplish one huge goal, especially if the best outcome has to occur within one short day.

2. An example of a "Measurable" best outcome would be "I will get to work on time today and will make a list of priorities for the day before I start working."

    This is typically more effective than writing down something like "I will accomplish a lot today." It's more effective to say what you want to accomplish because this enables better focus and clients will know exactly what they need to focus on getting done.

3. An example of an "Attainable" best outcome is one that the client is fully capable of achieving in a specifically allotted time period. The level of attainability will be specific to each individual client and situation. For example, you would not want a client to write down a best outcome that he or she was not likely to be able to pull off.

4. A "Realistic" Best Outcome Statement would be one that is both Attainable and Realistic given both the particulars of the situation and the mood, energy level, and motivational level of an individual on any given day.

5. A "Timely" Best Outcome Statement involves choosing a discrete time frame in which the desired behavior or outcome is to take place. We are more likely to follow through with a plan if we give ourselves a basic time frame in which the outcome is expected. In addition to following the SMART approach, Best Outcome Scenarios should have more to do with actions that the client has some control over vs. things that the client cannot control, such as the weather, the mood of their boss, or whether or not they are going to win the lottery.

5 Tips for Clients and Journal Keepers

1. Use the "SMART" guidelines under the "Tips for Coaches" section to formulate Best Outcome Statements that are S (Simple), M (measurable), A (attainable), R (realistic), and T (timely). (See the previous section for more precise explanations of how to construct SMART goals).

    In addition to using these guidelines, you need to make sure that you are focusing on outcomes that you have some control over, such as how hard you work, or whether or not you maintain a positive mind set. If you focus your "Best Outcome Scenarios" on outcomes that you have little control over, such as getting a raise or getting a certain attractive person you know to ask you out on a date, you will be less likely to achieve success.

    In other words, you will need focus your energies on figuring out the best way that you can behave in order to be successful, vs. trying to outline the best external circumstances that might "happen to you."

2. It is typically more effective to write out your "Best Outcome Scenario" in your own handwriting in a journal versus a file on your computer. This is best because the act of writing down goals by hand has been shown in research to lead to greater achievement of goals than merely typing goals into a computer file.

3. To make this technique even more effective, you might consider handwriting your Best Outcome Statement onto a Post-it note and placing the note either in your desk drawer or right on top of your computer where you can be reminded of it throughout the day. This will help you to keep the best outcome in mind throughout the day and will make it more likely to occur in real life.

4. Another way to make your best outcome more likely to occur in real life is to visualize the outcome happening while you meditate right after you write it down in your journal. There is also a lot of research that supports positive visualization as a tool that helps people to accomplish goals that they can imagine happening on a visual or visceral level.

5. A final tip for clients is to practice writing Best Outcomes on a daily basis and to evaluate which of the outcomes actually happened and which ones did not happen at the end of the week. Did the ones that happened more strictly adhere to a "SMART goal format," or was there something else about the way they were constructed that led to your being more likely to make them happen?

Each person will benefit from different types of Best Outcome Scenarios. By practicing this technique regularly, you will be able to identify the types of Best Outcomes that will work best for you!

3 Journaling Prompts

1. It would really make me feel good if. . .
2. I would be really happy if. . .
3. The best thing that can happen today is that. . .

About the Author

Steevie Jane Parks, PhD is a certified creativity coach, a licensed clinical psychologist, and a visual artist. She lives in Carrboro, North Carolina and provides both individual and group creativity coaching online to clients all over the world. She can best be reached through her website www. steeviejaneparks.com.

The Power of the Weekly Check-in   **8**

Sheryl Garratt

I've always kept a journal, but my weekly check-in is a more recent activity. The journaling check-in is more structured than my usual daily writing, and is surprisingly powerful. It's helped me stay focused, get more done, and have more time to do the things I enjoy.

As a coach working with creatives of all kinds, I've also taught this journaling method to clients, helping them adapt it to their own needs and goals.

I tend to do it on Sunday, when I find it's easier to think and plan. I've come to look forward to that quiet, contemplative hour at the beginning or the end of the day.

Armed with my journal, my calendar, a cup of coffee or a glass of wine, I assess the week just gone, to see what went right, what I've achieved—and what could improve. Then I plan the week ahead, keeping longer-term goals in mind.

You will adapt yours to fit your goals, and the habits you want to track. But here's mine, step by step, as a guide.

First, Celebrate the Wins

As soon as we solve a problem, most of us tend to forget it ever existed. It's easy to forget what you've actually completed, especially when your to-do list never seems to get any shorter. Just taking five minutes to go over your task list and realize how much you have done can be uplifting.

Then, if there are items that have been lingering on your list for a while, assess how important they really are.

- Could you get rid of it or delegate it to someone else?
- Is it relevant to your current goals and priorities?

- Do you need more information, or could you break the task down into smaller, more manageable steps?
- Or are you delaying it because it's difficult or scary?

If it's the latter, put the task on the following week's list as a priority, and make sure it gets done first. The whole week goes better when the hardest thing is already done.

Then Get Down to the Numbers

Just the act of recording your output tends to improve it. Last Saturday, for instance, it was cold and wet outside, and I had a good book to read. But I still went to the gym to do some weight training followed by 30 lengths of the pool, because otherwise I'd have to record, in my check-in, that the only exercise I'd done all week was a long walk.

At the moment, I'm counting the hours I spend on three key work activities: coaching conversations; writing (because I'm a writer, as well as a coach); and marketing. I'm building my mailing list, so I'll count how many new subscribers I have. I'll check my fitness app to see how many steps I've walked, and record any other exercise. And I also track meditation sessions, because I'm trying to get back into the habit of doing that daily.

After recording these figures, I write in my journal for a while, assessing what they *mean*: what worked, what could be improved, what I've learned. Analyzing which list-building activities have been most effective, for instance, has meant I can gradually focus on creating systems for the things that *do* work rather than forever taking new courses and chasing after the latest new tip, trick, or app. Keeping track of meditation has helped me realize that I'm more consistent if I do it first thing, and so I'm now starting to cement that into my morning routine.

Gradually, this tracking has also given me a much better idea of how long it takes to do certain tasks. I'm starting to realize that I never get to the end of my to-do list for the week, because I constantly underestimate how long it takes to get some jobs done. The check-ins have helped me become much more realistic about what to add to my list for the following week.

How Are You Feeding Your Mind?

As part of my weekly check-in, I now keep a note of the films and TV shows I watch, books I'm reading, any performances / art shows / events I've attended, and what I've studied or learned.

It's made me much more deliberate about what I consume. I've always kept lists of books I want to read, but now I also list films, TV dramas and documentaries, talks, podcasts, courses, and so on. This means I'm actively choosing what I want to focus on, rather than listening to a talk because it popped up in my feed, or lying on the sofa with the TV remote in my hand, mindlessly channel hopping.

I'm taking online courses that fit closely with work goals or personal projects rather than just dipping into random webinars. Even my reading has become more deliberate, as the check-ins make me much more aware of upcoming travel and projects, or articles that might be useful to read before a meeting.

How Are You Feeding Your Body?

Menu planning has become another part of my weekly check-in. Knowing what we're eating every day makes it easier to pick up anything we need during the week, use up any leftovers, or know what to get out the freezer the night before.

It has reduced our grocery bills and our food waste dramatically. It's also much easier for the rest of the family to pitch in and take a turn cooking dinner if they know what's on the menu.

It's not rigid. We often switch things around, or change our minds at the last minute. But having a meal plan for the week frees up a lot of mental energy and time. If we order takeaway now, it's because we want to. Not because it's too late to put together a dinner.

How Are You Managing Your Energy?

Before the weekly check-ins, I rarely looked ahead in an organized way. Now I check my work and personal schedules, looking for potential clashes and energy drains—and for opportunities.

If I'm going to be out late with friends, for instance, I might reschedule an 8 AM work call booked in for the following day. If I'm traveling to London for work, I might also plan to do some chores, book tickets for an art show, or arrange to meet up with a friend.

Once these fixed appointments are in place, I block out time for the other things I need to do that week. Batching tasks really helps. You're not wasting energy switching from admin to creative work, phone calls to deep thinking. I try to clear two-hour stretches for uninterrupted writing, if I can. I also make sure I have a weekly "date" scheduled: at least an hour to do something interesting, new, or inspiring, and keep the creative juices flowing.

It's easy to get over-enthusiastic about this, and plan out every minute. But buffers are crucial. We all need space to think and generate new ideas, or simply to deal with whatever life brings. If I have back-to-back meetings, for instance, I'll allow time to walk the scenic way between appointments, or to just sit in a cafe and gather myself. Even on a normal day, there should be space to walk or read, to nap or do some chores.

Are You Staying on Track?

This is where you check your priorities, and make sure you're doing something every week to move towards your goals. It's easy to get pulled off course by events, your in-box, or the demands and priorities of others. Your weekly check-in is a chance to get back to what *you* want to achieve.

I always have clear monthly and quarterly goals for my business. But it's easy to forget them, as I deal with the day-to-day demands of life and work. The weekly check-ins ensure that at least some of the tasks I'm adding to my list are furthering my longer-term intentions.

Who Are You Connecting With?

Finally, I look at connection. I work from home, so it's easy to go weeks without seeing anyone other than my family—especially when I have deadlines. So now I make sure I include reminders to call friends I haven't spoken to in a while, to chat with other coaches or writers, or organize a coffee date or a virtual get-together at least once a week.

I also make lists of new people I'd like to connect with. I then make a point of reaching out to some of them, even if it's just interacting with something they've posted on social media. That has often led, over time, to deeper relationships.

5 Tips for Helping Professionals

1. For clients with creative blocks it helps to commit to a minimum time at their desk, in their studio, doing their work—however badly.

It can also help to keep a log in which they can note what they've achieved, when and how they got into flow.

2. Encourage your clients to find patterns, and create rituals to get them into a flow state more easily. But often simply tracking the time and doing some work every day is enough to get them unstuck and into action again.

3. Make sure clients are building in sufficient time for rest and recuperation.

4. Tracking and journaling on what worked and what could be improved is a great way of establishing new habits, and finding ways to efficiently integrate them with existing habits.

5. Ensure that the check-ins are aligned with the client's values and long-term goals.

5 Tips for Clients and Journal Keepers

1. Track actions, not results. If you want more income, count how many proposals you send out, or the time you spend marketing, not how much you've earned, because the money might not result immediately. If you want to be slimmer and fitter, track exercise, or count how much water you drink or the portions of veggies you eat, not your weight. It really helps to focus on what you *can* control, and build habits that will lead to the results you want.

2. Over time, you'll build up data that helps you see that your weight always increases at a certain point in your monthly cycle (for women), or that there are slack times of year when work just doesn't come in at the same rate. You can plan for this, and enjoy those rhythms and cycles rather than fighting them or getting depressed by them.

3. It's important to look at everything. A few weeks ago, I was surprised how little work I'd done. But going over my calendar, I saw I'd had a day off to celebrate a friend's birthday with a long lunch followed by a brisk country walk. It was a good day. I'd reconnected with old friends, laughed a lot, spent some time in nature, and walked over 20,000 steps. Another day I'd had a medical check-up and while I was in town, I'd also scheduled in a meeting and visited an exhibition I wanted to see. So suddenly the work I *had* done didn't seem so bad at all.

4. Take time, at least once every three months or so, to assess your long-term aims, and adjust what you're tracking accordingly.

5. Once a new habit is established, you might want to stop tracking it. And it's important not to track too much at once. You are human, not a Tamogotchi toy!

3 Journaling Prompts

1. What questions would be useful for you to ask every week?
2. What will you start tracking?
3. What will your key focus be within your unique weekly check-ins?

About the Author

Sheryl Garratt is a writer and a coach helping creatives of all kinds get the success they want, doing work they love. She also enjoys a healthy, balanced life! You can find her at thecreativelife.net.

Mindfulness Writing 9

A Background for Coaches

Beth Jacobs

Most of us have a definite sense that mindfulness is a helpful quality but have only a vague sense of what it actually is, much less how to cultivate it and manifest its power. To understand mindfulness, it is best to look to its roots. The concept was developed in early Buddhism, almost 2,600 years ago. Your impressions of mindfulness, and of Buddhism for that matter, may be that they are ethereal and blissful, but actually early Buddhist work was quite scientific and exacting. The Buddhists systematized and developed mindfulness as a core of the religion's therapeutic and spiritual methodology.

The early Buddhist teaching that lays out the theory of mindfulness is *The Satipatthana Sutra* or *The Foundations of Mindfulness*. This teaching outlines the methods of mindfulness as well as a series of objects of concentration to develop the skill of mindfulness. Mindfulness is described as both a heart and mind activity: it is an ardent, careful, and dispassionate attention to the current moment, centered around a capacity to monitor itself.

The sutra lays out four basic areas of mindfulness content (body, feelings, mind states, and phenomena) and four basic areas of mindfulness monitoring (observing from internal and external views, observing both arising and falling away, observing just enough and not overdoing it, and observing independently or without trying to manipulate what is observed). In the sutra, 40 objects of meditation are taught in these categories, and the meditator works until each object can be held in the mind while balancing the four angles of view. This training is detailed and rigorous.

The point of this intense mindfulness training is to use the skill in service of reducing suffering. A great deal of Buddhist philosophy explains how mindfulness translates into this simple and core Buddhist purpose. In Buddhism, suffering is seen essentially as an inability to perceive and accept plain reality, as an overwrought effort to impose permanence and our own judgments on events.

When we accept that everything changes and our own self is never rigidly defined, we move more easily with what is and base our intentions more solidly. This capacity of awareness and acceptance is trainable. Mindfulness is a quality that is more like cleaning and clearing consciousness than elevating it and the more we remember to return to where we are, the better and easier life feels.

Almost any regular activity can increase mindfulness through repetition and focus. The more we practice specific skills, the more we become aware of the small differences that are highlighted in routine. Writing as a regular practice is an automatic tool of mindfulness. The paper or screen is a model of an accepting and neutral container, unaffected by the content it holds and perfectly reflecting all that is placed in it.

A regular journaling practice and mindfulness reciprocally build each other. More mindfulness leads to richer and deeper writing with a wider range of available techniques. Regular personal writing cultivates and encourages qualities of mindfulness by careful examination and freedom from evaluation.

A few specific aspects of writing as a practice aid mindfulness development. Writing slows down the pace of thought. Even with great keyboard skill, thoughts have to move more slowly to stay within the confines of written production. This gives us a sense of calm and a kind of physical release in writing. We feel the flow of thought more and can immerse in it with some leisure and pleasure.

Writing also forces completion of thoughts in a way that doesn't happen when we think to ourselves or even speak. Our thoughts usually come in fragments and bits and we don't notice how choppy and broken our internal mental world can be. The forced completion, even of a word sometimes but certainly of a phrase, a sentence, or a paragraph, flushes out ideas that can slink to the corner and hide. We get a fuller and more whole sense of internal process through writing and this refines our mindfulness skills.

Writing also synthesizes various modes of experience, including sensory, emotional, spiritual, and cognitive, through the mill of language. Combined with the physical activity of writing, this produces a whole-brain absorption, which cuts down distraction and interference. Like digestion, different aspects of experience are broken down into smaller and mixed pieces that are useful for creative and interactive processes.

Finally, writing automatically allows us to see internal process with dispassion and less clinging. We become more aware of thoughts as mental objects, as our productions and not as us ourselves. The thoughts laid before us in our writing are both ours and outside of us. The neutralization and perspective-building processes that are a part of mindfulness are increased by this distancing. Today's urgent feeling can disperse and yesterday's emergency might be forgotten. Writing holds the awareness of how much awareness can shift.

Because writing is such a good match with mindfulness building, a coach can always include it as part of a protocol of self-improvement. If a person has a regular writing practice, mindfulness can be introduced as a concept and developed by focusing on increasingly refined topics and manners of observation.

Writing can bring mindfulness to specific problem areas or areas of striving. For instance, a five-minute writing requirement before an anticipated obsessive behavior can lead to interruption of the behavior and increased awareness of its triggers through a deeper attunement to internal process. Another example might be a daily list of personal goals. This assessment over time brings the vision of improvement front and center and also illustrates its flexibility and the fact that we are often aiming for moving targets.

Specific writing techniques highlight aspects of the qualities of mindfulness. These can be used if clients seem to draw blanks when trying to develop a capacity to observe internal states or to forego evaluation of them. By demonstrating and developing these qualities in written exercises, the qualities take hold and start to bloom in other settings.

A first technique is a way to separate process from content. A focus on process leaves room for adaptation without getting stuck on the content. To experiment with this, you might have your client do a freewrite on their current state for two minutes. A freewrite relies on the physical momentum of writing and you ask the writer to just keep the writing moving and not to let it stop. A freewrite foregoes evaluation of everything, from legibility and spelling to good manners or even kindness. Just let the writing flow.

After doing this freewrite you can alter the process of writing with a prescribed focus and do a few more. One focus is to shift to the visual and write for two minutes completely watching the writing evolve, either at the nib of a pen, tip of a pencil, or fingertips on a keyboard. Have the writer continue to write freely but watch it carefully. Next, the writer can focus on auditory perception by either speaking aloud as they write if they are in a private setting or listening to the words inside their head as they pour out on the page.

Other ideas might be to write while focusing on the breath or the temperature of the air on the face, and you can tailor ideas to your clients' learning and sensory styles. Early Buddhists were very interested in the powers of sensory perception and by using these ideas, you can help a client experience the simple fact that a different focus produces a different event and that focus can be manipulated.

Another writing technique emphasizes what is called "a choiceless object" in Buddhism. This means that we can notice what is inside our minds without picking and choosing, just allowing whatever arises. In this technique, meditation is modified to try and capture raw observations. You can have your client sit quietly in any form of meditation with a journal, a pad of paper, or a keyboard on their lap.

If they don't have a particular meditation practice, just have them focus very simply on breathing, on following the in and out of the air they breathe. As the mind settles, ask them to jot down one word or a short phrase capturing a particular thought or sensation that arises. Then they repeat with another line, when something else catches their attention to the point of being defined. Stay with this for about two or three minutes. This exercise allows the process of experience to be literally noted without judgment and that can be a powerful mindfulness demonstration.

One other important Buddhist principle about mindfulness will help the coach and writer. Cultivating mindfulness often means working to eliminate its blockages. Writing explores and releases negative feelings and evaluations of the self that carry us away from the current moment. Staying in the present is mostly about not regretting the past or fearing the future while we are here. If problems are getting in the way of mindfulness, then turn to the problems using the power of written expression. Mindfulness does not mean never having bad feelings, life problems, and useless old patterns, because those are all part of being human. Mindfulness means seeing these as they arise and viewing them as the arena of our work, not what carries us away from the beauty of the present moment.

5 Tips for Helping Professionals

1. Mindfulness is not a magic quality but a skill that can be developed over time.
2. Help clients understand that the heart of mindfulness is a dispassionate global awareness in the midst of the mindfulness process.
3. Writing and mindfulness can augment and build each other.

4. Encourage clients to do something regular but not too rigorous with writing, so that they can see how their mindfulness processes grow.
5. Tailor different writing techniques to reduce particular deficits in your clients' capacities for mindfulness, such as distractibility or negative self-evaluation.

 5 Tips for Clients and Journal Keepers

1. Find an easy way to journal and do it regularly, so that you can see what is different within the framework of repetition.
2. Think of your journal page or screen as a blank witness of your process, catching everything, changing nothing, with neither reaction nor evaluation.
3. In your regular practice, also experiment with different writing techniques. If you write with flowing grammar, try lists. If you write pages and pages of feelings, try an analytic flowchart of your situation. Different forms of writing develop different mind skills.
4. Mindfulness is not about remembering the past but remembering to come back to the present. Give yourself a cue that reminds you to refocus where you are in your body and senses in the moment. Periodically write down what you are experiencing physically.
5. Don't try to make your writing good, your thinking clear, or your feelings pretty. Just try to let "what is" be expressed fully.

 3 Journaling Prompts

1. Write one sentence about how you feel about something in the past, one sentence about how you feel about something coming up in the future, and one sentence about how you feel about the present moment. Consider how those three feelings are actually all present feelings when you write about them.
2. How would you define mindfulness? How does your own idea of mindfulness contribute to an ongoing sense of well-being?

3. List five things that you can focus on that actually stop you from thinking, such as sensory experience, engrossing activities or healthy distractions. Keep one available if you notice that you are spinning out into unproductive thought.

 ## About the Author

Beth Jacobs, PhD, is a writer, clinical psychologist in private practice and transmitted lay teacher in the Soto Zen Buddhist lineage. She is the author of *Writing for Emotional Balance*, *Paper Sky*, *The Original Buddhist Psychology*, *A Buddhist Journal*, and *Long Shadows of Practice: Poems*. She facilitates expressive writing groups for children, teenagers, and grandparents.

Patricia's Bold Journey From Confusion to Clarity Through Journaling

10

Coleen Chandler

Patricia's tone was somber and her voice flat on the phone.

> Coleen, I am a mess. I'm scattered, tired, bored. I can't seem to muster up any energy to move forward. I have no vision, my goals don't excite me, my relationship is on its last leg, and my children tell me I'm no fun to be around. Even my work, which I love . . . I feel I've plateaued. I am not developing any new business and nothing gets done unless it's an emergency, so I'm constantly stressed. Oh, and I hate my body. I've gained weight, I'm out of shape. It seems like every part of my life is falling apart and I have no clue what to do. I am so confused and I feel I am driving in thick fog with no lights on. It scares the heck out of me.

There was a long silence.

"Well," I said, taking a deep breath, "Welcome to coaching, Patricia. What can I do for you?"

She burst out laughing, and so did I. "My friend told me you were funny. It feels good to laugh. But, really, I'm a mess, aren't I? Can you help me? I'm desperate for some clarity. Where do I start?"

I enjoy clients like Patricia, eager for solutions and willing to try new things. They come to coaching with so many challenges, on so many levels. They are typically bright, successful, educated, creative, and most likely high achievers who demand a lot of themselves and those around them. They've often been stuffing their emotions for years and can be unaware of their impact on others. Ah, yes, where to start?

After years of coaching creative high achievers, I have discovered that pure process coaching is slow going *at first* for this clientele, even downright frustrating, as they feel they need concrete actions to move forward. Focusing on their internal experience of what is happening at the moment is a skill they may have not developed yet, and it may sour them on coaching. Patricia was no exception. She had tried a couple of coaches and quit.

On the other hand, buying into their "I want it fixed and I want it fixed now" approach is counterproductive as well—a short-term fix that does not provide the deep transformation they are yearning for.

How to unravel this tangled ball of yarn? With a powerful ally—one of my favorite action-oriented coaching tools—journaling.

I introduced the concept to Patricia. She was not impressed ("Not for me, too woo-woo, no time") but she said she would give it a try for a few days. It took more than a few days. She tried and stopped many times. She felt she was wasting her limited time writing about inconsequential things. What was the point? Nothing exciting was happening in her life, she pointed out. If anything, journaling was reinforcing her conviction that her life was at a dead end and that was depressing her.

"Why don't you write about that?" I suggested.

"It feels weird writing intimate stuff on a piece of paper . . . it's so indulgent."

I proposed that she imagine herself writing to a loving friend or a trusted confidant. What would she want to share with that person? She chose to write to me.

A week later, she had her first breakthrough:

> *Why am I so scared of writing down my thoughts? Come to think of it, why am I so scared of sharing my thoughts? I don't remember the last time I talked about me, what I really feel, who I am, what I would like. I don't remember anyone asking me either. I give, give, give, take care of the household, make sure everyone is okay and has what they need. In between, I go to my office, close the door and work. I've done that for 14 years, every day, EVERY FREAKING DAY! And for what? God, I'm pissed.*

She read me this paragraph two times, choked up. She had just discovered two of the greatest gifts of journaling. One, it's a safe space to lay down one's thoughts. Two, thoughts become tangible—fully formed and independent sentences, extracted like gems from our confused minds. These thoughts do not fly away or churn endlessly; they are transformed into words that can be read, shared, and reflected on at a later date.

"That's powerful, Coleen."

Her surprise was genuine. "I just realize I wrote down what I'm not able to say aloud."

We stayed silent for a few seconds.

"My words. . . . They are so . . . angry," she sighed.

Over the next few weeks, Patricia's writings became more open as she became more vulnerable. Using her own words, I helped her explore and clarify her emotions and—her favorite—we worked on separating truth from fiction. Who was she, really? What did she truly want?

One morning, she sent me the excerpt that she wanted to be coached on:

> I've built walls around me, a fortress. It's tall, thick, impenetrable. I am the only one who has the key to the gate. I feel safe inside but I am so lonely. There are no windows, no light, no sun pouring in to warm the rooms. I think Robert does not love me anymore . . . or is it me who does not love him anymore? I don't know that I loved him when we got married. I think I was flattered that he asked me to marry him. Is my Yes 16 years ago still a Yes today?

The last question became our coaching focus for a few sessions. As she continued to pour her heart into her journal and do her coaching homework, she came to the conclusion that it had been a long time since she had been happy with Robert. It was a sad revelation. They eventually talked and came to the painful but mutually agreed upon conclusion that the relationship was over.

From that moment on, she journaled on each part of her life (family, spirituality, health, finances, her business, leisure, and more) using the image of various rooms in her fortress to represent each aspect of her life. My role was to be the flashlight that would guide her whenever she felt scared or stuck, and encourage her imagination to take her to unknown places.

By now, journaling had become a habit and I'd receive several days' entries every five days or so. Patricia was creating a new life for herself and reflecting on every bit of progress, every setback, and every aha moment. Her writings went deeper and became bolder and wiser each passing week. Her creativity and trust in herself flourished.

After a few months, I introduced Patricia to the notion of free flow journaling—to no longer have a direction while journaling but to simply let it rip, and whatever comes, comes. She took to it like a fish in water.

One year into our coaching, Patricia wrote:

> *I am in awe of the power of journaling. It has become a daily ritual where I talk to my sacred source and to my confidante. It's my safe space and though I am now living alone, I am not lonely anymore. I am learning the language of emotions, which gives me the courage to share my thoughts with others and make new friends. Most importantly, the fog has lifted. My fortress has become a welcoming hostel with cushy sofas, large windows and warm, bright colors. I walk outside and I see the sky, the trees and the long winding road that invites me to explore. This journey has been life changing.*

5 Tips for Helping Professionals

1. Don't give up on your clients if journaling does not seem to catch at first. Point to the smallest progress: a few lines of daily writing in a row, a tiny opening in self-reflection, or a catchy image (the fortress). This is the time to go to bat for your clients, especially if you believe journaling works. Colluding with your clients in their resistance is taking away their chance to discover this empowering practice.
2. Help them connect to their journal. Make it personal. Ask them to write to someone they trust and encourage them to send their new pages at least once a week. They usually write to me and that's fine. It focuses their writing and mirrors back that someone values their efforts.
3. Provide guidance. At the beginning of the coaching relationship, when clients are still tentative about journaling, ask them what they would like to journal about. Give them a few ideas if they are stuck and ask them to choose. It provides them with agency and direction. Later on, when they trust the process, introduce them to free flow journaling.
4. Journaling is not a substitute for excellent coaching. Use the journal as a window to insights, while diligently being curious about what's around and under their writings.
5. Encourage your clients to finish every journaling session with a super positive statement about what they wish for their day. If they journal in the evening, have them end with a statement of gratitude, no matter what their day was like. Here is an example from Patricia who,

while going through the most turbulent time of her life, ended every morning session with, "I wish myself a day of joy, lightness, hope, trust and harmony."

5 Tips for Clients and Journal Keepers

1. Don't stress if you did not journal today. No journaling patrol will give you a ticket. Relax and trust that you will get back to it tomorrow and set a reminder to do so.
2. Journal according to your circadian rhythm. Everyone has a preferred moment to journal in a 24-hour period. Learn yours and create a ritual around that time. This will help with consistency.
3. Be gentle and compassionate toward your writing. Your words are your authentic expression of the moment—let them flow however they choose to come out.
4. Find five creative ways to journal other than writing on your page, like drawing your emotions, sticking colored Post-its with various words or ideas, etc.
5. Celebrate your journaling successes with friends. Your successes deserve air time and you deserve the boost of endorphins.

3 Journaling Prompts

1. When I give myself the gift of unconditional love. . .
2. Today, I will practice being vulnerable by. . . (The client can substitute words like creative, adventurous, sexy, etc. for vulnerable)
3. What is the one courageous action I will take today and why?

About the Author

Coleen Chandler, PCC, CPCC, is an internationally accomplished creativity and success coach who coaches leaders, creatives, and entrepreneurs out of confusion and overwhelm, into a path of clarity, creativity, and mindful achievements. She's passionate about the creative mind and the intersection between the arts and business, believing that both thrive when synergistically linked. She offers programs on The Art of Mindful Leadership, Mastering the Stage, The High-Performance Life, and The Creative Mind at Work. Coleen is a Professional Certified Coach (PCC) through the International Coaching Federation (ICF) and currently serves as the Credentialing Director of the Sacramento Chapter of the ICF. She would love to hear from you at coleen@coleenchandler.com.

The Conflict Coaching Road Map for Journaling **11**

Linda Dobson

It's difficult to experience our powerful reactions to conflict—the intensity of anger, the overwhelm of sadness, the vulnerability of loneliness. When we feel disconnected from those important to us, whether the betrayal of a friend, misinterpretation of a family member, or comments from a dismissive colleague, we experience the acute impact of conflict.

By the same token, when we find a path that will help us gain greater awareness of the situation and secure relevant resolutions, we restore our sense of well-being. The Conflict Coaching Road Map for Journaling provides that path. It consists of four phases, Preparation, Focus, Discovery, and Action, that serve as bearing points on the journey to resolution. In what follows, you will learn a useful process and encounter powerful questions that have helped thousands of people find authentic, workable resolutions.

Before diving into the Conflict Coaching Road Map for Journaling, let me introduce you to Megan, a self-described "mess." Megan's 25-year marriage was ending, and she knew family and friends were growing tired of listening to her stories. Megan also knew that she had to address the conflict with her husband, which was very brave of her!

Megan and I used CCRMJ in a hybrid method, combining coaching conversations with her "fieldwork" of personal journaling. Megan's first opportunity to use the CCRMJ as a journaling tool occurred when she and her husband were meeting to talk about dividing their assets. This was the first time they had seen each other in months and Megan feared her chaotic feelings would sabotage her desire to speak clearly and listen carefully, compromising their, and their children's, future relationship.

To prepare herself for this encounter, Megan focused her journal writing on the CCRMJ's four steps.

Step 1. She examined her beliefs about conflict and became aware that her conflict style accommodated the needs of others before her own.

Step 2. After several attempts, she could write a vision that worked for her and then developed goals that would support her vision.

Step 3. As Megan journaled about what was important to her, she understood why some topics were more significant, while others decreased in emphasis.

Step 4. As Megan reviewed her entries, she developed solutions that would meet her needs. She could even consider her husband's potential responses and needs. Megan examined how to communicate her needs in a way that was consistent with her values.

How did it work? Megan reported that although there were triggers and tears, they did not distract her. She exercised compassion and thoughtfulness (strong identified values) and accurately and assertively asked for what she needed. Journaling with the CCRMJ framework resulted in her feeling more prepared and confident.

Conflict Coaching Road Map: The Four Phases

Phase 1. Preparation

This phase examines two key questions: how we "see" conflict and how we behave when we face challenging disagreements.

How do you see conflict? The phrase "What we think is what we do" addresses how thoughts influence how we approach conflict. For many of us, we learned conflict strategies from our families (few of whom had opportunities to study effective communication, especially during conflicts!). Role models might have been Aunt Martha, who didn't talk to Uncle Steve for decades, or Uncle Ken, who would shout his views until all were subdued. And then there was Gramma—she just stayed silent.

During the preparation phase, you journal your beliefs about conflict from the perspective of the wise, competent person you are, leaving behind that scared little kid of yore. When we take time to reflect upon how we have managed conflict in our lives, using our life experiences and personal strengths, we find that our perceptions about conflict have changed.

How do you respond to conflict? Ron Kraybill, creator of the Style Matters Conflict Style Inventory, suggests that there are five primary conflict responses: Directing, Avoiding, Harmonizing, Compromising, or Cooperating. Directing is task-oriented, while harmonizing is more relationship-oriented. Avoiding is . . . you guessed it, not engaged. Cooperating focuses on task and relationships, and compromising gives a little to get a little. The CCRMJ provides an opportunity to examine our conflict styles. As we journal, we can watch for language or phrases that illustrate our conflict style and decide if that style is the best fit for this conflict.

Journal Prompts for the Preparation Phase

- How would I like to redefine conflict from the viewpoint of the competent person I am today?
- What is my general conflict style? Do I get directive and task-focused when I am threatened by differences? Do I avoid talking about challenging issues? Do I harmonize and give up my needs to ensure peace at all costs, or am I intent on cooperatively talking things through? Is my style to "give and take" and seek compromises in conflictual situations?
- What conflict style have I been using in this conflict and is it the best choice for this situation?

Phase 2. Focus

The Focus phase highlights two key tasks: constructing a positive vision of the preferred outcome and establishing clear goals. Having a powerful vision and establishing strategic goals concentrates attention on the points pivotal to your resolution.

Vision: "If you know where you're going, you will get there." When emotions are high, it is easy to get stuck thinking about what you DON'T want to happen, and difficult to determine what you DO want to create. When visioning your preferred future, put on your imagination hat! What could resolution look like for you?

Journal Prompts for Focusing on Your Vision

- What would I like to achieve by resolving this conflict? What would a satisfactory resolution look like?
- If I had a magic wand and could create resolution, what would I do? How would I feel? What would I see? What would I hear?
- If I resolved this conflict, how would walking into the office (or home, or meetings) be different?

The second task in the Focus phase directs you to goals, the steppingstones for achieving your vision. Big, audacious goals (BAGs) stretch us to accomplish a dream, and small, achievable goals (SAGs), nudge us toward solutions. Well-written goals capture the hoped-for resolution in clear, behavioral terms. For example, instead of writing your goal as "talk about money" you might change it to describing specific behaviors, say, "To design a strategy that will meet our financial needs."

Journal Prompts for Creating Goals

- What goals do you need to address to achieve your vision?
- What is a BAG—a big, audacious goal that would resolve these differences? What is a SAG—a small, achievable goal?

Phase 3. Discovery

Discovery requires you to get intensely curious about your conflict—your responses, thoughts, feelings, assumptions, and triggers. Think of embodying Sherlock Holmes as you probe "What is happening and why?". This phase also surveys your values, acknowledging where and how values were compromised, and deciding which ones strengthen your creativity and resilience.

Journal Prompts for Discovery Phase

- What is important about this topic, and why is it important? (You can ask yourself this many times to deepen your understanding)
- What strengths do you bring to your resolution process? How will they show up?
- What values support you to be your best self as you seek resolution strategies?
- When you get triggered, what can you do to manage the trigger?

Phase 4. Action

"The only impossible journey is the one you never begin."
Tony Robbins

Action is the phase you've been waiting for: the time to write options and actions for resolving the dispute based on your thorough understanding of the needs, hopes, and vision of your best self.

Take a moment to review your journaling and become an "objective observer" of your conflict. Note changes in perspective, what you have learned about your thoughts and feelings, and where you have made assumptions.

Completing your review, assess and decide on straightforward actions that involve slight changes that will make a big difference in the conflict. Look further down and be sure to answer the last questions to reinforce your commitment to change.

Journal Prompts for Action

- Given your new insights, what stands out for you as ways to create action?
- How do your actions align with your values?
- What will you do?
- When will you do it?
- What will sustain your decision?
- How will you know if you are successful?

5 Tips for Helping Professionals

1. Never ask someone to do something you wouldn't do yourself.
2. Explore your own relationship with conflict, asking, "Do I think conflict is destructive or constructive?" and "Do I move away from it or do I approach it?"
3. What is your conflict style and how does it influence your questions or responses to client conflicts?
4. Conflict is a normal and natural part of our lives. Learn as much as you can about how to negotiate in a value-based way.
5. Know that your clients are creative and resourceful, even if they forget that they are.

5 Tips for Clients and Journal Keepers

1. Write your strengths and ask how they will serve you as you try to resolve your conflict.

2. If you could resolve this conflict, how would you approach your day tomorrow? What would be different?
3. Imagine that you have a good relationship with the person. What actions will have changed?
4. What are the values that will help you find a resolution that makes sense for you?
5. You are creative, resourceful, and whole. How would you like to embody that statement?

3 Journaling Prompts

1. Review the Conflict Coaching Road Map for Journaling. Which phase is most important for you to write about?
2. If you could resolve this conflict, what would your morning feel like tomorrow?
3. How would you like to hold space to feel or think all your thoughts about your current conflict?

About the Author

Linda Dobson, MA ABSc, MCC, is an executive coach, and has been mediating and conflict coaching for over two decades. She is passionate about changing our perspectives about conflict from fear and avoidance to . . . drum roll . . . creative opportunity to learn, grow, and expand what is possible. She established the award-winning "Conflict Coaching" program at the Justice Institute of BC and her teaching takes her from JIBC and University of Calgary, to Mumbai, India (master's in Mediation and Conflict Resolution) and Uganda (Peace Keeping and Reconciliation). Linda is completing her book *The Conflict Coaching Road Map* due 2021. You can reach Linda at lindadobson1@gmail.com or www.coachtheconflict.com.

Ideal Conversations 12

Kim Ades

As president and founder of an executive and leadership coaching company since 2004, my team and I have been coaching business owners, executives, and highly driven leaders to look closely at their thoughts and beliefs in order to understand how and why their behaviors lead to the results they are generating.

As a central part of this coaching process, we ask our clients to journal online with their coach daily. At the beginning of the week they receive a journaling prompt designed to trigger a flood of journaling. On a daily basis, their coach reads and responds to their journal with questions, inquiries, and comments, often igniting a back-and-forth dialogue exploring and unveiling their deeper values, beliefs, perspectives, and priorities. This leads to a very intense, intimate, and powerful coaching experience that creates a transformational impact for our clients.

At approximately week nine in the coaching process, they receive the following prompt:

Your Ideal Conversations

This is the week that you get to write and design the conversations that you want to have in your ideal life.

Each day choose a different person in your life to have a new conversation with (the person does not have to still be living). You can pick anyone who has had any degree of impact in your life—from the very significant to the more minor. It can even be with a person who has not yet crossed your path (like a new client, or a new life partner, or a new friend) and it can be with a group of people or someone famous. You can even go back and rewrite a conversation that you have already had but would like to design differently.

Write it as though you were writing the dialogue in a play. The most important part of this exercise is to create a conversation that is ideal for you.

The Surprising Discovery

When I first started using this prompt in the coaching process, my expectation was to gain specific insight to help our clients create a set of poignant and personal goals for the future. I was stunned to find that this prompt revealed so much more.

One of the first memories I have of the Ideal Conversation assignment is of a client who chose to write a conversation between herself and the Obama Administration. In this conversation, she was applying for the position of Secretary of State and she decided to script out the interview. It went something like this:

Obama Admin: Thank you so much for submitting your application for this position. We've seen a lot of candidates and we are very excited about your application. Tell us in your own words, what qualifies you for this position?

My client continued the dialogue with five long paragraphs describing her qualifications. She wrote about her cultural background and family history. She shared the story of how her parents immigrated to the United States and started a business and contributed to the local economy. She spoke about her education and work experience. She explained her personal values and ethics. And she continued with an elaborate description of all the initiatives that she would implement if she were to be chosen for the role of Secretary of State.

Obama Admin: My goodness! You are certainly more than qualified for this position and at this point, you are unequivocally our top candidate. As soon as we have completed all of our interviews we will reach out with the results.

At the bottom of her journal, she wrote me a personal note: "How's THAT for DREAMING BIG???"

Certainly, applying for the position of Secretary of State is a big dream. However, what kind of big dream ends with *"As soon as we have completed all of our interviews we will reach out with the results"*? In her Ideal Conversation, she created a situation with a less-than-ideal outcome. She still had to wait for the interviewers to screen all the remaining candidates before giving her the job. Why would someone create a situation like this? What was really at play?

Upon deeper investigation, what we discovered was that this client, who also happened to lead the digital marketing efforts for a large-sized company, often handed over final decision-making power to others. This showed up in her relationships with her coworkers, her communication with potential clients, and even in her relationships with friends and significant others. This was a pattern about which she was unaware.

Why did this happen? Because she believed that she did not have the authority to make decisions on her own and because she believed that taking the initiative to make decisions independently was disrespectful to others. Imagine being a leader without the confidence to make decisions. This was a serious hindrance to her leadership effectiveness, not to mention a source of stress in her personal relationships.

Once she understood how far-reaching this pattern was and how many areas of her life it affected, she was open to challenging some of the beliefs that interfered with her ability to make decisions for the company and for herself. This was a game-changing discovery.

A More Ideal Outcome

I have often thought about how this story could have turned out if I were writing the script:

Obama Admin: (calls me on the phone) Hello? Is this Kim Ades?

Me: Yes, it is!

Obama Admin: It's Brian White from the Obama Administration, we met a few weeks ago when you came in for an interview. . . .

Me: Yes! Of course!

Obama Admin: I just wanted to let you know that we've interviewed all the candidates and there is no question that you were by far the most qualified candidate for the role of Secretary of State. So—I am excited to let you know that you have been granted the position. However, before you begin, we'd like to send you and six of your closest friends on an all-inclusive paid trip to Italy!

Remarkably. . .

Looking back on nearly 20 years of coaching, it turns out that the way my client concluded her Ideal Conversation was not an isolated incident. I estimate that 95% of my clients have scripted an Ideal Conversation with either a less-than-ideal outcome or a dialogue laden with beliefs that were heavily grounded in "reality," limitation, or restriction. While this exercise seems to offer a blue-sky journaling opportunity, what it often reveals are the current-day struggles that individuals continue to carry with them that have strong implications in many key areas of their lives.

Another Interesting Development

Another client wrote a dialogue with Judge Clarence Thomas (JCT). My client "asked" JCT for his opinion and guidance regarding his career. JCT responded brilliantly and offered my client a great deal of insight. JCT's words of wisdom were written by my client. Inside of him lived a great amount of clarity and perception that was only accessible to him when he stepped into the shoes of someone that he considered to be valiant. He saw this quality in others but did not realize that he too had this quality in abundance. It's funny how sometimes our strengths and abilities are hidden to us until we are asked to speak in someone else's voice.

5 Tips for Helping Professionals

1. Ask your client to journal about an Ideal Conversation, situation, or circumstance.
2. Look for words, perspectives, emotions, and storylines that are even slightly less than ideal.
3. Ask your client what makes their Ideal Conversation ideal. Look for the instances where your client describes things, people, or situations as "realistic." For example, I have often heard clients say something like: "Realistically he will never apologize."
4. Identify the beliefs that compel the client to be realistic about their ideal situation—and challenge them. Explore other areas where these beliefs might come into play for your client and might cause pain or struggle.
5. Remind the client that the exercise was to write an Ideal Conversation—and share that ideal outcomes can never happen if they cannot be conceived. Ask your client to try again by writing another Ideal Conversation. Once they get the hang of imagining ideal scenarios, this practice can be as powerful as keeping a gratitude journal.

5 Tips for Journal Keepers

1. Identify a person with whom you would love to have a conversation.
2. Give some thought to why you want to have that conversation. To heal a past relationship? To achieve a lifelong dream? To acquire some knowledge or wisdom from the individual?
3. Determine the goal of the conversation—what do you want to walk away with at the end of the conversation?
4. Think about how you want to feel at the end of the conversation—peaceful, inspired, excited, proud. . .?
5. As you script the conversation, notice if you feel discomfort when you write something that feels "unrealistic"—this is precisely where your limiting beliefs exist. Explore these feelings further by journaling about these beliefs and challenging them (and yourself) in your journal.

 3 Journaling Prompts

Journaling Prompts for Ideal Conversations:
1. If you could have a conversation with anyone in the world, who would you choose and why? What would you discuss?
2. If someone could grant you an extraordinary wish—who would that wish come from and what would it be?
3. Is there a conversation that you've had in the past that you would love to redo? How would it sound now if it unfolded in an ideal manner?

 About the Author

Kim Ades (pronounced add-iss) is the president and founder of Frame of Mind Coaching™ and JournalEngine™ software. Recognized as an expert in the area of thought mastery and mental toughness, Kim uses her unique philosophy and quirky coaching style to help business owners and leaders identify their personal blind spots and shift their thinking in order to yield extraordinary results. Author, speaker, entrepreneur, coach, and mom of five, Kim teaches her powerful Frame of Mind Coaching™ process to leaders, coaches, parents, and influencers worldwide using journaling as the foundation of her process. You can learn more about Kim's work at: www.frameofmind coaching.com.

Journaling for Mental Health and Wellness

Creative Journaling for Self-Care

13

Nicolle Nattrass

Journaling and cake. I love both and if I had to give one up, it would undoubtedly be cake. That truly testifies to how much I believe in the power of journaling to transform and improve mental health and wellness.

From the very first journal I ever began, the "Dear Diary . . ." that came with the adorable key, journaling was a soft place for me to land. I could listen to myself, put pen to paper and say, "I matter, my feelings and thoughts matter."

Journal writing came easily because I enjoyed writing and in Grade 9, I actually won a Creative Writing Award. I enthusiastically embraced writing as an imaginative, creative outlet. It was a way to sort out my own emotional and mental states. Therefore, you may be surprised to hear that journaling does not come easily to the majority of clients and journal keepers that I work with. Truly, this surprise became the biggest influence in my work as a counselor and workshop facilitator, working on the frontline as an addiction counselor in a 21-day residential treatment center for women and men from 15–99 years old.

I very much admire this group of clients who were often in the throes of detox, facing recovery from drug and alcohol addiction as well as suffering complex trauma. For most of these clients, journal writing was challenging and I learned very early on that I could not make any "assumptions" that it should be easy. In fact, making any assumptions while working with clients is detrimental.

The process of connecting to self through journaling is complex and can elicit many different reactions. As a coach, when working alongside first-time clients or journal keepers, it is not unusual to hear, "I can't write," "I hate writing," "I am not creative," "I haven't written since Grade 5," and "Someone read my journal, no way I am going to let that happen again."

It is a common experience for clients and journal keepers when starting to journal to be faced with negative self-talk, perfectionism, criticism, creative blocks, and possible triggers from school.

Journaling for mental health and wellness can be a powerful tool for healing for clients and journal keepers, as it is a window into our relationship with self. In my work, my primary purpose is to embody a trauma-informed lens in order to create and support an atmosphere of safety, trust, and respect. I create a soft place for clients to land.

Within a treatment center or institution-type setting, maintaining safety, trust, and stability for clients is key. The role of the facilitator/counselor in this setting requires not only organizational preparation, such as gathering materials (being mindful that certain materials may not be allowed, for example, scissors or felt pens) but also requires mental preparation to be grounded and fully flexible. You, as a facilitator, should be prepared for anything to show up in the room. In most instances, I am not given any knowledge of those attending, other than certain vital issues that might be present.

Rather than using a directive instructional approach, I have discovered that this environment calls for an open, invitational style which is more likely to engage in participation. The former can trigger authority issues, shutting down, fear, and/or further resistance. At times, there can be a great deal of tension. The priority is to hold a nonjudgmental space, listen, and be present to support the client's feeling of ease, trust, and sense of security. Modeling a calm, welcoming demeanor establishes rapport and encourages engagement, whereas moving too quickly into directives may not be suitable.

To begin a session, I like to give a brief overview of what the group can expect, including talking about what the group experience will NOT be. This can help to alleviate initial fears and set clear guidelines. For example, I remove any expectation that there will be reading or sharing of journal entries and give the option to stop journal writing at any time. Rather than sharing their journal entries, clients are encouraged to share direct feedback about what the experience of writing is like for them. The emphasis is on process, not product.

In my *Creative Journaling for Self-Care* program, the focus is on creative freedom. There are no rules and no right or wrong in terms of expression on the page. Whatever shows up on the page in whatever medium, whether pen, pencil, felt, stickers, images, crayons, leaves, etc., is enough. Drawing and doodling can replace writing. Whatever form helps the client to connect with self is welcome.

For example, at one workshop focused on health and wellness, a client felt embarrassed and frustrated because she wanted to journal. But whenever she picked up a pen, she would experience painful numbness in her hand. She described it as freezing up and she was able to connect her current experience to a past experience when she'd been forced to stay after school to write lines to improve her handwriting.

Another client I worked with could not pick up a pen in a workshop setting, as she had been traumatized in residential school by her fingers being slapped by a ruler. The journal writing triggered further memories of physical abuse that she had endured as a child.

For those who face barriers using pen/paper, I offer flexible activities, for example, using smaller-sized paper, index cards to reduce blank space, writing with pencil which allows erasing, playing with words on the page, doodling or drawing in response to a writing prompt, or creating a collage using images or stickers.

This work can prove uncomfortable, raw, and, at times, unsettling for those who have trauma directly related to self-expression or writing. The experiences I witnessed as I worked with clients led me to believe that there was a need for a more "tender-hearted approach" with clients as they explored their creative self-care. This approach encourages a nurturing atmosphere and empowers the client to better self-regulate by offering a variety of alternative options, opportunities to opt out and make choices that support their autonomy.

Clients are encouraged to become conscious and/or curious about imposing rules about "right" and "wrong" on themselves as they explore. I often remind them that journaling for self-care is about finding what works for you. I use this example: if you want to buy a new car, chances are you are going to try out a few models to see what's a good fit. Similarly, finding your style and process takes time and a trial-and-error approach.

Working with groups of clients, there are sure to be many different learning styles present. Particularly with clients in treatment centers and institutional settings, I have discovered that giving frequent breaks and adjusting the pace by shortening exercises makes the information more digestible. My goal is to address as many different learning styles as possible so as to increase client engagement. For example, we might start with a short discussion, then move to a short two-sentence writing exercise, then read together a few pages from my workbook *Creative Journaling: The Promises of Recovery*, and then move on to a hands-on activity.

I put out a variety of journals of different sizes and colors, some lined and some blank, and give the clients time to choose their own. I have discovered that having a table nearby with an abundance of creative materials, like images, stickers, and decorations that they can use to personalize their journal, is useful. These materials increase interest and boost motivation, as well as giving clients the opportunity to interact and communicate.

This engages the senses, promotes discussion of likes and dislikes, and opens a pathway for creative flow. A sense of play emerges that allows hope and connectivity to enter. Time spent doing this can vary from 15 to 30 minutes. The results of this activity have surprised me time and time again, as I witness clients who are experiencing a great deal of reluctance or hesitation towards journaling relax and settle in. This is often a turning point that frees the client to risk and invest in their own process of self-exploration. Incorporating creativity of this sort can activate the journaling process in a way that engages clients and journal keepers more fully in their own creative alchemy.

I am grateful to have the opportunity to work with such a beautiful variety of clients and settings. I want to emphasize that journaling for my own self-care, both professionally and artistically, has given me rich insight into understanding and empathizing with clients. It may seem simple but it is crucial to treat a client's journaling process with the same care that I treat my own.

5 Tips for Helping Professionals

1. Review Thomas M. Skovholt's "Cycle of Caring," where a self-care process for coaches, counselors, and other helping professionals is clearly defined. Practicing your own self-care is paramount.
2. Keep in mind that creativity is a powerful antidote for stress. Encourage clients to get creative in their journals.
3. Use your journal to dialogue with yourself after a day of work or after a particularly insightful or challenging session with a client.
4. Explore the following exercise: write a letter to yourself that you do not send and that honors closure. For example, if there is a client that you wish you could have spent more time with, take a few minutes to describe what you learned from the experience and what you wish for the client.
5. Be mindful of the dynamics of the client group you are working with, be flexible, tune in, and adjust your own delivery to what works best for them.

5 Tips for Clients and Journal Keepers

1. Take the time to make your journal your own, personalize it through decorating it with stickers or your initials or something else meaningful to you. Let it be aesthetically pleasing to you, choose the type of paper you love to write on, choose what makes you feel good and makes you smile. The more you enjoy it, the more you will want to spend time and write in it.
2. Use index cards to write affirmations that you can paste into your journal or dedicate pages in your journal for positive messages. Have fun with it!
3. Find a special spot in your home to journal, a soft place for you to land. Create a nurturing space and add a favorite chair or photograph.
4. Need writing prompts? Google a writing prompt around a theme, print those prompts off, cut them into individual strips, place in jar, and *voilà!* Makes a great gift!
5. A busy schedule? Take a moment to write down one word in your journal. At the end of your day, go back to that word and reflect on it with writing or doodling.

3 Journaling Prompts

1. If I didn't have to do it right/perfectly I would. . .
2. I'd like to do a little less of _____ and a little more of _____.
3. It's been a long time, but I'd like to. . .

About the Author

Nicolle Nattrass is a Certified Addiction Counselor (CAC II), playwright (PGC), professional actress (CAEA), and workshop facilitator. After a career of 20 years as a professional actor, followed by years of frontline work as an addiction counselor, she developed courses and coaching in Creative Journaling for Self-Care that use both a therapeutic and creative approach for clients, journal keepers, and that utilize mental health and wellness for helping professionals. Courses offered include the CACCF-approved course Creative Journaling: Self-Care for the Helping Professional. She is also a member of the International Association for Journal Writing (IAJW.org) Journal Council and offers online courses. You can learn more at www.nicollenattrass.com.

Writing Through Recovery

14

Gail Heney

I need to confess that I journaled daily for many years before I got sober. I would awaken and sit with a foggy head and shaky grip on my pen, staring at the faint blue lines across the empty pages of my notebook. Hoping to summon the energy to capture and release the shame and self-loathing, so familiar and yet so raw, I would record that I felt "so blue and low energy."

I might say something about the day before that had been productive or for which I should feel the requisite thankfulness. I would skirt any mention of the evening before. I would then shift to a list of "things to do today." I would make written commitments that would keep me busy and tick the boxes of daily productivity: go for a run, fold the laundry, make chili, write notes for three clients, return phone calls. There would be the occasional day when the pain and hopelessness were too great to override. The entries those days were short: "On my mind today, I dunno, I'm sad, I have a black hole in my soul."

I still have the journal with my daily entry of writing 100 times: "I will only drink one glass of wine tonight." That was on May 11, 2002. I got sober in 2006.

In my experience, recovery is a lifetime of process. The bad news is that it never ends. The good news is that you can start over every day. It took years of daily writing during my active alcoholism to shift from lists of accomplishments and rationalizations, to admissions of deep sadness and nameless fears and shame, to naming humble truths and surrendering.

It has been my experience, both personally and as a helping professional, that the foundation for recovery is made of honesty, humility, and courage. I have a dear friend who's been sober for many years. He often shares that his problem wasn't the alcohol, it was people. It was his relationships. I believe that addiction is a symptom of underlying mental, physical, and emotional pain. I believe that addiction loses its power to control when we can talk to it and about it: honestly and openly with ourselves, then with another, and ideally with a spiritual third party as a companion.

The potential for journaling in recovery lies in its role as our mirror, our best friend, and our spiritual advocate. For most of us (read all of us), we have either lost or never had the ability to form a trusting connection with another human being. Our substance or activity of choice in addiction became our everything. Our world became small.

The framework of recovery requires us to go into the darkness we addictively avoided. It requires a leap of faith that scares away many. It has been my experience, as a person in recovery and as a mentor and coach for others, that the initial connection and willingness to be completely honest is a challenging threshold to overcome. Introducing a daily journaling practice as a means to enter into the chasms of our fear, shame, and sadness opens the door to dialogue and healing.

Entering into recovery requires that we admit that we have no power or control over our addiction. It requires that we admit that our lives were unmanageable. It requires that we admit that without a connection to something outside of our own warped perceptions of self and others, we will remain in the insanity of addiction. The necessity of making these admissions keeps many looking through the bottom of the glass, without having the willingness to put it down. The fear feeds the hopelessness.

The value of structure and routine to support those in early recovery is a well-known fact. A daily journaling practice will address the tangible as a means of getting to the untouchable, unspoken truths. There is power in routine: to settle a chaotic mind, to inject into a day where empty space and time feel like a sentence, to promote stillness and safe disclosure.

The daily routine can start with a donated lined notebook or a purchased fancy journal. The key is that it lies flat when open so that there's easy access to the whole page. In my experience, the physical act of writing with a pen provides a more meaningful process than typing on a keyboard. That sets the stage that daily writing is the beginning of a new relationship, with the page and with oneself. Having a discussion with yourself about when you will write, your physical environment for writing, and your ability to keep the journal safe and confidential are keys to overcoming early concerns and barriers.

For many in early recovery, the flood of emotions, with nothing to numb them, is overwhelming. Focusing on the act of journaling, so as to get the pen moving and so as to shift out of fear, is recommended. The goal is to let what's going on inside the mind, body, and spirit be released through the end of the pen. Grammar and spelling corrections and edits are all strongly discouraged.

I spent ten years trying to control my drinking, looking at myself in the mirror and asking what was wrong with me, and refusing to accept that I had no power to stop my gin habit. In my recovery community, I witness this over and over again. I hear from those trying to abstain for the first time and from the many chronic slippers (as we call them): "I thought I could manage it this time." Without accepting the insanity of this thought, there is no long-term sobriety.

Once on the road to surrender, which is the beginning of physical sobriety, the next potential obstacle has to do with emotional sobriety. In the early stages, we have to manage the hurdle of becoming humble and developing an open mind. It has to do with trusting what we cannot see. Before I stretched my mind to include invisible forces in the universe that would become my spiritual talisman, my yellow Labrador retriever was my higher power. His was unconditional love.

In early sobriety, building a foundation of honesty, humility and willingness is critical to the journey of recovery. The following suggestions may be helpful in putting pen to page and starting on the path of healing.

5 Tips for Helping Professionals

1. If the journal is to be shared with you, the client should read it aloud. Insisting they use their own voice gives them greater ownership and responsibility for the words written. It also deepens confidence and trust between the two of you.

2. Recommend that daily journal writing become a routine. Turning it into a daily habit eliminates negotiation and questioning. Encourage them to create a safe space and protected time of day if possible.

3. Hold them accountable for their writing practice. "What got in the way?" "What are you avoiding?" "What is more important than your recovery?"

4. Guide them to create a bond with their pen and page and address the page each day as though it were a trusted friend. Remind them that the page accepts unconditionally everything that is written. There is no need to edit, correct, or spell-check.

5. Provide an optional structure through prompts, readings, a podcast, or a question to consider. Those new to journaling will find the structure helpful and perhaps even necessary to get the pen moving.

5 Tips for Clients and Journal Keepers

1. Establishing a daily routine is key to developing confidence and willingness to write about your thoughts and feelings and to unlock the unspoken.
2. Writing longhand in a notebook specifically designated for daily journaling provides an uninterrupted and portable outlet for your words. Unlike using a tablet or laptop, there will be no distractions or interruptions from the 24/7 cyber world.
3. Resist the temptation to make it perfect. The entries are for you only. It will be your choice if you ever wish to share them. Practice no judgment, no corrections, no edits.
4. Set aside a specific amount of time or a specific number of pages you will commit to as your daily practice. Stick to it. There will be an ebb and flow to the nature and depth of your journaling. Just do it every day.
5. Use prompts, recovery literature, and your own emotional energy to access your voice, your thoughts, and your feelings. Let them flow from the end of your pen. If you are stuck after having written something, ask yourself, "What's the truth about that?" and write some more.

 3 Journaling Prompts

1. List some examples of what you did or things that happened when you were drinking/using. These are events that you wish hadn't happened, that you regret, and that you don't wish to admit or share with anyone.
2. Write a letter to a spiritual being, entity, or energy of your choice. In the letter describe what you need from them to support you on your journey of recovery.
3. Write a letter from your spiritual support entity/energy source expressing unconditional acceptance and support for who you are.

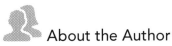 About the Author

As a natural seeker, teacher, and communicator, Gail Heney has been adventurous and atypical. A science education and a start as a health care professional, some solo travel, and then a 16-year career as a financial markets trader carried her into her mid-40s. During that time she married, and together with her husband built a loving household and active family life with three children and an endless variety of usual and unusual pets. At the age of 44, in what she calls an epiphany of the mind and body, Gail left her senior leadership position in banking and began a career shift to executive coaching.

As a daily journaler, an avid leadership coach, and an active participant in all aspects of her recovery, Gail confesses to having evolved through significant shifts in her emotional, intellectual, and spiritual realms. She shares her discovered wisdom and experiences in work with clients, women in recovery, and her weekly blogs.

Journaling to Manage Anxiety   **15**

Nick Lazaris

As you will discover in this chapter, the daily practice of encouraging your clients to write their personal story through journaling can become a valuable part of the commitment and accountability necessary to live their life without fear. I'll share with you the core components that can turn journaling into a self-directed tool to help clients take charge of both their mind and body when they are faced with the challenges of severe anxiety or panic.

There are 4 Power Skills that are a vital part of the path to less and less anxiety and that are strategic to the daily practice of journaling. These skills are: Positive Self-Talk; Focused Breathing; Muscle Relaxation; and Visualization. Each page of an Anxiety Journal would include a commitment to practicing each of these Power Skills. By using an Anxiety Journal, and by committing to practicing each of the skills on a daily basis, your clients will begin to gain freedom from fear and move towards the dreams and goals that matter the most to them.

Commitment to Journaling

Achieving the commitment necessary for the journal writing process to be effective and valuable for your client is encouraged by the following initial writing prompt:

I commit to write in my Anxiety Journal every day, starting today ___/___/___, and work towards creating a fearless life.

Signed, _____

5 Daily Journal Entries

A key to success when journaling is to write down the date of each entry. This allows for a visual reminder of the daily commitment to overcoming fears and anxiety while also being a way to hold oneself accountable should the client miss a day of journaling. It is important that the person journaling NOT beat themselves up if he or she misses an entry; instead, a simple recommitment to the next day of writing, while moving forward, is encouraged. This is a long-term game, not a short-term sprint.

Journal Entry #1—Gratitude

I suggest that journaling begins at the start the day with a reflection on things that the client is grateful for. Those who struggle with the challenge of anxiety know how easy it is to focus on things that they are afraid of or things that are coming up that scare them.

Being grateful for those things and people in their life that matter and make a difference can be a very powerful way to refocus their thinking, especially as they start their day. The task would be to write down one to three things or persons that they are grateful for, that they appreciate having in their life. By doing this every day, even in the midst of a struggle with anxiety, this will begin to get your client out of overthinking and into the reality of what truly matters to him or her.

Journal Entry #2—If I Were Fearless. . .

In this part of the daily journal, clients will write down what they would love to do if they were not anxious or afraid. Ask them to let their mind think and dream outside of the box of fear that they have found themselves in. This is not pretending, but should rather be focused and clear statements of who they would like to be as a fearless person living life to the fullest on that particular day.

A negative mental "picture" of what they are afraid of or want to avoid keeps the cycle of stress and anxiety going. By breaking into this cycle, first thing in the morning and with a new picture of who they desire to be that day, allows for the negative picture of fear to be replaced with a picture of them being fearless and achieving their daily goals.

Journal Entry #3—My Commitments

This is where clients will state their commitments for the day, commitments to the specific skills necessary for them to move past their prison of mental and physical anxiety and into a new world of freedom from fear.

Each day clients will write down a commitment to each of the 4 Power Skills (*Positive Self-Talk, Focused Breathing, Muscle Relaxation and Visualization*) required to take back control over their life.

Journal Entry #4—Capture Your Victories

Every evening, your client will take some time to reflect upon any and all victories that she experienced during the day. Whether these victories are small or large, she is to write down any positive thought, behavior, or achievement that she experienced. She is to do this as a way to capture her "wins" and validate and solidify her growth, as well as to remind herself what she is capable of.

Most people keep track of their "losses" or negative experiences and later use them as evidence against themselves of how incapable and hopeless they are. Encourage clients to take charge of their victories and begin to build real evidence of what they are able to achieve. This also allows for a review of their victories, especially when they get discouraged.

Journal Entry #5—Set Goals

The final task for clients, prior to the end of the day, is to take a moment to list what your clients would like to accomplish tomorrow that would make a difference in gaining control of their anxiety and fears. For example, they might set a goal of practicing their Focused Breathing exercise three more times tomorrow than they did today, or listening with more awareness to their negative self-talk in order to slow down and not create more negative evidence about themselves.

Another goal might be to take a small risk or try something new in an area that has caused anxiety in their life up until now. Again, whether big or small, setting positive, achievable goals that slowly take them out of their self-imposed comfort zone are steps to gaining emotional freedom.

Example of a Client Journal Entry

Today I am grateful for...
My loving family and the support of my spouse.
If I were fearless, today I would...
Accept the invitation from my friend to go to lunch, even though I am nervous about it.
Today I commit to...

- Being aware of and quieting my inner, critical voice
- Breathing deeply and slowly four times a day
- Practicing my relaxation exercise two times a day
- Practicing mental rehearsal once a day

My victories today were...

- I returned the call that I have been putting off out of fear of being rejected.
- My goals for tomorrow that will move me towards my dreams are...
- Take a drive with my husband that I have been putting off.
- Continue my breathing exercise practice and increase it to six times a day.
- Take a short walk to begin exercising as my therapist/coach recommended.
- Listen more closely for that negative, inner critical voice that triggers my anxiety and fear.

5 Tips for Helping Professionals

1. Encourage your clients to commit to writing in their journal on a daily basis (both morning as well as evening entries). The development of such a habit is a key to producing effective results.
2. You might add to, or possibly delete, any of the Power Skills that are required in order for your clients to take action on a daily basis, so that they can overcome their anxiety challenges. The key here is to create accountability for the basic behavioral skills necessary to manage and eventually overcome their anxiety.

3. Remind clients that journaling is not a pass/fail activity, but rather is an adjunct to the work that you are doing together. They are maintaining the journal for their own benefit, and not to please you.
4. Assist your client in creating specific examples of short-term achievable goals.
5. Capturing daily victories in the evening entry, no matter how small or seemingly insignificant, is crucial to building a sense that they "can do this."

 5 Tips for Clients and Journal Keepers

1. Commit to each of the skills, and the commitments within each skill, on a daily basis.
2. Believe that it is possible to gain freedom from your fears.
3. Write authentically and honestly—this is for YOU, not anyone else.
4. Take charge of your day through your journaling. Overcome hopelessness and helplessness by utilizing your journal on a regular basis.
5. If you miss a day of journaling, simply get back on track the next day—do not shame yourself!

 3 Journaling Prompts

1. *Today I am grateful for. . .*
2. *If I were fearless, today I would. . .*
3. *Today I commit to. . .*

 # About the Author

As a performance psychologist and creativity coach, Dr. Nick Lazaris has specialized for 38 years in helping creatives, performing artists, entrepreneurs, and business professionals overcome anxiety in their art, writing, public speaking, or while on stage. Dr. Nick coaches those who desire to increase their self-confidence, overcome fear, and create at or near their personal best. You can contact Dr. Nick at nick@drnicklazaris.com or go to www.drnicklazaris.com to receive your free *Performance Anxiety Road Map*.

When the Words Won't Come—Journal Keeping Without Words

16

Maureen Szulejewska

My own well-established journal practice is one that crept unobtrusively and uninvited into my life during a period of personal crisis. By the time I became fully aware of its incursion, it had not only carved out a niche for itself but also firmly established its credentials as a valued and indispensable confidante, always available, always receptive and infinitely wise.

Words are my medium and it is with words that I have filled the pages of the many journals that nestle comfortably on my bookshelves. They remember, celebrate, and mourn times that have passed; but they also bear witness and give voice to dreams, hopes, and ambitions for the future. Moments of pain, vulnerability, anger, hope, and excitement mingle with prosaic to-do lists, progress reviews of projects in hand and plans for future ventures. Journeys in the physical, external world share space with journeys of exploration into the very depths of my being.

Reflecting back on the stealthy incursion of journal keeping into my life, I am struck by the realization that one of my first volumes of journal entries is almost entirely wordless. It is housed in a large 12 x 12-inch scrapbook and contains pages of what in hindsight I now refer to as "nonverbal entries"— pages of patterns and images, collages created from a variety of embellishments, colored paper, and ephemera. Like the pages in written journals, these pages supported and accompanied me throughout a period of time, exploring past, present, and future but in a way that makes no use of words. An exuberant multi-colored design bedecked with sequins and glitter celebrates the exhilaration and joy of a weekend break. Lines of bunting crafted from ribbons and paper flags display the steady sequential stages in my life. A people-tile mosaic explores the history of my relationship patterns.

I started other pages in response to a question or journal prompt—a thought hovering on the edge of my consciousness, an insubstantial, ephemeral shape glimpsed indistinctly at a distance through swirling, shifting mists. Insubstantial wraiths that slowly and tentatively allowed themselves to be viewed with increasingly clarity, until I was able to capture something of their essence. Whatever materials came to hand were incorporated into these pages. The interdependence of experiences, roles, relationships, and places in shaping the person I had become was explored through weaving strips of paper, thread, ribbon, wool, and raffia. The parts of myself that I chose to keep hidden and those which I allow to be visible to others were explored and illustrated using paperclips, buttons, and matchsticks to represent porous and impermeable boundaries between these different parts of myself.

Some page layouts allowed themselves to be created very quickly but others became absorbing and time-consuming creations, centering and grounding activities in their own right. Starting with a sheet of cardboard as my blank canvas, I would select materials to incorporate one by one—buttons, feathers, leaves, ribbons, raffia, cotton wool, fabric oddments, scraps of paper in variety of color, texture, size. These were tried out, moved around, discarded, replaced in ways which continually changed and shifted until finally assuming the shape that satisfied intuitive, subconscious promptings. Even then I would leave the final version for 24 hours before finally consigning any component parts to a permanent abode. I always recorded the dates and the circumstances of each creation on the back; sometimes I would give the piece a title such as Childhood Memories, My Life in Doors, Portrait.

Today, my primary medium is words but this is often supplemented or primed by the creation of something visual. As I have no skill in drawing, sketching, or painting, I continue to explore other possibilities—a collage using pictures or words cut out from magazines, a richly colored and decorated image using scrapbook embellishments, a woven piece fashioned out of paper, ribbon, or raffia.

I believe a number of factors contributed to this embracing of a visual rather than verbal means of expression. It occurred at a time when my personal landscape was in disarray following a rapid series of major changes. Inability to find structure in my life was mirrored by an inability to use the highly structured medium of language in which to express myself.

Language relies not only on structure but also on words to convey meaning, and every individual develops their own lexicon specifically tailored to unique needs and interests. However, the personal crisis that had engulfed me was unprecedented in my experience and consequently the vocabulary at my disposal lacked words that could adequately convey the essence of this new reality. I had needed to find an alternative, effective way of capturing meaning and making sense at this time.

My first language is English but for almost 20 years I had lived in a non-English speaking country. This period of crisis coincided with a move back to a life that took place exclusively in the English language. Many of the memories I needed to process were rooted and encoded in memory in a different language and working with them in a nonverbal way enabled me to bypass the need to locate them in the vocabulary of a specific language. Indeed, translating an experience from the language of its original experiencing into another language can adversely affect a person's ability to access in full the details and emotional resonance of that original memory.

In my work as a pluralistic counselor, the therapeutic relationship which develops between myself and a client sits at the heart of the counseling process. The building of this relationship relies heavily on language, a limited and fallible tool of which we make use to build a bridge between our individual and unique inner worlds. I am fortunate that my experience with nonverbal journal keeping has enabled me to catch sight of ways to access and capture elements of that inner world without employing language. These ways have broadened my way of thinking and enriched the toolbox of skills and techniques I bring with me into each counseling relationship. I hope that what I have shared in this article has afforded a glimpse into these possibilities.

5 Tips for Helping Professionals

1. Try creating a nonverbal page. Start with a simple and concrete idea. Experiment with different materials and develop a feel for the possibilities. Make a book of samples from your experiments that you can show to clients. Be willing to be surprised by those clients who embrace the possibilities but remember it will not suit everyone.
2. Keep your sample book and some materials in a box file in your workspace for possible use by a client during a session. There

should be enough material to provide choice but not to overwhelm. Ten pages taken from different magazines can offer more variety than one magazine on a single subject. Include safety scissors, glue, and cardboard for a base.

3. Sometimes, it is helpful for a client to record achievements during challenging times. A verbal record is often not revisited once the entry has been made and the notebook closed. Visual creations of achievements produced by clients include scouting-style achievement badges sewn on a blanket, cardboard medals mounted on a pinboard, and 3-D decorations hung from an artificial tree.

4. Be curious about a client's language history. There may be significant memories that were experienced in a language other than that in which counseling is taking place. A multilingual client may not have an equally extensive emotional vocabulary in each language. Remember that the language of childhood is often the language of emotion.

5. If a client has a problem with remembering everyday events, a collection of items acquired during the course of a day such as shopping receipts or tickets could be glued in a notebook to offer a physical memory. The pages and ephemera could be colored and decorated.

5 Tips for Clients and Journal Keepers

1. Put together a collection of supplies—buttons, paperclips, colored paper, cardboard, wool, ribbon, string, lace, and anything else that catches your eye. Cut out shapes and patterns from empty carboard packets or magazines. You also need something for a base—I use 12″ x 12″ cardboard. Keep all these in one place along with glue and scissors.

2. Think about the presentation and storage of your finished pieces. Will you use different sized sheets for the backgrounds? How will you store them—in a ring binder or a box? Or will you use a scrapbook or a notebook?

3. Start with one simple prompt. Think about the idea, let it percolate, and then allow your subconscious to guide you. You might find you want to sketch out a preliminary outline to guide you. Don't be afraid to experiment—there is no wrong way to do this.

4. The time required is the time it takes—a few minutes or a few hours. Sometimes you might want to develop an idea, expand the way in which you represent it. It's okay to leave something and go back to it. But beware of ruminating on something negative. If you find yourself becoming trapped in negative thinking, stop what you are doing and do something positive instead.

5. Date everything you do. Consider giving each piece a title. On the back, record briefly the question/prompt/idea that you have explored. Take a moment to reflect on the experience and any insight or awareness you have gained. Record this in as few or as many words as you wish.

 3 Journaling Prompts

1. If your life is a path that passes through many different environments, what is the surrounding landscape like at present? Depict those surroundings on the page.

2. If you were a house, what kind of house would you be? Large, small, welcoming, forbidding, isolated, easy to reach? Memorable or easily overlooked? How can you illustrate the spirit of that house?

3. Choose a cherished memory—a person, a place, a feeling, or an event. Spend a few minutes bringing to mind as many details as possible. Then allow your subconscious to guide you in capturing the essence on the page.

 About the Author

Maureen (Mo) Szulejewska is a qualified pluralistic counselor who lives and works in her native Scotland. Her academic qualifications include BA (Hons) in English, MBA and MSc in counseling. She has a lifelong fascination with words, language, and communication as well as both personal and professional experience of the positive contribution writing can offer in supporting emotional well-being. A seasoned journal keeper, she has also facilitated writing for well-being and journal writing groups.

Journaling for Dating Anxiety · 17

Nefeli Soteriou

Dating anxiety takes many forms regardless of one's mating habits or sexual preferences. More often than not, dating anxiety appears as *procrastination*. One's hesitation to pursue relationships is most likely caused by discomfort at trying to overcome habitual ways of being. Simply put, it is easier to be single nowadays. Not only does a person have to commit to their goal of finding a partner, they will need to do the work to keep the promises they make to themselves, face their fears and doubts as they actively pursue dating and relating, recognize past relationship triggers, learn to move beyond the feelings of rejection, and perhaps realize how the whole process calls for an upgrade of their personality.

Here are some client examples that highlight some of these common dating challenges, while also showing how journaling can be helpful in dealing with dating anxiety.

One client was Sarah, an athletic woman in her forties who was proactive with her dating life. She was selective with who she would date and was very clear that she wanted marriage and family. Sarah was well read on the psychology of relationships and followed the most popular love coaches' blogs. Although Sarah went on thousands of first dates, nobody seemed to be a match.

Sarah's girlfriends commented: "I thought I was picky, yet you are impossible" and "You will slim him down honey like I did with my husband, just say yes!" That advice made no sense to Sarah, as she knew herself well and trusted her own opinions. However, over time, self-doubt started to creep in. Sarah sought professional help after an incident over a stranger's picture on a dating app. She reacted to this picture with anxiety, sharing, "I had an increased heart rate, everything was caving in on me, I started to cry, I became very emotional. It could be that I don't know how to talk to him, I might ruin it."

One of the first things we worked on together was learning to make the best out of a situation that she did have control over. She had to move forward in the direction she wanted to go in her life and believe unequivocally that the right person would join her.

When I proposed an exercise in journaling, Sarah opted out. "I don't like writing," she said firmly, brushing my suggestion aside. "I am almost fifty years old, set in my ways, I am not going to change now," she insisted. To further my point, I explained how I use journaling in my practice as a form of expressive writing. Trying to ease her concerns, I talked about how journaling has been linked to mental and physical health benefits by pioneering research.

I shared my own experience with journaling from my early teens to illustrate how it can affect individuals differently. At first, I jotted down daily events like most young girls do in their diaries. Over time, however, thoughts and feelings were expressed and "shy" poetry popped up, which guided me to a deeper connection with my own creative essence.

Apparently, it was the physical action of writing that bored Sarah. "What if you voice record your thoughts and feelings instead of writing?" I asked her. In finding a middle ground, which was customary for her line of work in public defense, Sarah agreed to complete voice recordings as her way of journaling.

A valuable journaling exercise tailored for Sarah was *Establishing Boundaries*, a 12-minute voice recording with three prompts for her to record in consecutive order. Sarah needed to learn to fearlessly articulate her needs and maintain strong boundaries.

Establishing Boundaries

Step 1: I don't like or I don't want. . .
Step 2: I want. . .
Step 3: I'd love it if you . . . and/or Would you. . .

I asked Sarah to do the recording with a stopwatch. She would start the watch and speak her responses to each individual prompt into the microphone for a maximum of four minutes. This allowed her thought processes to unfold naturally.

In my opinion, journal writing and voice recording are simply different processes to discharge one's thoughts and feelings. Voice recordings can be easily completed on a smart phone device; everyone has them nowadays.

A ten-minute voice recording is more than sufficient; however, I suggest that before you assign voice-recording prompts, you practice them and time yourself first.

Another set of voice recording prompts that empowered Sarah to learn to express her emotions and her innate sensitivity were the following:

Explore Emotions and Process Them

I suggested the following sentence starter prompts for exploring and processing emotions:

- I am feeling hurt. . .
- I feel disappointed because. . .
- I want. . .

The assigned length was up to 12 minutes altogether: four minutes tops to respond to each prompt.

A second client, Rea, was not legally divorced when we started to work together. "I was in it for life, he asked for the divorce," she said, bursting into tears. A sentimental woman in her early sixties, Rea was experiencing high levels of emotional pain. Not only was it difficult for her to accept that her 15-year marriage was over, but she held resentment against her husband because of her role as the breadwinner for her family. Though curious and willing to work in our partnership together, Rea expressed low confidence after my suggestion that she try online dating. "Who is going to want to look at me at this age? I am not that smart!" Rea felt this way despite being an accomplished Academic Dean at a university.

Rea completed the following first journal exercise regarding her self-concept:

Enhanced Self-Concept

What I love about myself includes these 100 things . . .! (For example, caring, loyal, kind, consistent, mother, designer, cook, friend, gardener, yogi, dancer, lover, cyclist, pet-sitter, knitter, hiker. . .)

The purpose of this exercise was to remind Rea of the many qualities and skills she possessed. I explained that she could develop the list anywhere that was convenient, from using the spare time while commuting to work or at her favorite bench at the local park.

This journaling activity was to be the preliminary work for a new journal entry regarding Rea's doubts and fears around online dating. I believe that online dating resembles selling: one must stand out from the competition and market themselves appropriately. Many people are uncomfortable unwrapping their own gifts and sharing them with the world. The journal prompt was: "To sell myself at an online dating website means . . .".

In advising Rea to write this journal entry for a maximum 15 minutes, I also pointed out how this exercise could bring up her own inner challenges in acknowledging and promoting her gifts to a wider choice pool of dating partners. This expressive journal entry was another small step that motivated Rea towards starting over.

I also invited Rea to engage with the following two-step prompt:

Explore Emotions and Process Them

Step 1: I feel . . . because . . .
Step 2: I want . . .

The prompt helped emotions to surface: being hurt, angry, scared, being resentful and even ashamed about mistakes Rea may have made in the relationship. In sharing her response, Rea described the break-up as "an excitement of chaos, things being in disarray and out of control." As a result, we worked on adaptive thinking strategies and distress tolerance for better self-management.

As Rea worked steadily to alleviate her emotional distress, she made notable progress. She moved from acknowledging her pain to resolving the frustration about having to decide to file for a divorce. Finally, Rea received a new understanding about the way forward in the relationship with her former husband, since they had to co-parent their two children together. Rea started to go on dates online. She was excited to simply have some fun with this new-to-her approach.

5 Tips for Helping Professionals

1. Establish professional rules of conduct with clients and patients and maintain ethical practices. I can't stress that enough.

2. Your clients' path to success is indicative to their readiness. Assess it early on. You might consider providing a questionnaire form to fill out with a 0–10 ranking scale, with number ten the highest level of commitment. Alternatively, listen deeply during an introductory interview to understand their short-term and long-term goals.

3 Guide your client to identify their own thinking patterns, reasoning, beliefs, and judgments. Innate client wisdom makes it a win-win for everyone involved. After all, your client's success is your reward.

4. Know that your encouragement and motivation may be faced with resistance. Never take it personally. Returning to old habits is part of the process. What are some of your ways to encourage and motivate your client and/or patient to start again the next day?

5. Care for but do not carry your client's load. Practice self-compassionate detachment once you leave the sessions for the day. Move your body. Either take a walk at the local park to change scenes, clear your head and smell the fresh air, or dance at home to your favorite songs.

5 Tips for Clients and Journal Keepers

1. Some of you may journal to find relief through stressful life events, others as a spiritual practice, and others as a form of creative expression. Know that you are significantly benefiting, even though the gains may be subtle to notice at first.

2. Consistency in journaling does pay off. I speak from personal experience from being drawn to the practice as a teen. Although I learned to document first my daily life, I then explored my creativity, which led to deeper self-awareness.

3. Journaling doesn't have to lead to your next great novel or to your new screenplay. Accept that sometimes the practice simply will serve to promote self-awareness.

4. The urge to journal may come up quite suddenly. Have a notepad and a pen handy or a personal computer notebook to jot down your responses.

5. Choose whether or not to share your journaling with others. After all, it is your intellectual property!

3 Journaling Prompts

1. SETTING BOUNDARIES (with families, friends, lovers)

   Step 1: I don't like or I don't want. . .
   Step 2: I want. . .
   Step 3: I'd love it if you . . . and/or Would you. . .

2. EXPLORE EMOTIONS AND PROCESS THEM

   Step 1: I am feeling hurt. . .
   Step 2: I feel disappointed because. . .
   Step 3: I want. . .

3. ENHANCE SELF-CONCEPT

   What I love about me are these 100 things!:

 About the Author

Nefeli Soteriou is an independent filmmaker and a professional coach with a humanistic approach to psychology and with additional training in cognitive behavioral therapy. In integrating coaching methodologies in her private practice, Nefeli helps bright minds thrive in life and well-being. Learn more about Nefeli at www.nefelisoteriou.com.

Amplified Journaling   **18**

Francesca Aniballi

Reading and writing have always been in dialogue, since I learned to practice them. They naturally complement and supplement each other. Thus, the stories, novels, poems, and essays I read soon prompted me to engage in a written response.

My first outing in the world of writing happened through poetry and journaling. Years later, when it was clear to me that journaling and writing were essential both to my personal practice and to my work with people, I developed amplified journaling serendipitously.

During a summer abroad, I was working at a nonprofit project involving orphan youth and childless or abandoned senior citizens. I read poetry selected on the basis of free-text responses to a questionnaire I had submitted to the groups I served.

The main themes that emerged were fear, rejection, abandonment, anger, loneliness, and grief. After some reflection, my choice fell on poetry because of the immediacy of the form and its emotional charge, while being open-ended enough to encourage individuals to reminisce and to make meaning for themselves.

The compressed and intense experience given by the reading of short poems was the invaluable asset I was looking for. I wanted to find ways to stimulate cross-generational communication and emotional healing. Thus, I started out by reading poems on those themes to the young and the elderly in two separate groups.

In the second stage of the project, the youth met the elderly and read out their favorite poems to them. Little by little, their responses emerged: casual remarks, occasional memories, full-blown narratives.

It was then that I decided to introduce a third stage and have the whole group journal together in response to the poems read. I asked them to visualize the poet/narrator/character first, and then start journaling from there. They would answer back to characters and to the poets, continue or contradict a line of thought, express their emotions, and tell fragments of their stories through journaling. This way "amplified journaling" was born.

There was a young man who was enthralled by the scene (Act 1, Scene 5) where Hamlet talks to his father's ghost. Because of his personal history, he responded to that scene. He developed a written dialogue with Hamlet. He wrote that at least Hamlet had known his own father and that was also fortunate to have his ghost appear before his eyes and talk to him. He wished he could say the same about his own father, whose face and life deeds were completely unknown to him.

He then concluded that because that part of his history was denied to him, he had to invent himself anew and make his own history by other means all by himself. He compared himself to a peregrine falcon surveying the lay of the land from above, with indifference and detachment. He had been like that for most of his life, because it helped him cope. Yet, it had also cost him a sense of connection and aliveness. He had always covered his interactions with others with a veil of impenetrable distance and aloofness. Amplified journaling helped him take notice of that and to admit his own pain to himself.

Among the women I worked with, I remember Monica (not her real name), a retired teacher in her late sixties. She responded to a poem by Mary O'Donnell, called "Antarctica," whose first line is "I do not know what other women know." The poet goes on to describe her yearning for a child and her jealousy of the young women who have conceived. Ironically, they tell her that she is free because she has no child, as they are "grafted willows forced before time."

Monica responded to the poem line by line. She journaled deep and wide in her story and she dipped her toe in a possible future for herself. Here is a page from her journal (reproduced with her permission), where she answered the first line of the poem:

> *Right, I do not know what other women know. That's a fact. I know other things; a knowledge I've always crossed out as unimportant. I know that I love opening my eyes in the morning and looking out of the window for the robins and sparrows, I enjoy sitting with my cup of coffee waiting . . . waiting . . . what for?*
>
> *Nothing ever happens; yet, in a way, everything goes on happening all the time. I do not know what other women know. I do not know their animal-sure right-thing-to-do with their children.*

I do know what loving a child is, though. And because I have no children of my own, yet I pined for years longing for one, I have that distance that helps listening to a child and brings respect for its soul to the table.

Through amplified journaling, Monica was able to find some inner responses that empowered her to look her pain straight in the eye.

In the same way, you can respond to any poem or quote. You can either pull lines from their context, or keep quotes in context by reading the work that contain them, and start a written conversation with the character or the narrators, thus exploring issues and themes that resonate with your own life experiences.

---

5 Tips for Helping Professionals

1. You can choose to have people work with poems, excerpts of short stories, tales, parables, or quotations that deal with specific themes, relevant to the circumstances and issues of the people you are serving, leaving the development of the journaling session free to evolve as an exploration.

2. For a more structured approach, you can ask clients to choose a poem or text from a select handful and to pick a character or object depicted in it to develop a conversation or to dialogue with them in such a way that their personal concerns and potential solutions or resources can emerge from the journaling process.

3. It is helpful to pace the session, allowing enough time for each stage, but not too much. I suggest the following: reading (ten minutes), quiet reflection (five minutes), amplified journaling (30 minutes), optional sharing (15 minutes). The reason for these particular timings is that the reading should be focused and intense for maximum impact; a five-minute reflection time allows the reading to land in the reader's consciousness and to seep through their memory bank in search of associations; 30 minutes of journaling is enough to dive deep and also to sustain the practice over time; and 15 minutes of optional sharing helps people to focus and to share only the most relevant, incisive parts of what they wrote. You can repeat this format with two in-between breaks, particularly in settings that require structure.

4. When working with a group, you can ask clients to bring their favorite poems and quotes to work from and you can also involve a different person as a co-guide for each session, if you want to give the group more autonomy and allow them to participate in the conduct of the sessions.

5. You can also make clear that clients may practice amplified journaling not only in a traditional journal but also in other formats that work well because they have a nonlinear structure or nonsequential content presentation. For example, you can suggest the use of a filing box, where clients will organize their journal entries by theme and cross-reference them, or a vision board where they can map visually the movements and associations that emerge in their journaling process.

 5 Tips for Clients and Journal Keepers

1. Use the internet to search poems by theme and poet. The World Wide Web abounds with good poetry websites. A dictionary of quotes also is an excellent source to practice amplified journaling.

2. Time the stages of your session. Pace yourself by using an alarm clock or by establishing a minimum page number you are going to write.

3. Use the line(s) from a story or poem that speak to you, that provoke you, that stir your imagination, or that catch your eye. This intuitive approach is good when you want to find out what you don't know that you know!

4. Supplement your amplified journaling with photos. After selecting the lines that you want to respond to, choose one picture that illustrates the point you intend to make, the thread you want to follow, or the theme that is emerging for you. The more symbolic the picture, the better it will help your process of excavation and meaning-making. It is better still if you take the pictures yourself.

5. When you have an issue in mind, set micro-objectives for yourself, such as "Through amplified journaling, today I am going to explore _____." Be specific and keep the focus on your intention.

3 Journaling Prompts

The following prompts are lines taken from famous literary works. Use them as a springboard for your journaling.

1. *Love is a growing or full constant light;*
   And his first minute, after noon, is night.
   John Donne, from *Songs and Sonnets* (1633), "A Lecture Upon the Shadow"

2. *Like all dreamers, I mistook disenchantment for truth.*
   Jean-Paul Sartre, from *Les Mots* (1964) "Écrire"

3. *It is the secret sympathy,*
   The silver link, the silken tie,
   Which heart to heart, and mind to mind,
   In body and soul can bind.
   Walter Scott, from *The Lay of the Last Minstrel* (1805) canto 5, stanza 13.

About the Author

Francesca Aniballi, PhD, holds a Certificate in Writing for Therapeutic Purposes. She is an Italian expressive arts facilitator and person-centered counselor, as well as a teacher and a certified ARTbundance coach. Visit her at https://blueplanetvision.com, where she offers coaching on personal development, goal achievement, and motivation, as well as courses about mindful creativity through journaling and creative writing, intuitive art-making, in combination with other expressive arts.

Journaling for Growth and Healing

PART IV

Journaling Your Stories for Growth and Healing

19

Sandra Marinella

We all have a story. Sometimes it is the story of being knocked to the ground—perhaps because of a cancer diagnosis or the death of a loved one. And if we aren't careful a story like this can become buried within us. We can deny it ever happened, and this might lead to physical or psychological problems. A journal can help us—*all of us*—to navigate the murky waters. I have seen this in my work as a writing specialist with thousands of students, professionals, veterans, and currently in my work with cancer patients at Mayo Clinic. A journal can help you change your story and change your life.

In 2012 I dug 27 of my old journals out of closets, nooks, and crannies hoping to reread them. I had just been diagnosed with breast cancer and the diagnosis shook me to the core. While I trudged from one doctor's office to the next, I scribbled copious notes in my journal. It proved to be a powerful companion. Somewhere along this unwanted journey, I realized my journal writing had always helped me navigate life's challenges and the thought took hold of me.

As I read my personal journals and began pouring over stacks of research, a geeky hobby of mine, I realized the power of telling our stories in our journals. I found that over 400 studies demonstrated that personal writing could improve physical and psychological health. Since journal writing had always been a bedrock in my teaching, I knew my journals would hold countless examples of how journaling had transformed a bad story into a manageable, even transformative, life experience for both myself and others too.

Here is one example I found:

Fifteen years ago, at the beginning of his senior year, Ben sat in the back of my high school writing classroom. Against the wall. Over his head was an imaginary sign that read "Leave me alone." But my job as a teacher was to knock down that sign. And while it took a few weeks, I did. On my third attempt at a conversation with Ben, there was a breakthrough.

Although he had few words for what had happened, Ben had scrawled pieces of a shattered story in his classroom journal. His painful story was stuck inside, but at this moment he would tell me. "Last summer . . . my uncle . . . my best friend . . . died." After several months, Ben had broken his silence.

While he continued to struggle with his words, Ben began to inch forward. In coming weeks, he chatted more freely with me and classmates. He even embarked on writing a personal narrative on his tragic loss. Sometimes his words came; other days he struggled. It would be a few weeks before he would share his story openly in class. Even then his story bobbed up unexpectedly. On the day narratives were due, I asked if any students wanted to read their work aloud. Ben's hand shot up— probably as much to his surprise as to his classmates'.

For a few seconds he sat staring at his essay, stunned that he had volunteered, but he found his voice. At first, he read haltingly about "his lost friend." But then Ben found his rhythm and read about the good times with his uncle—reading *Rolling Stone*, riding bikes, listening to U2, especially "Beautiful Day." He described a visit to a memorial in Washington, D.C., where he watched his uncle cry as he rubbed his fingers across a name. And he noted that Uncle Mark could neither forget the war nor talk about it. Then his voice softened, and Ben ended by describing a not-so-beautiful day when he opened the garage door to find his uncle shot to death. "Self-inflicted wound," he read. "A suicide." There was silence.

As students left my class that day, some paused to thank Ben for reading his story, and others paused to pat him on the back. While this story would never be okay, on that day, Ben began accepting his uncle's death and integrating it into his life in a way he could manage. In the coming year, Ben would attend a local college and turn the pain of his loss into a positive action by deciding to tutor veterans at his college. On one return visit to my classroom, Ben said, "Remember the words I poured into my journal . . . I think they helped save me at a bad time."

By the time I had read all 27 of my old journals, I knew I had countless stories like Ben's that demonstrated how journal writing had served as narrative therapy, even narrative medicine, in my life and the lives of the students and professionals I taught.

During my bout with cancer, I began sharing my writing practices with veterans and cancer patients and testing the impact. In the last three years, Dr. Denise Millstine and Barbara Thomley collected data on my writing to heal and transform program at Mayo's Integrative Health Clinic in Phoenix. Using stories and prompts from *The Story You Need to Tell—Writing to Heal from Trauma, Illness, or Loss*, I coached participants in finding, writing, and sharing their stories. The outcomes in this clinical setting were exciting. The writing methods proved to markedly decrease stress and pain and to dramatically improve moods and increase measures of well-being for the participants. This is a small step in our efforts to bring personal writing to the forefront as both narrative therapy and narrative medicine.

Amid the challenging times we face, it is no wonder many of us understand our need to write and rewrite our personal stories. Time and time again I have discovered there is incredible beauty in this process of journaling to understand the self and our stories. As professionals we can guide others through this as a healing process—or we can teach ourselves to embrace and undertake this journey in a search for transformative growth.

 5 Tips for Helping Professionals

In the course of working with writers in clinical and classroom settings, it became clear there were five stages of writing to heal and transform your understanding of difficult stories about the self. While the order can vary, usually the stages are predictable and understanding the process can help therapists, coaches, and teachers to help others to write their stories, and equally important, it can help each of us to find our stories and write our way forward.

The five stages of writing to heal and transform your story and your life—

1. *Experiencing pain and grief.* When you experience a trauma from a loss, illness, or any serious setback, you will experience painful emotions—perhaps guilt, anger, sadness, or denial. Your brain needs time to absorb and learn to live with the experience. Writing may be too painful.

2. *Breaking the silence.* At this time, you find your voice and begin to express your emotions and share what has happened.
3. *Accepting and piecing together a shattered story.* In this stage you begin to move your emotions into a logical framework and make sense of what has happened to you and what you plan to do about it. Writing is especially helpful in this stage.
4. *Finding meaning.* Here you make sense of your broken story and integrate it into your life. The story is complete.
5. *Rewriting or transforming your story.* With the pain of this experience behind you, you can move forward with renewed energy to live more fully.

---

 5 Tips for Clients and Journal Keepers

Here are tips to help you write the stories you need to tell in your journals—

1. Do not write about traumatic experiences until you are emotionally ready.
2. Find a comfortable place and time to write. Bring your water, tea, coffee, or a bit of chocolate!
3. Work to let your words flow, and do not worry about rules—grammar, punctuation, or spelling.
4. If your words need privacy, be sure to hide, secure, or shred them.
5. Most importantly, *ignore your inner critic* and focus on writing!

---

 3 Journaling Prompts

1. Choose a Word

Often a word can pull images, thoughts, and memories from deep within us. Choose one of these words: *fear. Anger. Pain. Hope. Appreciation. Peace. Resilience.* Write nonstop about this word for ten minutes or more. When done, review your writing. What thoughts, memories, or stories surfaced?

2. Song Lyrics

The music we love often frames our personal stories. Make a list of the songs you love. Then create a playlist. When you play this music, choose one song that currently connects to you. Then choose to write about the meaning of that song or write a poem about that song or create a collage that explores the memories evoked by these lyrics. You may want to share your creation with a friend.

3. Finding a Story You Need to Tell

If you have not written about a difficult experience, you may want to approach it first by doing a structured writing. By answering simple questions, you can explore your experience and decide if you are ready to move forward with an in-depth exploration. Begin by completing each sentence starter given here and follow it with a short paragraph of a few sentences. It should take about ten to 20 minutes.

- The story I would like to explore is . . .
- What comes to mind is . . .
- What bothers me about this experience is . . .
- What I would like to understand is . . .
- I am hopeful that . . .
- Perhaps it would help if . . .

Later come back and review this writing. At this time ask yourself: what have I learned? Is this a story I need to explore in more depth? Decide on your next step.

Reference

This chapter draws upon materials from *The Story You Need to Tell—Writing to Heal from Trauma, Illness, or Loss*. Copyright © 2017 by Sandra Marinella. Used with permission from the author and New World Library.

 ## About the Author

Sandra Marinella, MA, MEd, is an award-winning writing teacher and author. She has taught writing and story-sharing to thousands of students, professionals, veterans, and cancer patients. When she faced cancer, she wrote *The Story You Need to Tell*, an acclaimed and inspirational guide on writing to heal and transform. She teaches at Integrative Health at Mayo Clinic in Phoenix where a two-year project has established the effectiveness of her writing methods to reduce stress and pain and to dramatically improve moods and well-being. She speaks and gives workshops on the power of our stories and personal writing to heal and grow our lives. Learn more at www.storyyoutell.com.

The Dao of Expressive Writing to Heal

20

John F. Evans and Shu Cao Mo

An Evidence-Based Approach

Imagine a time when expressive writing for healing is universally supported to the extent that clinic managers, health care providers, hospital administrators, long-term care facilities, and insurance providers include it in their work as they now do with other therapies.

For this imagined scenario to become a reality, data must support the theory that writing is good for those who write, and the data must provide a protocol for practice. From our experience, universities, medical schools, clinics, and hospitals are open to evidence-based practices.

Quantitative Data Description

Enrollment and Retention

Of the 90+ participants who expressed interest in the study, 40 were screened and qualified. One person could not attend the first class, so was excluded from the study. Of the remaining 39 participants who completed baseline assessments, 38 completed the study, including post-study assessments (97.4% retention). It should be noted that the 39th participant attended all other classes, just not the final class. Also, there were no incentives or compensation for completing the study.

Pre-post Quantitative Surveys

Depressive symptoms were measured using the Center for Epidemiologic Studies Depression Scale Revised (CESD-R). Scores decreased from baseline (19.0 ± 13.48) to follow-up (12.7 ± 11.68), indicating a statistically significant mean decrease of -6.2 ± 11.98 points, 95% CI [-2.3, -10.2], $t(37) = -3.21$, $p = 0.003$, $d = 0.52$. These scores suggest a 32.6% decrease in depressive symptoms. Clinically, a score of at least 16 on the CESD-R may suggest a major depressive episode (although it is not diagnostic). Using this cutoff, 61.5% of participants endorsed symptoms suggesting a major depressive episode before the study; after the study, this decreased to 26.3% of participants.

Perceived Stress

Perceived stress was measured using the Perceived Stress Scale (PSS-10). Scores decreased from baseline (20.5 ± 7.43) to follow-up (14.3 ± 6.64), indicating a statistically significant mean decrease of -6.1 ± 8.03 points, 95% CI [-3.5, -8.8], $t(37) = -4.71$, $p < 0.0005$, $d = 0.76$. These scores suggest a 29.8% decrease in perceived stress. Compared to published national averages, scores represent a decrease from the 73rd percentile to the 42nd percentile.

Ruminative Symptoms

Ruminative symptoms were assessed using the Rumination Response Scale (RRS). Scores decreased from baseline (48.5 ± 12.56) to follow-up (39.8 ± 10.07), indicating a statistically significant mean decrease of -8.6 ± 10.58 points, 95% CI [-5.2, -12.1], $t(37) = -5.03$, $p < 0.0005$, $d = 0.82$. These scores suggest a 17.7% decrease in ruminative symptoms.

Resilience

Resilience was assessed using the Connor-Davidson Resilience Scale (CD-RISC). Resilience increased from baseline (64.3 ± 14.40) to follow-up (74.2 ± 13.15), indicating a statistically significant mean increase of 10.0 ± 13.33 points, 95% CI [5.6, 14.4], $t(37) = 4.61$, $p < 0.0005$, $d = 0.75$. These scores suggest a 15.6% increase in resilience.

Our data show that the expressive writing sequence in the workshop Transform Your Health: Write to Heal significantly lowered scores measuring depression, perceived stress, and rumination while it raised scores measuring resilience.

Writing Prompts and Qualitative Data Results From Post-Writing Reflections

The post-writing reflection tool (see Appendix) is useful for helping professionals and clients to measure the expressive writing process. The clients spend 20 minutes writing in response to the prompt. After each 20-minute session, they spend five minutes completing the post-writing reflection (PWR), which is then submitted to the facilitator for their response.

For the purpose of showing our qualitative data, we focus on only responses to question five in the post-writing reflection:

> 5. In the space below, briefly describe how your writing went. You do not have to share the content of your writing but reflect on your experience of writing and anything you associated with the process of your writing. (Write for approximately five minutes.)

Selected prompts are bold and post-writing reflections are in italics as follows.

Write your deepest thoughts and feelings about something you have never shared with anyone.

Going in, I didn't think I was ready to write about them. Again, I had some pre-formulated stories inside. But I decided to let go of the structure and simply to write whatever comes to my mind down. It was like a pressure valve that had been lifted off. More and more intense memories/stories came up. These pre-formulated stories serve as anchor/markers of the road path, enabling me to write. Instead of saying to myself that I don't have a story to tell, it has given me the permission/requirement to write them down, and use them to navigate further into the memory maze of my mind. At the end, I wrote about shame. I didn't expect it to flow so easily out of me because I never shared my side of the story—the inner thoughts and conflicts and desires—with anybody else outside me before. Writing that down makes me realize that, I was simply projecting and layering more shame onto myself. It affords me with a space to be compassionate toward myself, which is such a treasured thing to have. I feel like a part of the black hole inside me is being patched up as a consequence of that outpouring.

Using your name or preferred pronouns, write about something that keeps you up at night or that you think about more often than you would like.

I was expecting lots of dark matter to come back. Instead, I find how writing about it brings philosophy into life. Sometimes I describe my personal memoir writing as a mixture of pornography and philosophy. Responding to the first prompt helps me articulate why this is so. My deepest fascination with sex has to do with its relationship to the mind, the body, and the spirit. True that I have experienced some of the most unspeakable, grueling stories of abuse, self-sabotage, I also see the light/uplifting side of it. I find it fascinating how the entering into the abuse makes me come out the other side with so much hope, and appreciation for the beauty of life. Speaking about the scared and divine nature of sex also makes me appreciate what an expansive topic it is. It covers from politics, religion, to mythology to social studies. It is what humanity shares. Sex breathes life into stories, and vice versa. From nothingness comes everything.

Write a "selfie" in words of yourself six months from now, a vision of your optimal well-being, including especially your new perspective on your emotional and physical well-being. What is your vision of optimal well-being in body, mind, and spirit? Imagine yourself, your physical appearance, your stream of consciousness or interior monologue, your energy level, your interactions with others, your day, what you say, what you do, and how you feel. Looking into the future like this, write a descriptive paragraph, a "future selfie in words" using these questions to guide your writing.

. . . again, I feel that I am beginning to see a new self emerging. Someone who is willing to acknowledge her own energy in its fullness, no longer ashamed or embarrassed by the passions she feels toward life, and the risks she's willing to undertake. It's a deeply gratifying experience/moment to come to terms with the many sides of self. To see the light as well as the darkness. I have become more versed at shedding light into the darkness and imbuing that darkness with light. I am understanding how light is a quality of existence—feather-like, weightless, and the lightest of being where nonattachment is the key quality. I am understanding how positive energy exchange can be of deep rest, and that can be work or relationships. It's okay to always have more on the plate, and how I am interested in refining the containers/lens through which I communicate with the world. The form is not the message, but the form shapes the message. If our Being is like water, then the way we choose to live out our lives are determined by the styles/designs/questions we choose to engage with/others in. I am examining more deeply these systems of communications within my system/world/self.

5 Tips for Helping Professionals

1. Use expressive writing research to guide prompts and practice.
2. Use specific, evidenced-based prompts and sequences.
3. Use post-writing reflections to measure the process and progress.
4. Meet the clients where they are at. Allow anything new to emerge without expectation or judgment.
5. Share your own expressive writing to heal experience.

5 Tips for Clients and Journal Keepers

1. Take a courageous and open-hearted approach to journal writing. Stay open to whatever comes up.
2. Treat the writing prompt not as an assignment, but as a gift. Use meditation to help ground yourself before opening the writing prompt if needed.
3. Use the post-writing reflection to measure your journaling process.
4. Be your own scientist and pay attention to what works for you.
5. Observe the three-day rule (to avoid re-traumatizing yourself): stop writing if you write with the same perspective, tone, and word choice for three days.

3 Journaling Prompts

1. Write your deepest thoughts and feelings about something you have never shared with anyone.
2. Using your name or preferred pronouns, write about the something that keeps you up at night or that you think about more often than you would like.
3. Write a "selfie" in words of yourself six months from now, a vision of your optimal well-being, including especially your new perspective on your emotional and physical well-being.

Appendix: Post-writing Reflection Survey

Please complete the following questionnaire.
Put a number between 1–10 from the following scale after each question.

1	2	3	4	5	6	7	8	9	10
Not at all				somewhat				a great deal	

1. To what degree did you express your deepest thoughts and feelings? ___
2. To what degree do you currently feel sad or upset? ___
3. To what degree do you currently feel happy? ___
4. To what degree was your writing valuable and meaningful for you? ___
5. In the space below, briefly describe how your writing went. You do not have to share the content of your writing but reflect on your experience of writing and anything you associated with the process of your writing. (Write for approximately five minutes.)

 ## About the Authors

John F. Evans, MAT, MA, EdD, is a writing clinician and national board certified health and wellness coach who works with groups, individuals, and health care professionals, teaching them how to use writing for better physical, emotional, and spiritual health. Evans has authored five books and has taught journaling and writing for self-development for over 30 years. Evans often teaches at Duke Integrative Medicine and Duke's Health Humanities Lab. With James Pennebaker, Evans co-authored *Expressive Writing: Words That Heal* (2014). His book, *Wellness & Writing Connections: Writing for Better Physical, Mental, and Spiritual Health* (2010), is a collection of essays from the Wellness & Writing Connections Conference Series (2007–2010). At Duke Integrative Medicine, Evans has taught Caring for Caregivers, Legacy Writing, Transform Your Health: Write to Heal, Leading Patients in Writing for Health, and Writing as a Tool for Integrative Health Coaches. Evans blogs for *Psychology Today* in Personal Perspectives and is in a private practice at Psychology Associates in Chapel Hill, NC. www.wellnessandwritingconnections.com.

Shu Cao Mo, EdM, is a social entrepreneur advocating for individual and collective transformation through arts and education. She has organized student and teacher training workshops and has spoken on the future of education in China, India, Mongolia, Korea, and Japan. As a curator, she has presented public art productions in the United States and in China. Her work has been reported by the *Huffington Post*, and her social commentaries recorded on *Sydney Morning Herald* and *This American Life* (NPR). Born and raised in Hangzhou, China, Shu Cao Mo received an EdM in Arts in Education from Harvard University and a BA in Philosophy Theory and Theater Studies from Duke University. More information can be found at http://splash-institute.org/.

Writing to Your Future Self

21

April Bosshard

The human imagination contains incredible power. Using only our minds, we can project ourselves into alternate realities, including potential futures. Though we are still uncovering the mysteries of the human brain through ongoing neuroscience research, our imaginations can always be put to good use in support of our creative and personal well-being. One way to do this is to build relationships with different parts of yourself across time.

Your Past, Present, and Future Selves have wisdom and guidance to share. Journaling to tap into these inner resources can yield profound insights that can help you solve problems, heal hurts, and create more of what you want in life.

Asking for guidance from your Future Self requires a calm and open mind. Setting up a quiet environment and engaging in relaxing breathing techniques also helps deepen the experience. The intention is to reach across time to a future version of yourself—either to ask for help getting from "here to there" or simply to establish a line of communication between who you are "then" and who you are "now."

Freewriting in your journal, you can pose fairly simple questions, such as "What's one thing I could do today that could help me one year from now? What about five years from now?" Or you can hold an image in your mind of a desired future outcome, picture yourself living it, and ask that Future Self what series of decisions, experiences, and feeling states led to that outcome.

It's important to let the answers arise gently. Don't grab for the "shoulds" your ego-mind would like to burden you with. "Lose five pounds" might be something you wish for, but it's not the kind of demand your Future Self would come up with. "Walk often in the forest" or "laugh more" or "spend one day a month in silence" is more likely the kind of suggestion you'll get (and this would still end up having a direct impact on your health).

Short-term guidance is available too. You can journal on a question like, "What can I do today to help me get through tomorrow?" Or: "What few things this week will set me up properly for next week?" You might hear a whisper saying, "Get a good night's sleep" or "Call so and so for a supportive conversation." The advice is likely to come quickly and intuitively and you may resist it at first; but this type of inner listening and trusting helps you to build connections with yourself across time.

At the end of a writing retreat I taught in France, I invited each of the participants to write a letter to their Future Self. I had purchased fine French stationery and distributed a couple of pages to each writer. Everyone wrote to the Future Self that would receive this letter one day. Rather than asking for advice, this time their Present Selves captured their unique experiences so that their Future Selves could relive some of the richness of the summer retreat time.

Many months went by and everyone forgot about the letters, but one December day an envelope arrived in the mailbox. Each person said their letter arrived at exactly the right time with the exact words they needed to hear. They felt instantly connected to those retreat experiences, written by a Present Self (who was now a Past Self) to a Future Self (who was now a Present Self).

It turns out that we can move back and forth (and side to side) through time, accessing subtle inner resources that allow us each to be our own best friend, across time, if we choose. When people are asked to identify their primary relationship, they most often think of another person close to them, but the fact is *you* are your primary relationship—it's *you* who benefits most from your time, care, and attention.

Setting up a dialogue between your Present Self and your Future Self creates a connection to what feels like an inner mentor. This connection is supported by choosing, in the present moment, to develop a similar relationship to your Past Self and other Present Selves—other versions of yourself who might handle the moment just a little bit differently. You can tap into other Present Selves to help deal with problems and make decisions. I highly encourage people to thank their Past Selves for things they've done, thought, and felt that helped get them where they are now.

We all respond well to positive feedback, but we tend to look outward for this recognition rather than inward. Yet giving *ourselves* positive feedback sets up a trusting internal bond across time. Try thanking your Past Self for the goodness you're experiencing in your life right now. Maybe you once had the courage to talk to a stranger at a party years ago and that person is now your best friend or spouse. Maybe you worked hard to finish a project and are now reaping some rewards.

Thanking your Past Self for past efforts has an interesting impact on the Present Self. Registering the extra appreciation, the Present Self unconsciously engages in more efforts that will lead to more appreciation in the future. Another interesting twist occurs when the Present Self quite consciously makes an effort and devotes that effort to the Future Self (for example, "I'm flossing my teeth for you, Future Self"). The result is a lively and deep sense of harmony between who you are now and who you are becoming in the future.

Riding this wave of inner harmony, you are more able to support yourself in the present moment, too. At any given time, many of us are struggling with stressful situations or facing difficult decisions. It can be useful to reach out to an alternate Present Self. We always know more than we think we know, and consulting another version of ourselves—one who is less stressed or one who isn't worried about making the "right" decision—can give us access to more of our innate wisdom. What does the Present Self who isn't worried about losing his or her job have to say? What about the Present Self who knows that friend's remark wasn't meant to be hurtful? Pausing to consult alternate Present Selves can, with practice, connect us to more options for responding to life's problems and setbacks.

Exploring the connections between your various selves across time gives you access to profound personal wisdom and powerful creative energy. The following tips offer ways to help yourself and others solve problems, envision possible futures, uncover alternate ways of dealing with situations, and create lasting connections with who you've been and who you are, so that you can discover all you *could* be.

 5 Tips for Helping Professionals

1. *Write a letter to your Future Self.* If you have an ongoing relationship with a client, invite them to write a letter to their Future Self. Encourage them to write candidly about their fears, worries, hopes, and dreams, as if to a trusted friend. Provide a blank envelope into which this letter can be sealed and promise to send it to them after a decent amount of time has passed (say, three, six, or nine months). Address it yourself so they don't recognize their own handwriting when it arrives.

2. *Envision a desirable future.* Ask clients to write down some of the details of a desired future. Encourage them to see it in their mind's eye and feel it in their body, allowing all the sensations of this vision to amplify. Desires have *feelings* associated with them; the particulars of any vision include feeling a certain way. Ask the client to identify this feeling in a Future Self and then have them ask that Future Self which paths led to this feeling outcome.

3. *Solve problems creatively.* When a client's problem seems insurmountable, invite them to project themselves one year into the future, *after* the problem has been solved. Have them ask their Future Self how they got through this particularly difficult part of their life. What did they have to let go of, confront, nurture, and persist with to arrive at a solution?

4. *Remain calm, light, and receptive.* When encountering the Future Self, deep breathing, loose free-associative journal writing, and having zero expectations are key. We have tremendous wisdom within but it prefers to arise gently and does not respond to anxious demands.

5. *Listen for holistic guidance.* Our Future Selves have our best interests at heart and will provide general guidance. Messages received may advise you to relax, let go, or trust; or be strong, have courage, or endure; or simplify, help others, or turn away. Whatever messages arise, allow a few extra minutes to expand on them from the present vantage point. If needed, create a dialogue and ask your Future Self a few clarifying questions.

 ## 5 Tips for Clients and Journal Keepers

1. *Value your whole self.* We often look outward to others for answers about who we are on the inside, but when we do this we miss out on a deep reservoir of wisdom within. Who you are and who you've been are foundational for understanding who you *could be.*

2. *Appreciate your Past Self.* Make a habit of thanking your Past Self for things you did earlier that you're benefiting from now. Start small. Maybe you ate a delicious peach at breakfast. Say, "Thank you Past Self for deciding to buy these delicious peaches." Work your way up to larger things, such as applying to grad school, moving across the country, or getting out of a difficult relationship.

3. *Consult another Present Self.* Using your imagination, choose one circumstance in your life and change it. Then ask yourself how you might do things differently, how you might feel, how you might behave. If money weren't a concern, how might I deal with "x"? If I only had one year to live, would I still decide "y"? What if I knew I couldn't fail? These questions access parts of your mind that may be feeling stuck *because* of circumstances. By exploring alternatives our imaginations can offer new and unexpected solutions.

4. *Invite your heart to the conversation.* Before dialoguing with your Past, Present, or Future Self, take several deep breaths while focusing on the heart area. Tune into the deeper wisdom of the *heart* of your other selves. What used to make your Past Self's heart sing? What allows your Present Self's heart to expand now? Ask your Future Self's heart to tell you what it longs for.

5. *Write it all down.* Building a trusting relationship between your different timeline selves can be healing, insightful, and effective for manifesting new things in life. The process is perhaps more important than any outcomes, but you may want a journal record to refer back to down the road. Your Future Self will thank you.

3 Journaling Prompts

- What could I do today that my Future Self will thank me for later?
- What do I most appreciate about my Past Self?
- If my Past, Present, and Future Selves sat down to talk, what would they say to each other?

About the Author

April Bosshard is a writer, Story Coach, and creator of Deep Story Design. She helps writers all over the world navigate the personal and creative challenges that arise while working on long-form narrative projects, such as novels, screenplays, and memoirs. Find out more: www.deepstorydesign.com.

Journaling and the Reinvention of the Self One Loop at a Time

22

Meryl Cook

Journaling saved my life. It helped me to recover from breast cancer treatment and to reinvent myself after a 20-year practice as a homeopath. Journaling has become an integral part of my design process as a fiber artist. Now I'm using journaling and design at the corporate level for employee well-being and engagement.

My story began at age 59, just after I finished treatment for breast cancer. When I was diagnosed, I made the decision to leave my homeopathy practice. I knew that cancer was illness at a very deep level. I made myself a promise that I would allow the time and space I needed to heal and to figure out how to move forward.

When I was a homeopath, I saw far too many people who rushed back into life after a crisis like a job loss, an illness, or a period of grieving. They would have a wakeup call and make the decision to institute some changes, but they didn't allow space or time for this to happen. We need to be willing to step into the space of not knowing for the solution to arise.

An important component of reinvention is the ability to think and dream outside the box. The week I finished radiation treatments, I attended a workshop on journaling and yoga led by author Sheree Fitch and yogi Josette Coulter. I learned how writing can help to unblock the body, even just by the physical act of writing, and how moving the body can help to unblock the mind.

"What If" Exercise

An exercise I learned in this workshop is called "What if." Sheree suggested as a daily writing practice to write two or three "What ifs" a day. Writing a

"What if" is to write about possibilities and to dream wildly. Don't worry if some are silly or seem very far out. Write whatever wild dream pops into your head. I have added to this exercise a second component: imagine how your body would feel if your "What if" came true, and sketch or write about this.

The "What if" exercise helps us to get over blocks, opens up creativity, and also helps our body to begin imagining the healing flow it needs. After a period of writing daily "What ifs," my experience and the experiences of many of my workshop participants was that many of our wildest dreams and imaginings have become a reality.

From that day in 2016 I began my journaling practice. I wrote and wrote every day, and also spent time at my rug-hooking frame. Both the writing and the hooking were my way of holding space for myself, allowing my next steps to emerge. I found that the more I wrote, the more design ideas I had.

Journaling became an integral part of my design process. Prior to 2016, I had been rug-hooking and designing my own rugs for about seven years. I would be inspired by a scene or a quote and this would lead to a design idea. Once I began journaling about how I wanted my life to unfold, I started to sketch the sensations and the body feelings of my dreams and aspirations. These simple sketches became the design concept. I wrote phrases from my journal around the edges of the design. As I hooked, the phrases became a form of meditation.

One Loop at a Time

Each rug became the next step I needed in my healing journey. I wrote and hooked seven rugs. Their titles evoke the feelings I was trying to create for myself: Curvy Lines; Joy Releasing; Love Letter; Dancing Wildly with Joy; Breaking Open; Dancing in the Wind; and Abundance.

These seven rugs and the accompanying journal notes became my first book, which led to teaching others to write and hook themselves love letters and design their own healing mats. This led to my second book and to a career as a speaker and facilitator.

The title of my first two books and my approach to reinvention is *One Loop at a Time*. This refers to not needing to figure out all the details or to understand the whole process in order to begin making changes. When I began my reinvention after breast cancer, I didn't know where I was going or what I would be doing. I knew I needed and wanted to make a change. I made that decision and allowed myself the time and space to see what unfolded.

"One Loop at a Time" is a freeing process. It is the freedom to not have to have everything worked out in advance, the freedom to make changes along the way, and the freedom to get started without always knowing the end result.

Self-compassion Is Self-care With Love!

Each successful reinvention starts with self-compassion. One of the rules when I facilitate workshops is to leave your self-criticism at the door, enjoy the process, and see what unfolds.

How hard would it be for you to write yourself a love letter, a note of encouragement? I was surprised recently in a writing workshop I was facilitating. Several of the participants struggled with this "Invitation to Create" from my latest book *One Loop at a Time, The Creativity Workbook*:

> If you were writing yourself a love letter, a letter of encouragement and love, what would you say? What is the most loving thing you could do for yourself? How would your body move to express this quality? Sketch or write about this.

We are often good at writing short notes of love and encouragement to others, but find it difficult to do the same for ourselves. Perhaps you find it much easier to be self-critical. Treating myself with compassion and kindness is something I have been working on in recent years. I realized that my tendency to be harsh with myself was holding me back—from taking risks, from being audacious, from moving forward. In fact, I would say it was a block and a hard habit to break.

These things I know and . . .

When life is moving quickly or I have hit an obstacle that I don't know how to get around, I can become overwhelmed. At these times, I will first make a list of the strengths I bring to the situation. I call this "These things I know." Then I make a list of what I need at this moment to feel less overwhelmed and to feel better. Sometimes my "What do I need right now" is as simple as I need a nap, or a cup of tea, or to get out and walk my dog.

Three Essential Ingredients

There are three essential ingredients to journaling for reinvention of the self.

1. Space—allowing the time and space to journal and to imagine marvelous solutions.
2. One step (or loop) at a time—not trying to solve or figure out everything at once.

3. Self-kindness/Self-compassion—being gentle with yourself and taking time to encourage and praise yourself when you are struggling.

Regardless of where it leads me, journaling continues to be at the core of how I reinvent myself. I turn to the issue at hand using the process that works for me and write and design my way to flow and movement again. It has helped me change my life, allowed me to help others with their own reinvention, and now I use it as one of my main tools in the corporate work I'm doing.

5 Tips for Helping Professionals

1. Pivot. Encourage clients to express the problem they are experiencing in their journal, but then to quickly pivot to imagine the feeling they wish to create. I think it's important to acknowledge the negative emotions, but not to dwell on them.
2. Many of my writing exercises involve tapping into the body feeling. This practice trains the body and brain to look for and recognize positive sensations. It also encourages us to ground ourselves and be present.
3. Ground rules. I have found that my workshop ground rules (leave your self-criticism at the door, share only if you wish to, enjoy the process) create a safe space and encourage participants to open up.
4. Encourage clients to reinvent at any age. It's never too late.
5. Help your clients find a journaling practice that works for them. For some it is to set a regular time for writing, while for others it helps to carry a journal with them so they can write when inspired.

5 Tips for Clients and Journal Keepers

1. Carry a journal everywhere, so you can write when you have a moment.

2. Write freely, keep the pen moving, and don't worry about writing something profound. Let your thoughts and the ink flow.
3. Try sketching. If you usually write, try sketching sometimes to express what you are experiencing.
4. Use your journal to visualize where you want to be in your life or your career by writing three to five "What ifs" a day for a few months. Look back periodically to see what has developed!
5. Use the 80/20 rule. When I journal, I focus at least 80% on where I want to be in my life. It is important to acknowledge the negative, but don't give it a lot of weight. I try to write a few sentences about what is not flowing at the moment, but then I shift to imagining what flow feels like and how to get there.

3 Journal Prompts

1. What if? Write about three possibilities or wild dreams. Imagine how your body would feel if your What if came true, and sketch or write about this.
2. If you were writing yourself a love letter or a letter of encouragement, what would you say? Sketch or write about this.
3. "These things I know" and "What do I need right now?". When something is troubling you, write a list of the strengths you bring to the situation. Then write what you need right now to reduce your stress and feel better.

About the Author

Color, texture, joy, and self-compassion are the key features of Meryl Cook's beautifully crafted hooked rugs, her books about her journey from homeopath to artist and journal writer, and her journal writing practice. Meryl is the author of two books, *One Loop at a Time: A Story of Rughooking, Healing and Creativity* (2016) and *One Loop at a Time, The Creativity Workbook* (2017). What began as a way of holding space for herself following breast cancer treatment has led Meryl to a career as an artist and to working with corporate teams around well-being and engagement.

Mindful Writing for Transformation

23

Jen Johnson

When I write, I feel at home. When I do not write, I feel adrift in longing and searching for home. To write is to know in my body, heart, and mind that writing is healing. Each day, I pick up my journal and pen, and in that moment, I am already at home. Mindful writing allows me to make order from the chaos and loss that life inevitably brings, create a cohesive story from my experience, and make meaning from it. As I write, I shape the fragments of story into an integrated narrative, and I listen for the deeper meaning that emerges.

I have loved writing for as long as I can remember. I've been practicing mindful writing for transformation with committed regularity since my mid-thirties following my aging mother's relapse with addiction, near death by suicide, and eventual death from cancer. Mindfulness and writing have been two of the most powerful practices in my journey of healing from those losses.

Researchers have long emphasized that processing traumatic events requires creating a coherent narrative that changes our existing schemas, thus providing order and integration and encouraging healing. In considering ways to deepen the transformational experience of writing, Poon and Danoff-Burg (2011) found mindfulness to be a moderator in expressive writing.

Their study found that people who scored higher on a measure of mindfulness as a personality trait experienced greater benefit from expressive writing exercises that involved disclosing emotions and thoughts related to stressful experiences than people who scored lower on the measure of mindfulness. Therefore, this author incorporates mindfulness with transformational writing practices to facilitate greater therapeutic benefit from the writing.

Mindfulness is maintaining awareness of the present moment with curiosity and kindness. Mindful writing is a practice that involves allowing the narrative that emerges to be as it is and to meet it with curiosity and kindness. It involves also meeting our subsequent present moment responses to the writing—sensations, feelings, and thoughts—with kindness and curiosity. This practice allows us to relate with our experience, our writing, and our self with tenderness and compassion. And after all, isn't this quality of mercy and compassion what is most called for on the journey of healing from loss and other difficult times?

How do we treat ourselves in response to loss and other difficult experiences? Do we meet ourselves with judgment about how deeply we feel the loss or get entangled in regret over what we wish we had done differently? Or are we able to embrace our humanity and meet ourselves with an open heart and compassion?

As human beings, we are continually creating and revising our identity and the ways that we perceive ourselves through the narratives that we construct about the self. "Narrativity is a hallmark of postmodern theorizing about autobiography, that is, that identity is both declared and created with narrative" (Charon, 2006, p. 73). The theory of narrative identity suggests that we all create an evolving internalized story about our lives that weaves together our reconstructed past, perceived present, and anticipated future. Constructing a narrative identity provides a sense of purpose, meaning, and unity to the self, all of which positively impacts mental health (McAdams, 1996, 2001).

In *One Writer's Beginnings*, Eudora Welty (1983) describes herself as being a listener *for* stories: "Long before I wrote stories, I listened for stories. Listening *for* them is something more acute than listening *to* them" (p. 14). Listening for the narrative themes in our writing and in the writing of our therapy and coaching clients shines a light of discovery onto the themes of stories from the past and illuminates a way toward healing in the present and future. The stories that we tell ourselves and others about our identity and our lives determine how we will heal from the difficult experiences that we encounter—loss, illness, and trauma.

If you had to tell the story of your difficult experiences in one or two sentences, what story would you tell? What would be the plot of the story? Would those sentences emphasize the tragedy, or would they emphasize the ways that you have overcome the tragedy and the meaning you have made from it? How can we begin to shape our stories in ways that nurture healing? Mindful writing for transformation can help us to reshape our stories from chaotic narratives of loss or tragedy into narratives of healing, agency, and personal growth.

Therapists and coaches, what narrative themes do you hear in your clients' stories? One narrative element to listen for that points toward meaning is thematic content, and one of the central narrative themes associated with positive mental health is agency, or the ability to influence our lives (Adler,

2012). Another relevant type of narrative element to listen for is narrative coherence. Stories that include high levels of narrative coherence, including a sense of temporal coherence, causal coherence, thematic coherence, and coherence drawing from a cultural concept of biography, are correlated with positive psychological outcomes (Adler, Wagner & McAdams, 2007).

We can become more effective therapists by listening for the narrative themes in our clients' stories and using those themes to help guide the collaborative process of creating therapeutic goals with our clients. We can also use these themes to guide the choice of mindful writing for transformation prompts with which we invite our clients to engage.

As mentioned previously, the stories we tell determine how we will heal. And whatever we rest our attention on grows. Our thoughts shape our emotions, mental health, and physical health. Neuroscience research has shown that when we dwell on positive events and resources, even for 10–30 seconds throughout the day, it rewires the brain for happiness and resilience.

Active recovery of positive emotions such as peace, hope, joy, gratitude, compassion, and awe are important aspects of the process of restoration when healing from loss. The mindful writing for transformation model offers practices to support learning how to be skillfully present with the pain as well as practices for restoring positive emotions and experiences. In order to support the cultivation of positive emotional states and traits, the mindful writing for transformation model includes, but is not limited to, writing prompts that focus on cultivating inner strengths and resources.

Neuroscience research has shown that neurons that fire together wire together. Donald Hebb determined as early as the 1940s that

> when an axon of cell A is near enough to excite a cell B and repeatedly or persistently takes part in firing it, some growth process or metabolic change takes place in one or both cells such that A's efficiency, as one of the cells firing B, is increased.
>
> (1949, p. 62)

Theoretically, then, if we link a positive experience with a difficult experience, the neural network that has formed related to the difficult experience may weaken, and the neural network being formed related to the positive experience may strengthen.

In this author's experience, utilizing this process to assist the client in building inner strengths and resources can serve as a foundation of resilience that supports the client in moving forward in the additional tasks of grief work. Through mindful writing for transformation practices, we can teach our clients how to skillfully be present with difficult feelings without suppressing or indulging them while simultaneously making an effort to stay emotionally balanced by cultivating joy and other positive emotions.

What stories are we telling ourselves, and how will those stories shape our experience of healing? The story that I tell about my relationship with my mother is that she taught me how to find mindful refuge in nature. Another is that being her daughter helped me to learn how to more skillfully be present with pain while simultaneously cultivating joy. A third is that being her daughter helped me to become a more resilient person and a more compassionate teacher and therapist. Mindful writing for transformation helped me to reconstruct the layered and chaotic stories of loss into a cohesive and healing narrative. Narrative medicine is about storying our experience in a way that allows us to transform suffering into meaning. May we all offer our mindful presence to listening for the deeper meaning in the stories that we hear and tell.

Writing Prompt

I invite you to bring your attention to the breath, noticing the expansion of the chest and belly with the inhale and release of the chest and belly with the exhale. When the attention wanders, bring it back to the breath. Continue this practice for about two minutes.

For about ten minutes, write a cohesive narrative about a loss or other difficult experience. Focus on writing your deepest feelings and thoughts about the experience. Write about how the experience has affected your life and how it has shaped who you are today. Write about any ways you have become stronger or have grown as a result of the experience.

Now recall a specific moment when you felt peaceful. For about ten minutes, write about that moment in detail—where you were, what you saw, heard, and smelled. Write about how your body felt in that peaceful experience. As you recall the experience, write about how your body feels in this moment.

5 Tips for Helping Professionals

1. Practice being mindfully present with your clients.
2. Listen *for* the story that your client is writing or telling.

3. Listen *to* the story that your client is writing or telling.
4. Invite your client to identify the narrative themes in their stories.
5. Teach your clients mindful writing for transformation practices that both allow them to safely be with difficult feelings and create internal resources and strengths.

5 Tips for Clients and Journal Keepers

1. If writing about something makes you feel overwhelmed, put the pen down and stop writing.
2. If that happens regularly, consider seeking the support of an experienced licensed therapist before proceeding.
3. If you don't feel ready to write about the loss, you may find the second part of the writing prompt useful, writing about peace, as a way to begin to build additional internal resources for resilience.
4. Try to approach whatever arises in the writing practice with kindness, curiosity, and compassion.
5. If you are feeling hopeless, or if grief is keeping you from reconnecting with life, please seek the support of a licensed therapist.

3 Journaling Prompts

I invite you to begin with a brief mindfulness practice by bringing your attention to the breath, noticing the expansion of the chest and belly with the inhale and release of the chest and belly with the exhale. When the attention wanders, bring it back to the breath. Continue this practice for about two minutes.

1. A difficult experience that still needs my attention is _____. My deepest feelings and thoughts about the experience are. . . (five minutes)
2. The ways that this experience has affected my life and how it has shaped who I am today include _____ and the ways that

I have become stronger or have grown as a result of the experience include _____. (ten minutes)

3. A specific moment that I recall in which I felt at peace was _____. The details that I recall about that moment (what I felt, saw, heard, and smelled) include _____. As I write about that peaceful experience, in this moment what I notice happening in my body is _____. (ten minutes)

References

Adler, Jonathan M. Living into the Story: Agency and Coherence in a Longitudinal Study of Narrative Identity Development and Mental Health Over the Course of Psychotherapy. *Journal of Personality and Social Psychology*, vol. 102, no. 2, 2012, pp. 367–389.

Adler, Jonathan M., Wagner, Joshua W. & McAdams, Dan P. Personality and the Coherence of Psychotherapy Narratives. *Journal of Research in Personality*, vol. 41, 2007, pp. 1179–1198.

Charon, Rita. *Narrative Medicine: Honoring the Stories of Illness.* New York: Oxford University Press, 2006.

Hebb, Donald. *The Organization of Behavior: A Neuropsychological Theory.* New York: Wiley, 1949.

McAdams, Dan P. Personality, Modernity, and the Storied Self: A Contemporary Framework for Studying Persons. *Psychological Inquiry*, vol. 7, 1996, pp. 295–321.

McAdams, Dan P. The Psychology of Life Stories. *Review of General Psychology*, vol. 5, 2001, pp. 100–122.

Poon, Alvin & Danoff-Burg, Sharon. Mindfulness as a Moderator in Expressive Writing. *Journal of Clinical Psychology*, vol. 67, no. 9, 2011, pp. 881–895.

Welty, Eudora. *One Writer's Beginnings.* Cambridge: Harvard University Press, 1983.

 About the Author

Jen Johnson, MS, MFA, LCMHC, CRC, BCC is a mindfulness teacher, coach, and counselor offering an integrative approach to mind-body healing and resilience. Her areas of specialty include stress, grief and loss, illness, and trauma. Jen teaches online workshops on mindfulness, creativity, and mindful writing for transformation. Find out more on her website: jenjohnson.com.

Visual Journaling   **24**

How to Create a Dialogue With Your Subconscious Mind

Cherry Jeffs

In Athens one year, I waited for my boyfriend to finish his day's work so we could explore the city together. To fill the time, I experimented with a stream-of-consciousness drawing technique I'd recently learned. It claimed to help "make thoughts visible."

As I worked with the drawings, I began to realize that I was being mentally bullied in my relationship. As a result, I extricated myself from that damaging relationship a couple of years later. I never regretted leaving the relationship and I continue with this visual journaling practice to this day.

What Is a Stream-of-Conscious Drawing?

A stream-of-consciousness drawing (SOCD) is a nonrepresentational drawing. We can use it to interpret an idea or concept or to discover the kernel of a problem and solutions to it.

SOCD come from a part of us untouched by external expectations or ideas of right and wrong. They allow us to engage deeply with our subconscious and transfer what we learn to paper, literally making our thoughts visible. From there, we can interpret the insights further by writing or verbalizing.

Why Stream-of-Consciousness Drawings Should Be in Your Toolkit

It happens to me all the time as a coach. A client presents with a problem that isn't the real one, the one that's really affecting their situation. At times, it can be difficult to see past this and to get to the heart of what's actually going on. The client herself may struggle to find adequate words to describe her problems. Or, consciously or unconsciously, she may use words to mask her deeper feelings.

A Simple Technique to Help Your Clients Achieve Autonomy

Of course, your ultimate goal as a helping professional is to guide your clients towards autonomy. To enable them to navigate their problems without your help.

The simple SOCD technique can help your client become more emotionally self-sufficient and resilient by engaging with feelings of anxiety or dissonance and finding effective solutions to their problems.

No external help in interpreting the drawings is necessary. But you can use the interpretation stage of the SOCD process to dialogue with your client. And, as a client, you can use SOCDs even if your helping professional doesn't suggest them. It's up to you whether you share what you find. This technique is also a great supplement to regular journal writing.

The Benefits of SOCDs

SOCDs are quick to do and don't need any special tools or space. The technique is simple to learn and can be done anywhere. SOCDs are small and portable and to a casual observer they look like doodles.

This makes it an ideal technique for you to share with your clients. They don't need a private space to work and they don't need a lot of time—which lowers the bar to entry and makes implementation much more likely.

The Ability of Drawing to Clarify Complexity

As you will see in the exercise later in this chapter, the power of drawing lies in its ability to encapsulate a whole problem in a single, unified image. A drawing can reference past, present, and future all in one space. It can express complex relationships between different areas of our lives, emotions, and needs.

You Already Speak the Language of Line

Let's face it, a journaling technique involving drawing sounds "hard." But the SOCD technique isn't about being good at drawing. It's about using a visual language. A language made up of instinctive marks coming from the subconscious. A language we already know how to speak!

Even the simplest lines are full of information that our brains can interpret. Try this super-quick exercise yourself to understand what I mean. Then share it with your clients as a first step.

Simple Expressive Line Exercise

On a sheet of paper, close your eyes and draw three lines:
1. Draw the first line as quickly as you can.
2. Draw the second line at medium speed. Not as fast as the first but not slowly either.
3. Draw the third line really slowly. Take a long time to move your pencil across the paper.

Now look at your three lines. Which did you draw quickest? Slowest? What is it about the lines that differentiates them? You're witnessing the language of mark-making at work. The speed of the line is intrinsic to the line itself. You can't separate one from the other!

How to Do an SOCD

You'll need:

- A blank journal page or a sheet of paper (A4 / letter folded in half or quarters)
- A drawing pencil (not too hard) or a ballpoint pen

Instructions

1. Draw a frame or boundary to contain your drawing—a roughly drawn rectangle or any shape that feels right. Don't worry about straight or symmetrical edges. You are literally "drawing a line around" the problem to bring it into focus.

2. Close your eyes and visualize your problem or dilemma. Don't verbalize it too much before you draw. Limit yourself to open phrases like:

    - "What I feel about this situation is . . ."
    - "What's bothering me is . . ."
    - "What I don't understand about . . . is . . ."

3. Hold the problem or concept in your mind and body, as you begin to draw.

    Suspend your need to know what the drawing will look like. Trust it will be what it needs to be.

4. Instinctively draw marks and lines within your frame. Make many or few, heavy strokes or light, short marks or long. And any combination of these. There's no right or wrong here.

    Don't draw "pictures" or use symbols. (Raindrops, shooting stars, flowers, and the like.) Use only the language of marks. Enjoy and wonder at each stroke you make. Sense its impulse as it travels from your subconscious to the paper.

5. You're done when the image *feels* complete. You might sense a sudden "click" or silence in your head.

Grasping the Meaning of Your SOCD

Once you've finished your drawing, spend some looking at it. Hold it at arm's length to get a sense of the whole. Bring it closer and examine the details.

To Grasp the Meaning of Your SOCD, "Capture" It in Words

Do this by writing, voice-recording, or telling someone else about what you see. You don't need to write or speak in full sentences. Even single words are okay. Spend as much or as little time on this as you need.

Here are a few ideas to consider when looking at your drawing:

- What parts stand out most?
- What areas seem out of place or disconnected?
- What aspects are you attracted to?

You might find the interpretation difficult at first. But the more often you draw and interpret an SOCD, the easier it becomes. It might take a day or two to assimilate what you've discovered. And sometimes you'll need to do another drawing, or a series of drawings, to fully understand the situation.

5 Tips for Helping Professionals

You can help your client explore their SOCDs by talking through what they've discovered and suggesting related topics to go deeper into a theme.

Here are 5 tips to help them get the most out of the process:

1. Reassure your client that SOCDs aren't a "drawing exercise." You don't need to be "good at drawing" to do them.
2. Offer slightly provocative questions for your clients to address to help bypass resistance. As their confidence with the technique grows, they will be able to pursue their own line of investigation.
3. Help your client towards greater understanding of their SOCD, by suggesting statements such as the following as jumping off points:

   - This drawing makes me feel. . .
   - I don't understand. . .
   - This part reminds me of. . .
   - I see now that. . .

4. Don't let your clients procrastinate looking for the perfect notebook in which to do the drawings. A folded sheet of printer paper or index cards are enough.
5. Experimenting with SOCD drawings yourself will help you "read" your clients' drawings. They can also help illuminate the needs of a client you're struggling to understand!

5 Tips for Clients and Journal Keepers

How to Use SOCDs as a Coaching or Therapy Client

You can use SOCDs as part of your regular mental hygiene process to ensure issues and problems don't get buried or ignored. Especially if you aren't able to tackle them with your therapist or coach straight away.

How You Can Use SOCDs as a Journal Keeper

SOCDs are a great adjunct to any journaling practice. Use them to go deeper into something you've written that's puzzling you. Or continue to explore the ideas they spark in your written journal.

1. Remember to date your SOCDs so you can revisit them for extra insights. Or to see how your feelings and actions evolved due to the insights you gained.
2. You don't need to keep a special notebook for these drawings. They add an exciting extra dimension to a written journal. You can also take photos of your SOCDs and add them to a digital journal.
3. Looking at SOCDs upside down literally gives you a new perspective—often about the inner workings of the situation.
4. Although you didn't deliberately draw symbols, you might "see" symbols in your drawings. In the search for meaning, our minds latch onto anything tangible or identifiable. It's fine to go with that.
5. To use SOCDs when something indefinite is nagging at you, let your mind go blank and allow the drawing to discover and explore what the problem might be.

 3 Journaling Prompts

There's no "right" way to ask questions of your subconscious. One useful method is to pretend you're seeking answers from an oracle like the I Ching.

For example, you might ask:

1. How should I approach dealing with . . . now?
2. Why am I feeling so . . . about . . . at the moment?
3. What's the meaning behind my reluctance to. . .?

Open questions prepare you to receive the wisdom of your deepest insight and stop your conscious mind attempting to skew the answers before you start!

About the Author

Cherry is an artist who makes "artists' books." She's also a lifelong journal keeper and a writer about the creative process. During her first 40 years she had a tortuous on-off relationship with her own art-making, but remained committed to her calling as an artist. To overcome her creative blocks, she experimented with all sorts of techniques for building a resilient creative practice—including journaling of all kinds! She finally emerged as the joyous and productive artist she was meant to be. She now uses her writing, her compassionate and motivational work with coaching clients and her art itself to share everything she learned. Visit Cherry at https://www.cherryjeffs.com.

Creating Change in Three Steps

25

Aneesah Wilhelmstätter

This vision-led self-coaching tool for creative change will help you, the journal keeper, design your dreams and fulfill your wishes through the following game-changing three steps:

1. H = Heighten your hopes
2. O = Optimize for optimistic outcomes
3. P = Plan to prevail

Each of these three steps leads with a clear intention, offering a corresponding prompt to help us accomplish what we intend to accomplish. We get to choose whether we become pioneers of possibility instead of prisoners of the past. Hop on board to get your HOPES up in 3–2–1. . . we have lift off!

Step 1. Heighten Your Hopes

Step one invites you, the journal keeper, to envision yourself living as an exemplar of those cherished values you hope to stand up for. No matter what we intend to create and accomplish, it must be rooted in a clear, compelling, rich, and high vision of the Greatest Possible Self (GPS) we aspire to become. Holding to this aspiration as our highest hope and anchor, we can always allow ourselves to feel a replenishing and renewable sense of self-sufficiency, satisfaction, and success, in spite of objectively optimal and minimal outcomes.

When you are the coach, you can help your clients explore what virtues and values are particularly meaningful to them, as well as what their aspirations are, identity-wise, in each of the priority areas of their lives, including in their relationship with themselves. You can prompt your client to do this for the chosen priority domain of life, be that work, energy regulation, love, learning, or some other domain. Building up profiles for each of the three or four priority domains can provide clients with common themes for creating a master profile.

The aim of this exercise is to identify seven things a person can imagine "doing" that are pathways of showing up as the best version of themselves. These doable things that represent more "a way of being" can be expressed in terms of values, virtues, identities, strengths, and a self-care daily practice to "get into this greatness." A characteristic seven such things might be: wisdom, courage, joy of learning, heroic pioneering, tenaciousness, trustworthiness, and a daily "virtue meditation practice" where the client reflects on these qualities.

How I use it: first, I picture a situation where I need to follow through on some action to get a task done in service of my goals and objectives. I have found it particularly meaningful to use it with the help of this delightful trio: "I can hope to . . . I can hope for . . . I can hope that . . .". It's one way of saying: "I can always hope." I self-reflect as follows:

> *I can hope to become who I must become to live a full and fabulous life, joyful and free as I make myself into my own masterpiece. I can hope for the courageous generosity to give whatever I've got to become who I must become and do what needs to be done. I can hope that I can gather strength as I go, exemplifying trustworthiness, generosity, courage, wisdom, transcendence, justice and love.*

Step 2. Visualizing Benefits

Step two gives you, the journal keeper, a taste of the benefits you can hope to experience as you work towards creating phenomenal changes and tangible results. Look into the week ahead of you. What is one thing in that targeted area of your life that you really want to accomplish? What is this goal that is important to you? Now, lift your gaze beyond that horizon, say, four weeks forward. Still looking towards those dearest desires, imagining the forms that success can take that would feel satisfying for you.

If you are the coach, help your clients train their focus on how they want to feel when their wishes are fulfilled. Encourage them to give themselves permission to go towards what feels daunting, yet possible and plausible. Their goals should stretch their abilities. Ask your client: "How is your life changing as these miracles are happening for you?" It can also be useful to create mini guided visualization scripts of the following sort:

> Gaze into this great new life of yours and step into it so that you may feel it as deeply and as fully as you can. As you give yourself a sense of that pleasure, engaging all of your senses, continue to notice and name how you hope to feel when you work towards and create all that you want. Returning to the present moment, try to capture the sense you have of these benefits in seven words that are emotions and feelings. Now turn to your journal and write these words down.

Step 3. Strategizing for Strength-Building and Skill-Building

With the help of an action-oriented planning tool "Possibility in 21s," we can all strategize for strength-building and skill-building so as to move forward toward our goals. The great news is that you, the journal keeper, have already started doing this, in steps 1 and 2! This action plan list of 21 items is really made up of three lists, each highlighting seven doable things. You get to decide how to number it. The first seven items are your identified "highest hopes." Then, for items eight through 14, enter the seven emotionally beneficial states you hope to embody. In this third part of the transformation process, you design a when-I-can plan. It can be useful to determine three specific behaviors to implement. Then, for one of these behaviors, craft two expectations you can practice holding and two thoughts you can think to bring yourself in alignment with your intentions.

For journal keepers, here's one way you might do this. On a new (perhaps ruled) page, allocate seven lines for each of the seven things to do. On the first line, write down the word "WHEN." Leave room to fill in the time, place, and/ or situation when you will take this step. Draw a line down the middle of the next five lines to create a tactics table. On the left uppermost line, write down, "Instead of . . .". Moving over to the right, put down the words "What if, I CAN . . .". This is the planning pattern to apply to all seven items: three behaviors (B), two expectations (E), and two thoughts (T). I like to call this part of the possibility game, "Placing my BETS!". Every day, I ponder this possibility: "What if it's possible for me to do this thing, engage this new expectation, and think this new thought? Imagine how my life might change!"

Game on! The magic continues to happen when you, the coach, bring your creativity to the coaching work, helping your client address the obstacles they pose to themselves when it comes to putting those plans into play. The seven new choices can now be added to complete the list of 21 things they can do.

5 Tips for Helping Professionals

1. Experimenting with a provocative, passionate, and playful voice invites your client into awe. The added advantage is that it contributes towards enriching the relationship and the coaching experience for both you and your client. Clients are inclined to reciprocate.
2. Introducing ritual, perhaps by using a "prompt" that might include words, movement, breath, or a combination of these, serves as a useful ceremonial bridge that creates a smooth transition from one way of being present to another.
3. Invite clients to identify their top signature strengths. Engaging in active recall, such as when these strengths served their challenge-meeting efforts, helps them harness their inner resources and increases a sense of agency and competency.
4. Guide your client to make congruent and meaningful choices by encouraging them to redefine success. When setting their sights on certain objectives and outcomes, clients need to determine what their definition of true success is.
5. Building "relationship" is an invaluable contributor to a client's motivation and transformation. Creating a safe haven, inquiring into deeper underlying needs and encouraging the sharing of feelings with an attitude of unconditional positive regard help clients feel seen and supported.

5 Tips for Clients and Journal Keepers

1. Cultivating the skill of self-inquiry helps you focus on, clarify, and reinforce your intentions. It also helps generate insights that inform your implementation efforts. Looking within for answers generates hope through establishing a sense of direction, agency, and options.
2. You can upgrade your self-inquiry to include "Sleep Prospecting." By going to bed with a wonder-evoking prompt such as "I wonder

what new meaning I can invest in this?", you prime yourself to awaken, ready to receive fresh insight.

3. When you focus on your wins, and celebrate your heroic obstacle-meeting efforts, you are building up a memory bank that serves as a self-renewing Power Supply of encouragement and builds resilience.

4. An enjoyable way to call on your Greatest Possible/Prospective Self is to use an index card as a cue and a calling card. This VISA card (**V**irtue, **I**dentity, **S**trength, and self-care **A**ction), is a useful tool for making more congruent choices, choices that are more likely to lead to enduring and sustainable transformation.

5. Commit to regularly updating your prospectus (i.e., your H-O-P-E-S [**H**igh Hopes; **O**utcomes; (obstacle-meeting) **P**lans; **E**xpectations; and **S**trategies]). Doing this reminds you that this is an iterative process (i.e., one of trial and error).

 3 Journaling Prompts

1. I can always heighten my hopes *In This Picture of Possibility*, what greatness am I witnessing that inspires me to become all I must become?

2. I can always optimize for optimistic outcomes. In my *Greatest Possible New Life*, what bountiful benefits am I experiencing as I overcome obstacles and work to create phenomenal changes and tangible outcomes?

3. I can always plan to prevail. In my present *Great New Life*, what 21 possible, practical, plausible things can I do that signal my intention to play to my strengths as I move forward toward my desired outcomes?

 About the Author

Aneesah Wilhelmstätter identifies herself as a miracle worker and wish whisperer, painter, graphic artist, creativity and life purpose coach, herald of hope, writer, and course creator and facilitator. Still living the expat adventure, since leaving her country of origin in 1998, she has resided in Paris, London, and the Netherlands. Her international travels, with their consistent call to self-reinvention, sparked her passion for change, transition, transformation, and *The Hero's Journey*. She is the author of several books including *Passion to Performance*, *The Expat's Way*, and *The Thankful Way Journal*. She has also designed the *Tarot of Experience*. Aneesah graduated in the social sciences, worked in mental health at the Johannesburg General Hospital, before founding Creative Change Coaching in 2001. You can connect with her on Facebook at Creative Change Coaching (www.facebook.com/creativechangecoaching/).

The Trauma-Sensitive Writing Process

26

Emelie Hill Dittmer

The course *Writing for Healing Purposes* aims to find new paths that can help us discover and explore, through writing, the consequences of traumatic or significant life events.

Course participants need to have had, to some extent, worked on themselves through counseling and/or alternative therapy, as this process could be an upheaval if in an emotionally raw state.

One of my course participants reflects on the 20-week-long program I've been teaching at a Folk High School in Sweden, an institution for adult education. She writes: "My senses have become enhanced, I am heard and seen and feel more today. I now dare to trust my intuition, I'm stronger and more sensitive. My fear towards cancer and death no longer exist, I'm no longer scared."

The Writing for Healing journey has been profound for her and 20 of her fellow course participants. As a facilitator, I find it exhilarating to witness a client's reflections. She shares more of her experiences with me. . .

> Writing for me is a laboratory, experimenting with a situation in a past and present tense. I can express myself from the outside, as I wish, relating to the situation, instead of how I did at the time. I can test what it would be like if my heavy thoughts did not exist.

This method was developed by the Swedish writing movement called *Write Your Self*, which helps people reclaim their voices and stories after experiencing trauma.

It began in 2011 with its foundation in James W. Pennebaker's and Louise De Salvo's research.

Since my certification in this Writing for Healing method, I have facilitated many groups both in Sweden and England. I started at a charity that supports people with mental health needs where we explored intimate subjects, gradually integrating a trauma-sensitive writing program and protocol.

The key factors in trauma-sensitive writing are trust, patience, and resilience. Working through an eight-step foundational program takes participants to different times and places. Each process leads individuals safely through the turbulent waves of their past.

The eight steps include the following:

1. A Room of One's Own
2. Begin Writing
3. Self-Care
4. The Writing Body
5. Genres
6. Subjects
7. Creating Wholeness
8. Expressing the Wordless

I divide the facilitation process into three phases:

1. Reflection time, preparation, self-care, and trust.
2. A stage of deeper writing, flow, and everything that wants to arise.
3. Aftermath. You read through what you've written, read it aloud, and receive feedback, which you think about; and then you rest.

When we revisit trauma for the purposes of healing, what do we need to get there? This is a question I'm asked frequently, often at the beginning of the process. There is no simple answer, but I start by saying that we must embrace the notion of a gradual process, comparable to a meditative state.

We must practice deep listening, patience, and resilience during the initial reflection period, building a safe *room of one's own*, in preparation to return to uncomfortable places.

We must learn to trust that something valuable will take shape. This is possible when we respect ourselves and the writing process. It's important to take your time to feel everything, then you can gradually let go, allowing healing to begin.

Writing ourselves through our fears and expectations is challenging. I remind my clients that what emerges from their writing might not be what they had expected or even wanted, but it may actually be what needed to come out. We never know what will evolve. This usually baffles the writer and it is not until they have reached a certain point that they realize this truth.

We start by reflecting on the writing process itself and how to create a physical, as well as a mentally safe state for writing of this nature. What does this space look like and how does it feel to be there? This helps to achieve a relaxed state, where we can tap into the stories that we need to express.

We then gently move on to "writing in flow" through the use of imagery. At the end of the writing session, we ask ourselves "How do I feel?" and "What surprised me the most about the session?" Gentle free or flow writing is how we begin writing our most vulnerable stories and we follow up this writing with self-reflection.

Step four, *the writing body*, is a breakthrough for many.

By creating a dialogue with parts of our body that may carry our trauma, all the senses begin to awaken. The body thinks and feels to a much greater degree than we believe or are aware of and focusing on the body is a crucial part of the process. After this work, something shifts as we enter a new stage with a sense of flow and newfound curiosity. We are then more willing to go further into our memory archives, unlocking some of those tightly locked doors.

It is important to remember that writing about traumatic events is purely for your benefit. But what if you do want to share what you've written? Midway into the course, we carefully invite each other into our writing rooms, as we can heal on a more profound level when allowing others to be a witness. When we truly break the silence, a beautiful interplay and prerequisite for change occurs.

I often hear participants say, "I have realized that silence hurts me a lot." Some clients want to go deep as soon as possible in order to remove traumatic events from their system. However, by working gradually, we open up in a safer way, and it becomes less of an effort to remember.

Next, we channel our experiences through a fictive persona and write various key scenes, moving between past and present. We attempt to create a memory archive as this is a good system for collecting and storing subjects, topics, and the many details that may flood in and overwhelm us.

The more tools we use, the easier it is to find the answers to our questions and to make stories from our fragments, with the goal to *create wholeness*.

Once we are far into our stories, we are then ready to create a timeline focusing on significant and complex scenes, as well as what has brought us joy. A map of the past to the present day helps us notice what nurtured us and is a reminder that we are safe.

The final exercise is to write a different ending to our story. We now start to become more accepting and ready to review earlier writing, binding the story together and expressing the wordless as we enter the so-called "aftermath." During this time, it is very important to eat well, get plenty of sleep, and use the writing journal for self-care.

We can't erase what has happened to us but we can seek acceptance and profound meaning when reclaiming our voice, power, and strength. This writing technique is sustainable and brings us comfort. As one student put it, "Writing has given me acceptance, a deeper meaning and a certain distance. Everything has significance, even the most difficult experiences. To get all these stories out of me and my body has brought more harmony."

5 Tips for Helping Professionals

1. Always acknowledge the person first, then bring the focus back to writing.
2. Ask questions, but do not question; this helps to fill in the necessary gaps. Find the right way to communicate.
3. It is important to have a dialogue about what kind of feedback helps the client. Is there a specific focus? Assist with writing routines or a plan?
4. Early guidelines are important especially in a group context. Primarily, writing and the texts we are working with are the focus, not our lives. This creates a safe framework for your mutual collaboration and becomes a part of a sustainable writing process.
5. Maintain a diary, documenting challenging sessions with a client or group. Acknowledge your own reactions, feelings, and patterns. This can be a great source, as well as a release after a tough session.

5 Tips for Clients and Journal Keepers

1. Allow at least ten minutes reflection time prior to and after your writing session. Asking the following:

   What would you do before a session, to prepare yourself?
   What could you do after, to change focus and release or take care of feelings that came up while you wrote?

2. Remembering at your own pace can take different lengths of time. Remain observant and curious.
3. Document the process, your feelings, and reflections in a writing journal, before, during, and after the session.
4. Remembering what nurtured you through a difficult time is key to your safety in the present moment. Contemplate what brings you a sense of gratitude, appreciation, and joy now. What are your gifts and accomplishments, no matter how small?
5. Practice daily flow writing for any amount of time. Compare the first and last paragraph of your text; is there a connection? If so, how can that help you onwards?

3 Journaling Prompts

1. Find a picture that appeals to you and base your freewriting on this image for a five-minute period.
2. What have your hands been through or created? Use this focus for a ten-minute exercise.
3. Write about a past event, attempting to alter the ending.

About the Author

Emelie Hill Dittmer is a therapeutic writing teacher based in Sweden. She established a unique program in Writing for Healing Purposes, at an institute for adult education. She also offers online classes, workshops, one-to-one tutoring, courses, and lectures. She blends trauma-sensitive and expressive writing methods developed both in Sweden, the U.S., and England, along with her own material.

Healing Organs Through Nonverbal Color Journaling

27

Pragati Chaudhry

When someone undergoes trauma, the memory and language centers in their brain can become compromised. When this happens, they experience an inability to express themselves completely via words. Often one is not even aware of the impact the trauma has had on their emotional and physical body. Nonverbal journaling has been found significant in recovering this lost or subconscious information. Advancements in brain research confirm that instinctive, nonverbal insight can be helpful in healing negative and painful emotions caused by trauma.

Poorly managed negative emotions and attitudes create feelings of helplessness and hopelessness that begin to affect the physical body. Chronic stress upsets the body's hormone balance, depletes the brain chemicals required for happiness, and damages the immune system.

In order to change physically manifested discomfort, the body needs to release the stress that is causing discomfort. Releasing tension and stress through color journaling has the potential to bring the body back into balance.

The Relationship of Organs With Emotions

Many believe that every organ in the human body corresponds to the frequency of a certain emotion. When a given organ is exposed to repeated stress, imbalance begins. It has been found that many times a physical disorder linked to a certain organ actually stems from an imbalance in the emotion associated with that organ. Emotions are inevitable, but it may be that when they are repressed, disease occurs in the organs that process those particular emotions.

For example, it has been found that fear and anxiety are common emotions in people diagnosed with a chronic kidney disease. The emotion of anger is believed to be stored in the liver and gall bladder. Sadness is believed to affect the lungs, whose functions include respiration, oxygenation, and keeping a healthy immune system.

Breakthroughs in neuroscience are now confirming that the nonverbal portion of the brain plays a significant role in processing sadness, anger, fear, and other emotions. Awakening the sensory, nonverbal processor with a simple creative act, such as splashing color on paper, has given survivors of trauma a means for emotional release.

In cases of trauma-induced stress, verbal coaching and therapy typically can't fully assist clients because clients have trouble using language expressively. Trauma may well have affected their capacity for verbal expression. Engaging the nonverbal portion of the brain allows them to communicate more fully, release stress, and restore homeostasis.

Nonverbal Color Journaling Exercise

The following is a three-part exercise that helps a person release anger through color journaling:

Part 1. Preparation for the exercise

1. Plan for a 35- to 40-minute period of uninterrupted time.
2. Bring some liquid colors, Q-tips, and cardstock paper.
3. Have something with you that can help you time the sections of the exercise.

Part 2. Warm-up

1. Find a comfortable table and chair, and for a few minutes, close your eyes and notice what comes up. Simply listen within without judgment and write the first three words down that come into your awareness. These words don't need to connect or make sense together.
2. After you have written these three words, draw your attention to your first word and choose three colors. You don't want to expand the palette

of colors beyond three, because that will limit spontaneity and will bring attention to its visual appeal. The use of Q-tips is recommended for the same reason since artistic brushes or palette knives can limit the spontaneity of raw self-expression, so refrain from using those.

3. What does that word bring up? There is usually a visual splash of colors that comes up, which equates to feelings brought up by the word in your brain. Without effort, your brain begins to work accepting and acknowledging those feelings evoked by the first word.

4. Then think of the second word you wrote, and see or sense in your mind's eye what splashes of color it brings up. For instance, if the word is "angry," notice that engaging with its expression immediately starts the release of anger. You are allowing and acknowledging the stressful emotion and this allows its energetic and emotional charge to dissipate.

5. When you are done with the third warm-up word, please put your papers and Q-tips to the side. Now you are ready to dive into deeper waters!

Part 3. Diving into the issue

1. When you are ready, close your eyes and take a few breaths to connect with the anger issue (or other issue) that brought you to coaching. We will work with this issue now, in four parts, and include all of the color splashes on one sheet of paper.

    A. For five minutes, express through nonverbal color journaling your response to this question: "What is this anger really about?"

    B. On the same paper, engage with the following question for another five minutes: "How is this affecting my life?"

    C. Then tackle the following question for another five minutes, using the same paper: "What will happen if I let this anger go?"

    D. The last question to tackle is: "Where do I go from here?"

People have reported that engaging the nonverbal portion of their brain allowed them to release and heal their anger in a deeply transformational way.

Anger is a natural emotion that is characterized by the feeling that someone or something has deliberately done you wrong. It can be a good thing, and can motivate you to find solutions to problems. But if it is denied altogether, it has negative effects, not only on your relationships, but also on your body's health, in particular your liver. Anger goes hand-in-hand with resentment, and unless released, it hinders us.

There is amazing potential in the release of this emotion. People start by expressing what makes them angry and they then express how they respond to its consequences. Through the course of this nonverbal self-expression with color journaling, the emotion starts to take a turn for almost everyone: they begin to see beyond the anger, and start to experience some emotional ease. As this happens, locked up energy is released, and there is an increased feeling of peace and well-being. Nonverbal color journaling can help heal organs and bodies.

5 Tips for Helping Professionals

1. Sometimes, people are aware of the symptoms of a wound within, but are unconscious of its deeper cause. This is the place where energy can be blocked and it might affect their expression of health and vitality. Supporting clients with color journaling can help them discover what they might have suppressed and give them a way to express it.
2. The warm-up exercises are important for color journaling. It allows people to become comfortable with the unusual materials of Q-tips and make-up sponges. The choice of such materials is for discouraging representational expression. If engaged with representational forms, they would likely become engaged with artful depiction instead of healing.
3. Refrain from reading meaning into their creative expressions. The methodology of color journaling is unique, and self-revealing to every person. As a facilitator, I abstain from my inferences of others' works. I encourage them to share their own insights, and this brings them to a place of great confidence and peace.
4. While facilitating color journaling, adding background music isn't necessary. Music carries its own mood and can influence people in subtle ways.
5. Your clients, or you, do not need to have prior art experience for color journaling. People create from their inner guidance—the process is self-directed and deeply transformational.

5 Tips for Clients and Journal Keepers

1. Acknowledging emotional pain is a necessary step in healing. But sometimes, we are not even aware of what we may have buried

deep inside through the journey of life. When we live this way, denial stays in our energy field and between us and our life purpose. Engage your nonverbal abilities to release pain.

2. Everything is energy, including your thoughts and words. Scientists have found that the resonate energy of words directly influence the structure of the medium of water which incidentally constitutes much of the human body. We are creating our life with pure thoughts and energy and we can create differently from awareness.

3. Through expressive release, powerful questions, and energetic awareness, we can bring intention to our journaling. The expansive creative energy emanating from our beings loves to splash colors!

4. Start unlocking everything that is keeping you stuck in a limited reality. Through self-expression, arrive at a "lightness" within yourself. See how the issue served you, the gift in it, the story in it, the blessing in it, and move forward with the new energy that supports your well-being and life purpose.

5. While we have come to identify with the few aspects of our existence— our gender, our age, our nationality, our position in society, our personal preferences, all things that come and go—we may not have realized the gift of who we truly are. Journal to discover the gift you are!

 3 Journaling Prompts

1. *Trapeze Artist*
   Imagine you are a trapeze artist and have to let go of something secure and grab onto something new. You hold on to one trapeze and let go to catch the next one. Focus on what it feels to be in the space in between. Journal these feelings with colors.

2. *Skies*
   Close your eyes. Take a deep breath and relax. Imagine you are looking at a sky that is so colorful, it appears to be painted. As you scan your gaze across the sky, it appears to change in temperature as well as color. When you are done scanning, open your eyes and paint the feeling of the sky, in any color.

3. *Freedom*
   Take a deep breath and relax. Express what it feels like to be free, whatever "free" means to you in this moment. Choose any colors to paint your feelings about your freedom.

About the Author

Pragati holds a degree in Fine Arts (MFA), and in teaching Fine Arts (MST), and loves leading people to a space where they stop creating from struggle and start reclaiming their true power. She has had the privilege to work with extraordinary people from all around the world who have followed their calling to connect with their own creative alchemy. Trained as a creativity coach, and having studied trauma-informed expressive arts therapy, she offers coaching and workshops for deep transformation through art and writing.

Check out Pragati's offerings here:

Creative Alchemies, "Healing with Art" workshops:

www.creativealchemies.com.

Conscious Creation Energetics, workshops in "Writing with Awareness":

www.consciouscreationenergetics.com.

Journaling for Coach and Therapist Self-Care

28

Lynda Monk

Helping professionals are story keepers and due to the nature of our work, we are often listening deeply, with a desire to help and with empathy engaged. We absorb, in some ways, the various stories in our clients' lives. These stories are inspiring, traumatic, difficult, painful, or uplifting in nature—depending on who our clients are, why they seek our help, and our specific roles as helpers. These factors and many others can influence the types of stories we hear in our line of work.

As helpers, coaches, healers, and change agents, we are listening, asking powerful questions, being empathetic, nonjudgmental, and compassionate, while holding our clients as creative, resourceful, and whole, all in service to supporting their well-being, healing, growth, and goals that brought them to seek our support in the first place. Narrative and story are at the heart of our transformational work. Through the helping process, caring is at the occupational core. It is this very caring and commitment to helping our clients that can lead to the common occupational hazards in helping careers including burnout and vicarious trauma.

Early in my social work career, I worked in child welfare, children's mental health, suicide prevention and intervention, crisis response, and eventually health care. I quickly learned that if I buried every single painful or complex emotion I felt as a helping professional, it wouldn't take long for it to become overwhelming and to change my view of the world from a place of goodness and inspiration to a place of trauma, hardship, and risks. I did not want to pay that kind of price for helping others. I wanted to find ways to care for myself that would allow my health, happiness, resiliency, and optimism to thrive.

While I loved my work as a frontline social worker, I became more interested in how getting out of bed each day to help other people, often in very difficult circumstances, impacted the well-being of people doing this type of work. This question led me to direct my Master of Social Work (MSW) studies towards learning as much as I could about burnout prevention and self-care for helping professionals. During my studies and research, I kept happening upon mention of the importance of reflective practice, and I started noticing that journaling was often highlighted as an effective way to help prevent caregiver burnout.

This discovery was a light-bulb moment for me regarding the role that my journaling practice was playing in my own well-being as a helping professional. I reflected and recalled that I often had journaled after difficult days, after painful losses, after witnessing the hard situations my clients were in and so on.

Excerpt From My Journal

Here is an excerpt from a past journal entry, written many years ago, after reflecting back on the role my journaling played in my own well-being as a helping professional:

> *I filled journal after journal with the stories we did not speak. I wrote in the parking lot, sitting in my car, after the funeral of a thirteen-year-old boy who hanged himself in his family garage after the last class of the day. I wrote deep into and out of all this pain and suffering, his and mine. I did not know it then, as a 25-year-old social worker, that I was writing to keep myself whole, sane and observant of life bigger than all this blackness. I was writing to find and celebrate resiliency, mine and others. I was writing to construct meaning out of the most meaningless tragedies. I was writing to hold a positive perspective, to stay in touch with optimism. Writing allowed me to keep breathing when I was holding my breath for too long. Writing held me up, sat me down, kept me believing in the power of the human spirit and it still does.*

The breakthrough understanding was that my journal writing practice was a very important part of my self-care, leading to healing and renewal as a helping professional. A couple of years after completing my master's degree, I decided to leave my work as a medical social worker and start my own training and coaching business specializing in burnout prevention for helpers, healers, and leaders. Eventually, I also trained and certified as a professional coach. I offered training workshops, retreats, keynote presentations, and online courses for universities; and regardless of the specific topic being taught or presented, I always gave participants an opportunity to journal. While there are many, many things we can do for our self-care, I really believe having a regular, reflective journaling practice is the secret self-care ingredient that can really make a difference in nourishing the health and well-being of helpers.

Why Is This?

First of all, it has to do with the nature of the occupational hazards that are common risks for helpers, including, but not limited to, burnout and vicarious trauma.

Burnout is the accumulation of occupational stress over time. It happens to professionals who were once on fire with a sense of purpose in their work. Gradually, while serving this purpose, while serving clients in need, subtle deprivations of one's own replenishment and wellness needs can set in. This might look like skipping lunch, choosing to work straight through breaks, over-giving at the expense of one's own self-care, and so forth. Eventually the professional feels miserable and depleted, and can be suffering from many emotional, physical, psychological, and spiritual symptoms of burnout.

Vicarious trauma, unlike burnout, can happen in an instance when through listening and bearing witness to the traumatic stories that clients might share, helpers can become traumatized themselves. This indirect exposure to trauma experiences can begin to impact the helper's world view, sense of safety, and can trigger very similar symptoms to PTSD (Post-Traumatic Stress Disorder) in the helper himself or herself. It is imperative that helping professionals have self-care strategies that mitigate the risks for these, and other, common occupational hazards associated with the work they do. Journaling is one self-care practice that research shows can make a positive difference for the well-being of helpers. There are many studies that show the health and wellness benefits of expressive journal writing, for example, *Writing to Heal: A Guided Journal for Recovering from Trauma and Emotional Upheaval* by Dr. James Pennebaker; and an edited collection of research called *The Writing Cure: How Expressive Writing Promotes Health and Emotional Well-Being* by Stephen Lepore and Joshua Smyth.

Why Engage in Journaling for Self-Care?

1. *Process thoughts, feelings, and stressors*
   The journal is a place where we can process the stories we hear, and more importantly, make meaning out of all we witness. It is also a

place to track our personal stress levels, and engage in a healthy way to explore them and find solutions to the challenges and stressors inherent in our career and life. Journaling offers us pause, and allows us to notice and express our feelings and also make commitments to actions that flow from the self-awareness we gain from personal expressive writing.

2. *Cultivate personal and professional growth*
    Expressive writing through journaling is an empowering practice that can help us cultivate both personal and professional development. Journal writing, when used in this way, can be an enriching, contemplative, and reflective practice.

3. *Achieve greater coaching or counseling mastery*
    Journaling requires that we are fully present. Helping others requires this full presence as well. When we take time, on purpose, to journal—to be still, attentive, and reflect on our work and how our work impacts us and others—we are generating what Janet Harvey, MCC, calls the "artful pause that generates professional mastery."

4. *Tap into our inner wisdom and personal power*
    As human beings, we possess a personal power and wisdom that often goes untapped. This is true for coaches, helpers, and clients alike. In part, our role as coaches is to help others, and ourselves, to discover this potential and power within. To do this we must listen to our intuition and instincts about our own lives and our ways of being and doing, so that this self-awareness can infuse into success in all we strive to do. At the same time, we must also notice our resistance to doing this listening.

Self-Care Benefits of Journaling

There are many benefits to having a reflective journaling practice for self-care as a helping professional. These can include:

- Increasing your learning
- Taking action towards your goals
- Decreasing stress and overwhelm
- Accessing inner strength and resilience
- Improving emotional, physical, psychological, and spiritual health
- Deepening professional mastery

- Expressing gratitude
- Focusing on what brings joy, satisfaction, and meaning in life and work

Journaling is something that is easy to do. You can weave it into the natural rhythm of your days. You can journal for five minutes to transition between clients. You can start your day by journaling your hopes and intentions for the new day before you. You can write a list of things you are grateful for at the end of your day or before going to sleep. As we often say as coaches, what we focus on grows. Journaling is a self-care tool that can help coaches, counselors, and our clients to live more awakened, healthy, and conscious lives.

Author and journaling expert Christina Baldwin writes, "There is a Spanish proverb which says, there is no road; we make the road as we walk. I would say the same things about journal writing—we make the path as we write."

 5 Tips for Helping Professionals

1. Engage in reflective practice as part of your burnout prevention efforts. Be sure to have your own reflective self-care practice that you tend to on a regular basis. These might include mindfulness, meditation, reflective peer supervision, and, of course, journaling.
2. Prioritize your own purposeful renewal pauses in the midst of it all where you take time, daily, to pause, breathe, relax, journal, reflect, and renew.
3. When journaling to process your emotions or your reactions in relation to the client stories you are hearing, make sure that you are respectful of confidentiality in your journal too. In other words, write about how you are feeling and your own needs and responses, versus the details of your client's situations.
4. Balance your self-care with other-care. As helpers it is easy to fall into over-giving, over-caring, and abandoning one's own needs. This is an imbalanced trajectory that can lead to burnout. Explore what balance means to you within the pages of your journal.
5. Be sure that if you are recommending journaling to your clients, that you are also engaging with this transformational healing tool in your own life. There is an underlying synergy and strength that comes from all parties going to the page, even separately from one another.

5 Tips for Clients and Journal Keepers

1. Remember that whatever you write is right. You are always the expert of your own lived experience. In this way journaling is always a self-empowering practice.
2. Allow your journal to hold a balanced perspective. Write about the challenges of life, as well as the joys, beauty, and mysteries.
3. Cultivate resilience in your journal through writing about your strengths, your hopes, your optimism, and the goodness you see in your life and in the world. This can be especially challenging to do during difficult times, and it is this focus that helps uplift you and engage your resilience to thrive during times of adversity.
4. Be curious as you journal. Curiosity is the cornerstone to all learning, self-discovery, and personal growth. Asking questions in your journal is one way to invite deeper awareness so new insights, ideas, and inspiration can emerge.
5. The people who tend to get the most out of journaling as a tool for healing are those who are open to self-discovery and growth through self-expression. Give yourself permission to know, grow, and care for yourself through writing. Trust yourself and trust the process of writing about your thoughts and feelings to help nourish your own well-being and resilience.

 3 Journaling Prompts

1. What are the ways you currently care for yourself emotionally, physically, psychologically, and spiritually? Create a list of your current self-care practices, as well as a list of things you would like to do more of for your self-care.
2. What brings you joy, satisfaction, and meaning in your work as a helping professional?
3. What do you need at this time in your life and work? How can you meet that need?

About the Author

Lynda Monk, MSW, RSW, CPCC, is a Registered Social Worker and Writing for Wellness Coach. She is the Director of the International Association for Journal Writing (http://IAJW.org) and the founder of Thrive Training and Coaching (http://lyndamonk.com). She is co-author of *Writing Alone Together: Journaling in a Circle of Women for Creativity, Compassion and Connection*, as well as author *of Life Source Writing: A Reflective Journaling Practice for Self-Discovery, Self-Care, Wellness and Creativity*. Lynda has supported thousands of people to go to the page and write for personal growth and well-being through both in-person workshops, retreats, and online events.

Spiritual and Nature Journaling

PART V

Meditate on Paper   **29**

Kimberly Wulfert

Introduction

Meditate on Paper uses writing instead of silence used in traditional meditation, to act as the bridge to connect you to your inner wisdom or the spiritual. This bridge is made of unconditional love and acceptance. You may feel supported, heard, understood, and cared for when using this approach to journaling.

First, there are two common challenges to discuss.

Writing communication from spirit is not difficult, but it does take practice like in traditional meditation. Practice is repetition. This builds neuronal pathways that become entrenched as a memory and a mind-body mapping in your brain, and creates a muscle memory in your body making this writing flow more effortlessly over time. Think of yourself as the driver and writing as the transportation that wisdom or spirit uses to get the message to you. Just as you can drive your car to the same place repeatedly without much deliberate attention, the less attention to the writing you pay, the more it will flow without your opinion clouding the message.

Trusting your interpretation of the information received takes time. The key to establishing trust is in practicing, documenting, and mindfully following what occurs as you act or do not act in accordance with your interpretation of the guidance.

Meditate on Paper combines a way to connect and document these experiences over time. With this record, you build trust in yourself and the messages communicated to you. Although fun to receive, flashes of insight are not apt to be relied upon without established trust.

Focused attention, self-reliance, decisiveness, and mindful self and other compassion all help to bring strength and ease into your life. Engaging in this type of writing helps you cultivate these qualities and supports you to greet the mysteries of life as adventures to explore.

The Meditate on Paper Workshop

This workshop was developed for nonclinical groups of adults. Writing prompts are neutral or positive stimulants, and there is no reading of the journaling rather just discussion to process the experience and gain personal insights. I am not aware of negative experiences resulting from the methods I describe here. With individual clinical or coaching clients, I specify the dynamics of a situation for them to journal about and tailor methods to their state of mind. To journal writers reading this, I suggest you practice the methods in the order presented, choosing low emotion questions until you feel confident in the process.

I begin the workshop sharing much of what I wrote in the introduction. After that the participants share their names, where they live, and what they hope to get out of the workshop. This often gives me insight into what spiritual beliefs are present so I may adjust my language accordingly, and it provides a window into their expectations for the workshop at the onset which I can then address. People may bring in complex or longstanding emotional situations in hopes of finding answers. I remind them they are learning a new skill which takes time and practice before they can confidently probe more deeply through their written communication. I dissuade them from asking about highly emotional or traumatic events at this early stage.

Next, we discuss the handout which highlights key factors about the Meditate on Paper process for them to keep in mind. First is the approach to writing. In brief, be open and receptive, write down whatever comes through your hand AS IT comes through without editing, reading, or attempting to understand until the communication is completely done. Then read it slowly beginning with the question. It may take a few readings, days, or weeks for the intended message to become clear.

Second, how you phrase your question matters. Use exploratory phrasing and be specific rather than vague. Although yes or no questions used intermittently within the context of a long dialogue of writing can be successful, avoid them otherwise. Instead, use phrases that explore the situation and options such as the following:

* How can I best approach _____ .
* What am I missing in regards to _____

- What does my body want me to know about _____
- What am I not understanding about _____
- What will happen if I do _____

(Time: 35 minutes)

Next, I take them through a guided meditation to stimulate their chakra energy. In Ayurvedic medicine these are energy centers turning like wheels that connect your subtle energy bodies—the ethereal, emotional, and mental—to your physical body. In particular I focus on the Root, Throat, Third Eye, and Crown chakras respectively for grounding, self-trust and expression, intuition, and the connection to spirit in order for the clients to be aware of their highest good.

(Time: 10 minutes)

Then, using the warm-up prompts that I provide to them verbally, they journal to prime their mind, memory, and hand. We discuss their experience briefly after each prompt. The prompts are listed later in the chapter.

(Time: 45 minutes)

The Four Journaling Methods

I spend about a half hour with each of the following journaling methods and discussion. Participants do not read what they wrote aloud, but instead share what they learned or experienced using the method. All sharing is optional, but I find most participants do share. I answer any questions after each method is experienced.

1. **Nondominant Hand Writing**

   Chose something you are wondering about. Write it mindfully as a question. Then switch the pen to your nondominant hand and write, more likely print, whatever comes through to your hand. Usually, it is short. You may sense another question arising in response. If so, switch to your dominant hand to write it down and then switch back to the nondominant hand to write the response. Read only when completed.

2. **Body Wisdom Writing**

   Jot down a physical problem that has been bothering you lately. It can be any discomfort or pain, an illness, tension, fatigue, or headache. One at a time I will ask you four questions which, in turn, you will pose to your physical problem itself. Be the voice of your physical problem by writing what comes into your awareness in answer to these questions.

1. What purpose do you serve in my life?
2. Why are you using my body to talk to me?
3. Are you speaking through my body in any other way?
4. What do I need to do to help you to get better?

With an open and curious mind read the question and your body's communication back. If you want to know more or need clarification, continue with an inquiry, and receive the response in writing. I think you will discover that your body carries a deep well of wisdom.

3. **Dialogue Writing**

Think of a conflict you want to resolve. It can be a current conflict or a past one that keeps looping in your mind. Formulate a question that asks the other something you want to know.

When dialoguing in writing, place a colon mark after your name, and with a curious sincere attitude write the question to the person. Then, to signify you are tapping into their energy, on the next line write their name with a colon mark and let their response flow. Continue the dialogue using the name and colon mark to consciously shift the point of view. You will sense when the conversation is complete. Read it through entirely a few times. Journal your takeaway and any action you could take.

4. **Automatic Writing**

Automatic writing is energy "spoken" to you through writing. Begin visualizing your Source energy and open to receiving its wisdom and message with gratitude and curiosity. Before writing, intentionally relax your upper body and breathe, allowing letters to form onto the page. Continue writing whatever comes through until it naturally ends; avoid paying too close attention or censoring since this will stop the automatic writing process. Stay open and neutral in the spaciousness of the connection within or from the Universe, letting the pen be the voice of the message.

You can:

- Ask to receive whatever message is right for you now
- Choose a topic and ask what you need to know at this moment
- Ask questions about a current dilemma of yours

Conclude the workshop in a manner that suits your situation. Allow adequate time for sharing, comments, and questions.

5 Tips for Helping Professionals

1. Read them Mary Oliver's poem "The Journey" after the introduction.
2. To conclude the workshop, ask the participants to share their favorite writing method and why they chose it. This will usually indicate their biggest discovery.
3. Check in two days after the workshop with a general inquiry follow-up email because suppressed emotions or questions could emerge.
4. In private settings, choose the method and tailor it to the client. Specify the situation or question to focus on. Ask them to journal in this way on one or more occasions and discuss it with you next time. They may read it to you or share the result.
5. Take a 30-minute break midway, usually after completing writing with the nondominant hand.

5 Tips for Clients and Journal Keepers

1. Choose one writing method to focus on over time until you trust the process and have confidence using it.
2. Practice mindfulness by journaling what you notice internally and around you as it occurs without judging or analyzing it.
3. Journal at various times of the day. Notice how this affects what you journal about.
4. Save everyday papers and lists from your week to make a collage to express yourself in a journal entry.
5. If you are alone while journaling highly emotional things, keep it under 20 minutes in a sitting. You can come back to where you left off the next day.

3 Journaling Prompts

I recommend using these warm-up prompts in the workshop or to prime the client or your own connection to mind, body, and spirit.

1. Think back to a memorable getaway to somewhere you had never been before. What was special for you and how did you feel? What thoughts and emotions went through your mind and body?
2. Reflect on an award or recognition for something you had won or done that surprised you. How did you feel receiving it? What did your behavior convey?
3. What do you especially enjoy doing that brings you into a creative flow where time is forgotten and contentment deepens? Imagine doing it now. What is the experience like for you? Is there an intuitive aspect?

 About the Author

Kimberly Wulfert, PhD, is a California licensed clinical psychologist with a mindfulness-based private practice in southern California. In 2011 she began teaching Meditation for Mind, Body, Brain Health then developed Journaling after Meditation and Meditate on Paper workshops, and other mind, body, spirit workshops. After decades of personal journal writing, she began also creating the books she journals in and teaching others to develop their creativity further. Her website is KimberlyWulfert.com.

Journaling and the Shadow **30**

Heidi Hinda Chadwick

Most of our repressed, depressed, and oppressed self is hidden within and is "the not beautiful," a term that the Jungian analyst Clarissa Pinkola Estes coined in her book *Women Who Run with the Wolves*. This includes our jealousies, resentments, dissatisfactions, and self-loathing, all bound tightly together and hushed into the dark by shame. Shame's job is to hide us away from showing up for and engaging with life.

From a young age, we had parts of ourselves, our human nature, criticized as "wrong" by the world around us, perhaps by our caregivers, parents, older siblings, peers, and, as we grew up, by our "friends" at school, teachers, and those given the position and power of authority. Add to this the era we have grown up in, the prevailing culture, society, religion, environment, neighborhood, and geographical as well as political climate, and it's no surprise that once we are a "fully functioning" adult, we have split off or distanced from many aspects of our wholeness.

Our shadow includes those parts of ourselves deemed dark and un-holy (not whole). We will have squashed these parts so far down that we haven't even noticed their absence, but guaranteed it is exactly this absence that will be felt in our lives, as the presence of self-sabotage and self-destruction.

Journaling one's shadow is a potent practice that, if held tenderly, can be a life changer, where we make art out of our wounded places, and find the jewels within. But before we unravel what lurks in the closet of shadows, it is worth noting that every aspect of our human personality and character holds an exquisite amount of energy and power. This power is our life force, and it includes our sexual and creative energy. It's no surprise that feelings of shame can manifest in hiding or suppressing our creativity and sexuality. The expression of such may be deemed too much for some. But self-expression in all forms is ours to claim and foster—it is our birthright!

How can we create a safe and trusting space to explore our shadow side? First, we need a clear, strong, and healthy relationship to our "ground of being." This is also known as feeling centered, anchored, rooted, and "here." There needs to be a safe container so that as energy becomes freed it can be held and coped with. Our ability to bear ourselves, our emotional responses, our experiences, and the energies that move in and through us, is the reason "why" behind most Eastern bodywork practices. Consider yoga for example. This has become very body-centric, but the philosophy of yoga, the Yoga Sutras, notes that the purpose of the postures is to find a steady and comfortable seat. This seat represents the ability to move through life, centered and at peace; and, to create a firm and fired "pot" (physical body) to be able to hold the increase of prana (life force) that the practice aims to free up.

To bear life, live in freedom, and embody every single part of us, we need to have a strong enough "pot" in order not to collapse, be overwhelmed, become traumatized, or break down (apart) into pieces. We need, ideally, to be able to hold all the fragrant, fragile, and fierce fragments of who we are as we deliver these exiled (shadow) fragments back home, back into the body and heart, so we become whole, clear, and of substance. We want to be able to sit in the skin that we live in, and feel all of our human experience, the good, the bad, and the ugly! Any form of mindful and conscious bodywork practice can help give us this grounding.

Second, we need kindness. Shadow work can be both brutal and beautiful, but the mind, just like the body, has to be able to bear what is uncovered. There is great grace, tender forgiveness and acceptance available in facing these places when done so approached with kindness as an ally. Invite yourself, or the client, to imagine that it is a dear friend that is speaking. Listen and receive these words without judgment.

Shadow work is human unraveling and is deeply vulnerable and brave. For these parts of one's self that initially went underground coerced by shame, the last thing they need as they come to the surface for air, is to be shamed anew. Embodiment and kindness are pillars to prepare the way for shadow work.

Let me tell you a story of how I have found myself holding sessions exploring these edge-walking places, for it is edge-walking work no shadow of a doubt (pun intended!). I am offering writing as prayer, as a sacred and reverent practice of truth telling and liberation.

In 2019, I broke. It doesn't really matter how, but suffice to say that on an intense retreat something in me snapped. No amount of words on a page can recount the horror of a time when identity, self, and body fell to pieces. I threw myself into and grasped on to every single healing practice available to me. One of the most profound threads that I was given as I swung my arms and screamed out into what many a mystic has described as the dark night of the soul was the permission to write the unspoken. You see, what had broken in me was a survival strategy, an identity, that as a very young girl, I had taken on, as armor, to feel safe and survive an uncertain world around me. As this shattered and I had nothing to hold on to, what was underneath, trapped and frozen in time, was a well of deep disappointment, resentment, jealousy, and rage. No wonder the little girl in me had created a persona to live in. These places were strong and most likely would have destroyed her and I would not be writing these words to you now.

My teacher simply said, "give them full permission to be."

So, I filled four notebooks with the most vitriolic, poisonous, and darkest words. I can honestly say that as I let them take center stage and spew their monologues and rants all over the page, my pen as secretary, I could literally feel, viscerally so, the venom leaving my blood. I could feel my life force returning, my aliveness coming back, the pain of emptying myself of the secret places within me, as the numbing that I had lived as, began to thaw. It is painful, excruciatingly so, when we start to thaw out of the frozen we have been inhabiting and calling a life. It's almost unbearable. But bear it we must if we are to become free.

So how do we start to work with journaling the shadow?

I will take you through how to work with a client. Of course, do adapt this if it is for your own personal exploration.

Let's say that jealousy is present. If the client is willing to edge-walk with it, ask them to start to move around the room, and invite jealousy to join them. To inhabit them. They actually don't have to do anything as, like all of us, this is a part of our human experience. Ask the client to take the shape of jealousy as they move. The posture. The gait. Invite them to embody how jealousy holds its head. Its hands. How it breathes. Support them to really get into it, as if they are taking on the costume of this character for a play. As Shakespeare said, "all the world's a stage!"

Keep asking the client to relax into what they are doing. To lean in. Remind them that they are safe. Then ask them if jealousy has a catchphrase, a sentence, that maybe it likes to say.

Once the client feels the embodiment and energy of jealousy, they have shapeshifted. This is a powerful alchemical place to be in, when art becomes medicine. Invite them to take pen and paper and start to write out everything that jealousy wants to say. All of it. Every single damn word. Tell them that no one will see this. That even they do not have to read the words back.

Remind the client to stay in connection to their body including their physical, energetic, and emotional body. Encourage them to follow this connection as they write. If they are truly in connection and aligned with what they are writing, their experience will shift and change, maybe even surprisingly so. They may find that pleasure arises, an intense anger that's never been felt, grief or joy. Ask the client to stay and bear these, to breathe, and allow these to flow as the pen does. Keep going until something shifts and the emotional charge, and this is important, is gone.

The client may well find a deep tenderness in the words that jealousy shares. Unmet needs. Desires. Hopes. The human ache of a part that has never been listened to. Many things may be revealed and felt through embodied writing of this nature.

To close this practice, ask them to give thanks. To this part of themselves, and to their body and heart for the willingness to be so courageous to walk that edge. Afterwards there needs to be a period of grounding and nourishment. An integration. This can be supported by taking time in nature, perhaps having a comforting hot drink and some earthy food, taking a hot bath or shower. Some people also like to shake their body or dance during this integration phase.

The transformation from this process can be profound. Watch out for shame making an appearance afterwards. Let that go. Stay in the moment. Stay here. Trust. This can be repeated for each of the places or areas of their life and shame experiences that the client would like to explore.

A client might choose to work with one shadow experience for a longer period of time in order to get to know it more fully. Interestingly, the more we embody these aspects of ourselves the more they become integrated as healthy aspects of who we are. The intention is not to fix these parts. They may never go away. Rather, we are trying to take back the power that shame often tries to shrink or hide in us. Then we can play with these places; for instance, we can own our jealousy. In this, we become free.

As we own our shadow, we bring ourselves back to life. Maybe this is the greatest gift we can ever give to ourselves.

5 Tips for Helping Professionals

1.   Give the client full permission to welcome their shadow.
2.   Start the session with a loving kindness meditation.

3. If your client starts to dissociate, stop or at least pause. Signs that this might be happening include your client reporting that she feels disconnected or confused, that she has the sense of not fully being there, or that she feels that she's losing contact with her body.
4. Ask the client if they want to burn their words to release them.
5. Ask the client to write out, and share with you, what they think might happen if they were to reveal these parts of themselves to the world. For example, will they be rejected, abandoned, disappoint or hurt another?

 5 Tips for Clients and Journal Keepers

1. Light a candle beforehand to honor this work as a ritual and prayer.
2. Spend a day as that character and see what is revealed to you.
3. Make sure you have any extra emotional support that you may need.
4. Be willing to be surprised.
5. Claim aloud this part of you, maybe to the wind, the trees, the sky!

 3 Journaling Prompts

1. Try giving voice to your repressed anger, sadness, fear; for example, keep repeating "It's not fair that . . ." and write what wants to come out.
2. Carry your notebook with you and if you catch shadow's voice arising then capture it while it is alive in you, as if you're a secret detective!
3. Write from the place of "I am not. . .," for example, "I am not nice/kind/grateful," etc.

 About the Author

Heidi Hinda Chadwick is the creator of "The Creative Genius" and "Your Creative Voice." She is a creativity mentor and a writer. Heidi is a fierce proponent of living in radical honesty, freedom, playfulness, beauty, curiosity, and truth. She believes that life is art and art is life. To learn more about her work please visit www.heidihindachadwick.com and/or follow her on Instagram at @heidihinda.

Journaling Through the Seasons   **31**

Midori Evans

Why do human beings journal? What are we looking for as we grab our pens and dive into writing each day? The one constant in journaling is the relationship we have with ourselves and our inner worlds when we write. Writing in a journal reflects our passions, our struggles, the directions our lives are taking, and the stumbles we have along the way. We all also have a vital connection with the external world that is our home. The choices we face along whatever paths we may traverse are all mirrored in the natural world and its cyclical changes.

Using the astronomical seasons to frame journal writing helps ground us human beings. Perhaps you have heard your clients complaining about darker nights and shorter days. Imagine if you tracked the days together, watching for the equinox, holding space for the darkness while waiting for the spring to come?

The results of that can be transformational! Living and writing with the seasons provides a gentle background to the problems your clients may be facing. It removes the burden of diving constantly into problems and troubles; it offers a focal point outside of ourselves. Journaling with the seasons creates a living path of renewal.

What causes the seasons, anyway?

Seasons change because of how the planet tilts on its axis as it rotates around the sun. The seasons correlate with the amount of sunlight we receive where we live while the vernal and autumnal equinoxes are the days when the sun is exactly above the equator. The equinoxes mark the times when day and night are equal. In contrast, the solstices, summer and winter, celebrate the sun at its highest and lowest points in the sky at noon. The solstices welcome, respectively, the longest and shortest days of the year.

As you think about how to use this work with your clients, I would encourage you to begin to mark the dates of the solstices and equinoxes in your professional calendar. As you guide others through this process, you will notice more about the natural world as you go about your day. Welcome that awareness into your working life. Bring a few observations from your own journal writing to share with your clients in service to their learning and growth. Together, you can build a shared framework for meaningful reflection through journaling.

Winter

During the winter months, the hemisphere where we live is pointed away from the sun. Winter solstice is welcomed in the Northern Hemisphere on December 21 or 22 and in the Southern Hemisphere on June 20 or 21.

We dive into the darkness of winter, sometimes into the darkness of our own souls. This can be an intimidating time to write, yet can also reap huge rewards. What is it about the dark that scares us? The worry we will not emerge, that the spring will not come again? Or the recognition of the flurry of dark thoughts and memories that can emerge when we stop blocking them out?

We often name dark thoughts as demons, monsters, or gremlins. We name them so because the feelings they bring up in us are formidable. But they are not impossible to defeat. We might ask in the pages of our daily journal: who are these winter monsters that come to visit? How can I help my clients recognize them?

Winter prompts can celebrate the lights of winter! Frozen ice crystals. A morning coating of snow. Our frozen breath, that visualization of cold made manifest before us. Sparkling night skies and winter candlelight. Humans have always brought light into the wintertime. Explore in your journal ways to welcome light yet also speak to the darkness.

Spring

The vernal equinox on March 20 or 21 heralds the beginning of spring in the Northern Hemisphere.

The shift into spring is one of celebration! Plan to look together with your clients for the first crocus or snowdrop to poke its head up above the ground.

That day can launch the start of a rich and fertile exploration of the theme of rebirth.

Take a moment now to look at the light that is entering your home. Where do you sit when you write? Are you near a window? Do you know what time the sun illuminates your room? Bring that welcoming light into your office. Arrange furniture to make the most of natural light, or purchase a full-spectrum lamp to grace the corner of your office. Create a practice for both you and your clients of welcoming the day by journaling near a window with morning sunlight.

There are so many spring journaling prompts to choose from. Birdsong. The last flurry of a spring snow shower. Sunrise creeping earlier each morning. Walk the path of spring rejuvenation by waking just a bit earlier each day and marking the signs of new life that are emerging all around you.

Summer

During the summer months, the hemisphere where we live is pointed toward the sun. Summer solstice is welcomed in the Northern Hemisphere on June 20 or 21 and in the Southern Hemisphere on December 21 or 22.

Summer beckons us with its warmth and its long, leisurely days. Sunsets over the water, cookouts with good friends, the sun's warmth on our backs as we garden. It can be hard for some people to keep journaling through the summer. Though you and your clients may be tempted to set down your pens, it is that very warmth and the length of the days that can serve as germination times for some deep and healing ideas. Think of a summer writing practice as yeast bubbling away in warm water. Ideas that come to you in the summer can come to fruition in the later seasons, too.

Encourage your clients to head outside for their summer journaling. Or if easy access to the outdoors from your dwelling is a problem, open a window to let in the summer breezes. Our first attention as we start to summer journal is to notice the wind, the smell of the air, and how we feel letting the wind touch our face. Begin to write, talking to the wind.

Summer prompts can include a dive into water, campfire nights, the shouts and calls of summer baseball, glorious displays of brilliant fireworks. The laziness of long, summer nights, no school, and fewer responsibilities. Let the heat of summer permeate as you journal deep into that place where some of your most treasured memories live.

Autumn

The autumnal equinox on September 22 or 23 in the Northern Hemisphere shifts the season from summer into fall.

Where are you writing as we make this shift? Are you still outside or have you begun to move your life indoors again? Wherever you are, make notes of what is bountiful for you.

The only season that is graced with two names, autumn can be a time when clients both fear the upcoming seasonal changes and celebrate the bounty of their lives. The "fall of the leaves" season is a harbinger of the darker times yet its colors and gifts are glorious.

Some fear the upcoming darkness and shortening of days so focus on building continuity in the writing practice. The foundation can be added to by beginning an image collection. Assign a day for photography, with only a goal of capturing how the season feels without concern for perfection or photographic skills. Guide your clients through this journaling practice by keeping a dialogue open for whatever needs to emerge in this bridge time. Journal prompts can explore the variety of colors in the leaves, the transition into a new school year for children, or the holiday associations of the harvest.

Living in a Temperate Climate

People who live closer to the equator experience fewer shifts in seasonal temperatures and may not be as acutely aware of their effect on their lives. Yet seasonal shifts can be observed by watching the growth seasons of plants, observing harvest celebrations, and noting rainy seasons or other cyclical weather phenomena. The key is to pay attention to your environment and to allow your writing to reflect what you see.

5 Tips for Helping Professionals

1. Do this work yourself in your own journal writing! The more connected you are to seasonal shifts, the easier it will be to guide others, as your insights and experience will serve as a foundation.

2. This work is a commitment. Embarking on using these techniques will permeate all parts of how you work. You may find yourself changing the art in your office or using new imagery on your website. Let those changes arise.

3. Use the childhood references to ritual that are part and parcel of seasonal changes. Colors, holidays, life transitions—they can all be used in this work. Specific detailed prompts are best, rather than overall themes. For example, instead of Halloween, use pumpkins. Offering a childhood prompt can be problematic for some, though, so be prepared for unexpected responses and have backup ideas on hand.

4. Create a daily record of the natural world. Write a few words about what you observe each day in terms of weather, storms approaching, or increasing light and carry that observation with you into your daily work.

5. The tastes of the seasons are powerful! Use the richness of seasonal imagery—winter snow on your tongue, spring wild edibles, summer watermelon, and fall apples.

 ### 5 Tips for Clients and Journal Keepers

1. Be prepared for some rich imagery to arise as you integrate your writing with season-watching. Let your expressions of seasonal journaling take many forms, from poems to digital art to drawings with text.

2. Bring your writing practice outside. Look for a seasonally safe writing environment—or focus on finding a place with a view where you can still stay safely warm/cool! The quieter the better, to allow the sounds of the season to integrate into your observations. A favorite rock perch along a hiking trail, a park bench set back from the main path, or sitting in your car looking out at water or mountains are all great options!

3. Know that human cyclical patterns don't always mirror those of the world around us, especially now that we are so divorced from the rhythms of natural life. This is a process.

4. Be willing to dive deeper and learn more about the cycles of the moon or local growing patterns to provide even deeper frameworks for your writing.

5. Design a way of keeping track of the seasons. Draw a calendar or put a notation in your daily journal. Create symbols for moon shifts, sunrise times, or anything else that is meaningful for you.

4 Journaling Prompts

1. *Winter:* Write of the deep blue of the sky in winter, or of the blue of an icicle when it shimmers in the sunlight.
2. *Spring:* Return to a childhood memory of planting. How did it feel to hold the dirt in your hand, or to see the results of your first planting?
3. *Summer:* Remember a day lying out in a field or sitting on a park bench staring at the clouds. Write your cloud memories.
4. *Fall:* Write of pumpkins at a farm stand. How are they shaped? What is the variation in their colors? Do you picture carved faces or choose by instinct?

 ## About the Author

Midori Evans is the founder of *Midori Creativity*, a creativity-coaching business that helps individuals and businesses connect to their best creative selves. A lifelong creative explorer, she loves to travel and is a gifted writer, photographer, musician, and educator. Midori Evans draws on the inspiration of the natural world in her work as a creativity coach, writer, and landscape photographer. She is the founder of Creativity Abloom, a series of conversations about creativity and currently runs Artists Share!, a monthly artist critique group, and seasonal Artist's Way group classes.

The Elements of Journaling

32

Sasha Boyle

Keeping a sketchbook is an intimate, private, and tactile practice for an artist. The sketchbook is the place of secret visual formulas and sacred creative risk-taking, often connecting threads of an artist's curious inner dialogue. This unique part of being an artist perhaps lives in a similar internal space to keeping a written journal, yet is still very different.

In my 40-day creativity retreat, journaling is reframed as a tool for behavior modification, but with a dash of drama. I offer you here a journal technique to build a structural support to complement, not replace, the sketchbook in your life.

Designed to be a quick exercise in your morning and evening routine, you, artist and maker of meaning are asked to reimagine yourself as a creative person working with the planets in our sky. Like a role-play of an ancient Mesopotamian astrologer perched on a ziggurat, your job is to observe the seven wanderers and recognize what lessons they teach you each day.

Begin in the morning by writing down the date and the astrological ruler of the day. I am referring to the seven planets visible to the naked eye, otherwise known as the wanderers by ancient civilizations. You then have four journaling prompts for the day: air, earth, fire, and water.

AIR is your cue to contemplate how the planetary ruler of the day can support you. EARTH prompts you to consider what real-world allies can help you on this particular day. FIRE asks what actions are you taking today? WATER is left for your end-of-day reflection.

FOR EXAMPLE

[date] **Monday**
Sample journal entry: *Monday's ruler is the Moon. The qualities that thrive under the Moon have to do with emotion and the felt experience of life.*

Air

Contemplation

Sample journal entry: *How can I work with emotion today? I have a doctor's appointment in the afternoon and feel I'll need to do a creative visualization and imagine a personal shield around me to help with emotional boundaries.*

I have a guided visualization that I recorded where I am imagining sitting on a soothing mossy hillside and mentally build a boundary around me. I'll play this recording on the way to the appointment. This will keep emotions I want in and emotions I don't want out.

Earth

Allies

Sample journal entry: *Today my allies are the nutritious foods I put in my body. I have also been wanting to experiment with colors of silver, white and blue on paper in the studio so maybe today I'll try that.*

Fire

Action

Write a to-do list.
Sample journal entry:

- Walk two miles
- Write for one hour
- Doctor's appointment
- Enter the studio for three hours
- Make dinner + tomorrow's lunch

Water

Reflection

Sample journal entry: *Boundary visualization was helpful today, going to the doctor's was rough. Playing around with silver blue and colors was satisfying.*

Tomorrow I want to be very specific with what I am writing during my writing time, so many projects going on. I am so grateful no one was sick today so I had time in the studio.

On Planetary Rulership

Taking the position that you, as an artist, are your own best advocate, this journaling technique encourages you to play, and work dramatically, to creatively jump start your day. Like the Mesopotamians 5,000 years ago, we use the model of the seven visible planets to organize time, starting with the seven days of the week.

Does this mean you become superstitious about your daily activities? Not at all, this is just an exercise to play with. The act of anchoring your perspective from a different space in time, just for a bit, is a way to approach your day from an atypical and hopefully fresh perspective.

The ancients believe each planet is known for being particularly auspicious for particular tasks, which is outlined later. Could you possibly use this as a jumping off point in your journal? If yes, great! Have fun. If no, why? Start there.

Monday—Moon
Tuesday—Mars
Wednesday—Mercury
Thursday—Jupiter
Friday—Venus
Saturday—Saturn
Sunday—Sun

Monday is Moon day, Tuesday is the day of Mars, Wednesday is Mercury's day, Thursday is ruled by Jupiter, Venus rules Friday, Saturn governs Saturday, and Sunday is reserved for the sun.

As an interesting side note, the linguistic remnants of this planetary organization can be found today in Romance, Celtic, Germanic, Indian, Japanese, Classical Chinese, Korean, and Spanish languages. For example, Luna means Moon and Lunes is Monday in Spanish; Martes means Tuesday translated as Mars's day, etc.

The simplicity of honoring the planet of the day and the energetic quality offered by that planet creates a primal and basic tone to the organization of your day's journey. This offers a fresh way, a new type of discipline, in order to be curious and explore how you can support and inspire your creative actions.

How Do You Organize Your Week? You Plan It!

Planetary Rulers

Monday The Moon
White | Light Blue
Moon day is for creativity, receptivity, and self-care. It's time to watch your emotions, sink into the *feeling* of the projects you want to produce and join with their *essence*. Or a good day to wear light blue!

Tuesday Mars
Red
Mars day is a day of movement, desires, activation, unity, and expression. There is more energy available to help you take action and bust through your blockages. It is a day to be especially physical.

Wednesday Mercury
Green
Mercury and Venus are the planets associated with the arts and as artists they walk closely with you through your creative life. Mercury rules communication and curiosity while Venus knows how to make everyone look and feel good. Work with Mercury to sing, record, write, and use your hands.

Thursday Jupiter
Yellow
Jupiter, the planet of abundance. Good luck and creative expansion governs Thursday. This is a day to focus on the part of your creativity you would like to see grow.

Friday Venus
Pink
Friday is reserved for Venus, the planet of fertile restoration. Friday is a space in time to fall in love with what you have done so far and unapologetically care for yourself.

Saturday Saturn
Black
Saturn is the planet of karma, time, discipline, and form. Saturday offers a moment to do what was left undone from the week. Saturn governs our careers, ambitions, and how we are seen in the public eye. His influence helps you get real and honest with yourself.

Sunday Sun
Orange
Sunday is a day to welcome the sun's rays and invite that solar energy to your space on earth. This is the day to fill your cup spiritually and plug into something that recharges your battery, so you can be a lighthouse to others.

5 Tips for Helping Professionals

1. If astrology is not for you, I encourage you to rework this journal format for your general use with clients. Consider the "Planet of the Day" as a divination practice. Divination, not as a pseudoscience or a parlor trick, but divination from Plato and Aristotle's perspective as a prompt to the temporal window of intuition.

2. The concept of using divination is to encourage the journaler to utilize skills of resilience and respond to a cue that is not of their making. A less cathartic practice than sketchbook work, this elemental journal exercise is more about creating a unique and workable template for action.

3. Another popular divination practice you could substitute for a religiously sensitive client is Dictiomancy, the divination by randomly opening a dictionary and choosing a word to work with like the planet of the day.

4. Create your own type of divination, like an inkblot test (this is called Chartomancy, for the divinary curious!). Then ask your client to contemplate it (AIR), choose a few tools to use (EARTH), make a to-do list (FIRE), and follow-up to reflect at the end of the day (WATER).

5. Prolonged use of this journaling technique can affect positive behavioral change, if the client wants change.

5 Tips for Clients and Journal Keepers

1. Keep it playful by using tactile tools you love in the journaling process—colored sharpies, stickers, or a genuine ink quill.

2. Embrace play and be a secret agent. Up your game and learn the planetary glyphs, the ancient symbols for the planets. For example, instead of writing "Monday," use the moon glyph ☽. It'll make you feel like you are writing in code.

3. Know who you are. Learn where the seven wanderers are best positioned for you by getting a Natal Astrology reading.

4. Commit to journaling for a specific window of time, like three days, two weeks, 40 days.

5. Be consistent in both the act of journaling with the elements and also with the time of your journaling, if possible.

3 Journaling Prompts

1. Based on the descriptions offered here, what planet do you most identify with and why?
2. How do you honor the elements in your daily life?
3. What possibilities do you see for yourself and for your clients with this approach to journaling?

 ## About the Author

Sasha Boyle, BFA and Yoga Acharya, helps artists and makers get deeper insight into accessing their creativity. Her goal is to walk with a rising army of creative optimists who use their art making to uplift themselves and our culture. Sasha offers Artist Natal Astrology Readings, Virtual Creative Focusing Retreats, and a daily Astrology Subscription at sashaboyle.com.

Nature Metaphors for Journaling and Therapeutic Writing

33

Jackee Holder

How to Work With Nature and Tree Metaphors

We know from numerous research studies that spending time with trees can lower cortisol levels, boost the immune system and reduce anxiety. While this offers a huge green prescription for the body, mind and spirit, nature is also a bulging book of juicy metaphors. Take for example the weeping willow tree at the end of my road, pruned back once a year and left butt naked. Every year I think the same thoughts, "They've killed off the weeping willow tree this time for real." And every year I'm caught by surprise as green shoots appear at the knuckled edges of the tree's branches and the green mane grows back shaggy and wild.

Nature metaphors flow easily into coaching conversations. There's often a familiarity, a remembering of a time when we were once close to nature and to Mother Earth. What follows is a simple method of introducing how to work with nature and tree metaphors with groups or in a one-to-one coaching session.

This first exercise starts with brainstorming metaphors and sayings associated with nature, trees, and plants. Bring the exercise alive by drawing an image of a tree on a large sheet of flip chart paper and use this to pin the metaphors to as they are shared out loud.

Next pose a general question to your client or group: what sayings or metaphors do you associate with nature, trees, or plants? Allow time to gather thoughts and do share a couple of examples of metaphors as this often helps with generating ideas and contributions. If you are working with a group or team spilt them into smaller groups where they can bounce ideas off each other and if working online you can add the two groups to breakout rooms to continue with the brainstorming.

Over the years, examples of metaphors that have made it onto the list from both one-to-one sessions and group sessions include:

- See the wood for the trees
- Rooted
- Branching out
- Going out on a limb
- Blossoming
- Letting go
- Planting
- Seed
- Growing
- Leaf behind
- Thrive
- Grow
- Rest
- Grounded
- Flourish
- Harvest
- Incubate
- Fertilize
- Prune

Normally I pause at around 20 metaphors but if a group or individual is really in a flow you can run the activity for a couple more minutes. Circle or underline the metaphors you like and are interested in working with for the next stage of the exercise. Select three to five metaphors from your list.

The next phase of the exercise involves turning these metaphors into a series of nature-inspired coaching questions that can be used to explore a problem, issue, dilemma, or opportunity.

This exercise really came alive a few years ago on a well-being retreat for women. I was facilitating a session called Looking for Answers in Different Places. The purpose of the session was to explore how nature, and connecting with nature and all its hidden messages and insights, can connect you directly and indirectly to the landscape of your inner world, feelings, and emotions.

In small table groups women would collate sets of nature-inspired coaching questions based on the metaphors gathered from the earlier brainstorm. I started to notice how energized the women became during this activity. When they offered the questions created in each group, I would hear responses like, "Oh I like that," to "That's a really good question," or "That question made me think."

These questions were landing with the women in the group. I knew this for sure as they scribbled down the questions, and as they shared them across the tables copied them down into their notebooks and journals. It was clear these questions were making an impact.

The next step involves putting the questions to work. This requires the coachee or group member to highlight an issue they would welcome help or support with. It could be a question they needed answers to or an opportunity they want to explore. Take one of the questions from the newly created nature questions and use it to engage with a seven-minute freewriting activity.

Women wrote solutions, found perspectives they hadn't considered before, and evoked memories full of wisdom and promise. One woman remembered a striking memory of her grandmother gathering every vase and glass in her home and filling the house with bluebells from nearby woods. The memory was so striking that she could smell the floral aroma of blue bells in the air as she captured the memory on the page. This memory contained insight and meaning that was deeply personal and meaningful to her. By conjuring the memory onto the page in her journal she was able to self-prescribe her own natural medication for the issue she wanted to resolve.

What Would the Wise Ancient Tree Have to Say?

The ancient tree image is wild and feral in the imagination for many, providing a step away from the road well-traveled into new and different ways of thinking. Of all the nature-inspired questions groups work with, this question, "What would the wise ancient tree have to say?", is by far the most popular question accompanied by comments like, "I love what my ancient tree had to say," or "My ancient tree was so wise." Trees have been revered and celebrated amongst ancient cultures globally. In Africa, under the looming canopies of towering monolith baobab trees steeped in age, the elders and council would meet. Under the vine-like branches of aging banyan trees, sacred rituals and ceremonies, before dawn and dusk, would be performed in the presence of this sacred tree of India.

The use of the ancient tree metaphor is also a powerful way to connect with your own inner guidance system. Through the tree archetype individuals can evoke the wisdom of their own inner wise owl sitting on the branch of the ancient tree or draw directly from the wisdom of their inner mentor or coach.

Caring for a Plant

Once I was when facilitating a personal development program all the women participating were each gifted a small money plant. The purpose of the gift was twofold. One to connect the women to nature and second it was a natural nudge for the women to develop their rituals and customs of taking care of the plant. Our intention was that by taking care of the plant, it would be a mirror to taking care of self.

This simple practice of caring for a money plant evoked strong and varied experiences amongst the group. One woman parched her plant by neglecting to water it. She could see the direct relationship to where she felt parched in her own life. Another woman overwatered her plant which led to a surprise realization regarding how she was overconsuming in her life to overcompensate for a big void she was afraid to acknowledge. A third group member started a ritual of singing to her plant every morning. Singing was something she loved doing as a child but it was very absent from her adult life. This ritual was of great comfort each morning as she watched her plant develop new shoots and branches before her very eyes. Looking at plants closely through the use of metaphors is a natural and easy way of looking at yourself.

Lockdown was a stark reminder of the impending impact of climate change on the environment. We needed nature even if we weren't aware of it. Parks and green spaces became important places to escape to while dealing with the social isolation and devastation of COVID-19. Collectively the world was reminded that nature was our first home. Just the other day my daughter said to me out of the blue, "Mum, I've never told you this but whenever I feel upset, I always feel better when I go and stand on grass barefoot. It roots and grounds me." Not only do we long to be close to nature, we also metaphorically seek to find ways to be close to our inner nature.

It is my hope that developing and working with nature-inspired questions will help you and your clients ground into positive experiences in nature from the past, while also offering questions that can help individuals to think widely and deeply around who they are, what they want, and what makes them happy. Dance in the moment with these questions, encourage clients and teams to tap into the wisdom nature has to offer them both on and off the page.

5 Tips for Helping Professionals

1. This approach of working with nature metaphors leads to better observations of nature and the environment and can lead to a deeper appreciation and connection with your own personal nature. By having an integrative approach, you can use the questions to explore qualities such as empathy, generosity, appreciation, and gratitude.
2. These prompts can be used to help clients to reflect on personal self-care and well-being. Curiosity about clients' relationships with nature or the outdoors can be a natural catalyst for conversations about their inner worlds.
3. When it comes to the environment this nature-based practice has wider benefits. Beyond the coaching room, these metaphors can inspire individual responsibility for the environment at home and in the real world. By becoming more aware and relational with nature, clients can be empowered to take ownership and responsibility for the nature and trees on their doorstep.
4. You will create the right atmosphere and generate the best results when you work with these questions yourself. Take them into supervision or into your own coaching sessions. Use them as prompts in your own reflective writing.
5. Keep a record of questions that clients respond well to and create your own deck.

5 Tips for Clients and Journal Keepers

1. Metaphors can easily become a list of clichés. Create new words from your metaphors as a way of enticing your imagination to come out and play on the page.
2. Use the nature questions to get started but give yourself permission to not have to keep to the prompt.
3. Brainstorm questions with friends, colleagues or family members. Diverse groups often think outside of the box and come up with unexpected and surprising questions.

4. Get creative and create your own personal deck of questions. You might use paper luggage tags, a set of questions on quality card paper, or create your own hand-illustrated deck.
5. Reflect on the questions as a way of going deeper to see what else might be hidden from your awareness that wants to come into view.

 3 Journaling Prompts

1. A forest grows one tree at a time. What's the one thing you want to grow right now?
2. What would the big sky have to say about the opportunities available to you?
3. If you pruned away what was no longer needed, what positive would be left behind for you to work with?

 About the Author

Jackee Holder is the author of the *Writing with Fabulous Trees: A Writing Map for Parks, Gardens, and Other Green Spaces* (2016) bringing together the restorative benefits of nature, eco-psychology, eco-geography, and self-reflection through tree-inspired journal and creative writing prompts. Jackee is a leadership coach and coach trainer who lives in the heart of what was once the great North Wood that covered most of South London. She is the author of three nonfiction titles, a *Psychologies* magazine columnist and runs the online Paper Therapy Journal Writing course. You can learn more about her work at www.jackeeholder.com.

Journaling and Creativity

PART
VI

The Visioning® Process

34

Turning Dreams Into Reality Through Collage and the Creative Journal Method

Lucia Capacchione

Journaling has been an integral part of my personal and professional life. Healing from a serious illness by drawing and writing in a journal led to a career change. I integrated my skills as an artist and expertise as a child development specialist into a new career in art therapy. I pioneered Journal Therapy (1975) and Inner Child Work (1976). This led to developing the Creative Journal Expressive Arts (CJEA) Method, simple tools for any process of healing, creativity, and life Visioning®.

The CJEA Method is for everyone. If you can hold a crayon, you can do this work. It is for all ages, from toddlers to seniors. The Method has been used with all populations, regardless of zip code or community. Applications include mental health care, addiction treatment, body-mind healing, education, life and career coaching, creativity, and spiritual guidance.

The CJEA (Creative Journal Expressive Arts) Method includes:

- The Creative Journal Method (1976)
- Inner Child Reparenting Method (1976)
- Whole-Brain, Two-Handed Method (1976)
- Body-Mind Healing-Arts Method (1980)
- Visioning® Method (1994)

I co-founded, with Dr. Marsha Nelson, the Creative Journal Expressive Arts (CJEA) professional training program (1997). We have over 80 practitioners applying CJEA methods internationally. In our advanced Visioning® coach certification program, professionals learn to use the Visioning® process, as presented in my book, *Visioning: Ten Steps to Designing the Life of Your Dreams.*

Creative Journal Expressive Arts (CJEA) processes help clients uncover emotions, inner wisdom, and their true Heart's Desires. No talent or training in the arts is required. The practitioner establishes a safe, nonjudgmental atmosphere. They are given simple techniques to tame the inevitable negative self-talk. CJEA processes cultivate self-nurturing and healthy boundaries. Clients often break through creative blocks, stop procrastinating, and move forward in their lives with self-confidence and enthusiasm.

With these unique methods, clients gain insight through spontaneous expression in the arts: drawing, painting, collage, sculpting, movement, drama, music, and Journal Therapy. Clients often come for my Inner Child Reparenting Method, a process for healing early abuse, trauma, health challenges, addictions, and codependency.

I have always used a prescriptive coaching approach to therapy, encouraging personal accountability through journal prompts and expressive arts activities done by the client between sessions. Clients keep a journal using drawing, collage, and writing. Journal prompts are based on my Whole-Brain, Two-Handed Method: drawing and writing done with the nondominant hand (the hand we don't normally write with). There is also bilateral art (both hands drawing at the same time) and written dialogues (alternating between the hands). Journal prompts are assigned from my books *Recovery of Your Inner Child*, *Drawing Your Stress Away*, and *Hello, This Is Your Body Talking*.

As clients forge a deep connection with their own source of creativity and inner wisdom, they begin to discover their true selves. They learn how to listen to "that still, small voice within" and make more fulfilling choices. In response to my clients' desires to re-create their lives, I reapplied the CJEA process to *life design*, developing the Visioning® Method of life and career coaching.

To create a process for *life design*, I reflected on my earlier career as an artist and designer for Mattel and Hallmark, and consultant to Walt Disney Imagineering. Using a *Design Thinking* approach, I developed a process involving ten simple steps, starting with *The Creative Idea* (in the case of Visioning®, finding one's *Heart's Desire*) and ending with celebrating the dream come true. I eventually authored a how-to book on the method, *Visioning: Ten Steps to Designing the Life of Your Dreams.*

The Visioning® Method starts with a silent Creative Self meditation for tuning into one's *Heart's Desire*. This can cover any area of life: health, work, relationships, home, recreation, travel, spiritual life, retirement, recovery, etc. Once the true Heart's Desire is discovered, it is written down in a journal. This Heart's Desire declaration is called the "focus phrase." It is written with the nondominant hand because that hand taps directly into the right brain (regardless of one's handedness), accessing creativity, emotions, and intuition. This technique has been shown to bypass false logic and self-criticism associated with the left brain.

Often, the client is surprised by what they uncover. They often say things like, "I thought this was going to be about my career, but I wrote *internal peace and serenity* instead. Where did that come from?" The nondominant hand clears a path to our own truth while dodging the rules and expectations of others.

The nondominant hand circumvents the left-brain critic who limits our dreams, and hampers our potential. The inner workings of the brain-hand connection are documented in my book, *The Power of Your Other Hand: Unlock Creativity and Inner Wisdom through the Right Side of Your Brain* (2019).

The key to the Visioning® Method is the Vision Board. In a quiet space and time, the client begins the collage process, equipped with scissors, glue, magazines, colored markers, a journal, and large art paper or poster board. These art materials naturally evoke a creative place of make-believe in my client's hearts and imaginations. The Visioning® Method charts a course to turn dreams into reality.

Creating a Vision Board starts with images and words. We begin with searching through magazines for elements that illustrate the "focus phrase." The mantra is: "grab what grabs you." No editing or analysis. Never mind "practical" or "affordable." The idea is to reach for the sky, anything goes, as long as the images and words portray the "focus phrase." The goal is to picture the *experiences* we want, not just show *things* we want to possess. How do we want to *feel* when our dream becomes a reality?

As soon as clients start looking through magazines, they go to the place where daydreams live: the right-brain creative zone. It never fails. Time stops, an hour seems like minutes.

After they have collected a pile of images and words or phrases, clients make their final selections, based on the "focus phrase." Does the image or word illustrate their Heart's Desire? The final elements are laid out on the art paper or poster board. Often the Inner Critic surfaces at this point. Clients are assured that there's no right or wrong way to compose the Vision Board. We stop to confront the voice of negative self-talk. It says things like: "This is stupid. This will never happen. What a waste of time. Don't you have more important things to do? Who do you think you are? Getting a little grandiose, aren't you?" Or an "art critic" will trash-talk the design or esthetic. "This is ugly. You have no talent. What are you trying to do here?"

5 Tips for Helping Professionals

1. Do all the processes you are sharing with clients. You can't take anybody else to places you have not been.
2. Do a Vision Board, at least annually, to keep current with your Heart's Desires.
3. Scribble and draw difficult feelings out to clear stress in your personal or professional life.
4. Write dialogues with Inner Wisdom asking for guidance in your personal or professional life (Inner Wisdom speaks through the nondominant hand).
5. Write letters of gratitude.

5 Tips for Clients and Journal Keepers

1. To maintain a regular practice of journaling, choose a quiet, safe place and show up there with your journal at the same time each day or evening.
2. To spark creativity, scribble and doodle with both hands at the same time (use crayons or colored markers).
3. If you feel blocked or in a rut, confront your Inner Critic (see earlier prompt) with a two-handed dialogue.
4. Write dialogues with Inner Wisdom for guidance in your life (Inner Wisdom speaks through the nondominant hand).
5. Write letters of gratitude to your support system.

3 Journaling Prompts

1. Inner Critic Journaling

   With a colored marker in your dominant hand, write what the Inner Critic in your head says about your Heart's Desire and the images and words you selected. Use the second person: "*You* are wasting your time. This is a pipe dream; it will never happen. *You* should be checking your email." Do this for five minutes.

Using a different color in your nondominant hand, let your sassy creative Inner Child answer back. Be assertive; use four letter words, if necessary. Give your Inner Child permission to tell the critic off, in no uncertain terms. "SHUT UP. I'm sick of you. Stop putting me and my dream down. I'm having fun and you can't stop me. GET OUT! NOW!" Continue until your assertive Inner Child has gotten the upper hand over the critic.

This journal process usually works like a charm in breaking the spell of self-doubt and judgment. The client is asked to read their dialogue out loud. By this time, the client is laughing out loud. This clears the way to the next step: completing the collage in peace and quiet.

After completing the collage, the client is asked to display it in a place where they can look at it every day.

In the 12-week Visioning® program, the coaching client is advised to sit and look at the collage three times a day. Each week new Creative Journal homework prompts are assigned. These journal entries are discussed in the sessions. New processes are presented as well. For example, the client may be invited to role-play the dominant images or words in the collage. The client is asked to "Become the woman in the red business suit making a power point presentation." If the client has done a journal dialogue with "the woman in the red business suit," she is invited to read the dialogue out loud. She takes a position in the room where "the woman in the red suit" would feel most comfortable. She is encouraged to *embody* the woman in the collage. Perhaps she sits at a table or desk.

2. Telling My Story

Look carefully at your Vision Board. Imagine you are already living the life you pictured there. Open up your senses and ask: what do I see? What do I hear? What fragrances do I smell? Any tastes? Textures?

Write about "being there" in the first person, present tense. Using your nondominant hand, describe the scene.

3. Future Self

Project yourself into the future and imagine you have already realized your dream. With your dominant hand, write a letter to a friend and describe how it feels to be living your Heart's Desire as pictured on the Vision Board.

Finally, the key to success in Visioning® is letting it happen. We don't start worrying about how the dream will manifest. That's none of our business. Our job is to dream, to get really clear about what we want. We reinforce this daily by looking at the Vision Board, by journaling (using prompts from the book, *Visioning*). We deal with inner doubts that may come up by doing the dialogue between the critic and the Inner Child. Then we step aside and allow it to happen, in its own way. That last one is tough. Most people want to start strategizing, planning, *making* it happen. Big mistake. I have seen over and over, in my own life and the lives of my clients, that you don't *make* it happen. I always tell clients: when you go to a restaurant you place your order and then wait. You don't go into the kitchen and tell them how to prepare your meal. Instead, you let it happen. When you do that, the path becomes much more creative and surprising than you could have ever imagined. The Universe or Higher Power or whatever you believe in will do the work.

 About the Author

Lucia Capacchione, PhD, ATR. REAT, is an Art Therapist, Expressive Arts Therapist and Visioning® Coach. She is the bestselling author of 23 books on journaling for all ages, including *The Creative Journal, Recovery of Your Inner Child*, and *The Power of Your Other Hand*. Her signature techniques include bilateral drawing and writing with the nondominant hand. She was a weekly management consultant for Walt Disney Imagineering for over a decade and is Director of the Creative Journal Expressive Arts Certification Program and Visioning® Coach Training. Her coaching methods are used in corporations (vision statements, team building, product development and branding), group and organizational Visioning®, career programs in high school, and life coaching for individuals and couples.

Weaving the Net **35**

Journaling and Creative Productivity

Shannon Borg

Jump, they say, *and the net will appear.*

At 52, I jumped.

I saved my pennies, quit my full-time desk job in marketing, and, having never really painted before, I went back to art school to study oil painting.

It was scary, it was difficult. I felt like I was *weaving the net* as I was falling into it.

Now, three years later, I am showing and selling my art, teaching and writing about the creative process, and living in a "Paris in the 20s" of my own making. It was a dream that took years to follow. My journal became my trusted guide and mentor while making this dream come true.

I wrote my way out of creative paralysis, because, as Anais Nin said, "the day came when the risk to remain tight in a bud was more painful than the risk it took to blossom."

Creating Your Own System

Whether we are aware of it or not, we all already have a creative process. It is our job as artists to bring it into awareness for ourselves so we can work with that power, rather than allow it to work against us.

When I started to take my own artistic transformation seriously, my mantra became: *routine will save my life.* During a period of consuming books such as *The Artist's Way* by Julia Cameron, I started a daily routine of journaling every morning—writing my Morning Pages—that I had abandoned on and off for years.

I began to unpack my own creative process in my journal, identifying and examining its stages, figuring out what works for me, and discovering where I get stuck. I found that it is easy for me to get ideas and to do research. Oh, how we artists love ideas and rabbit holes!

However, it is much more difficult for me to actually originate a project and bring it to completion. The simple act of having a morning journaling routine helped me see and overcome some of these mental blocks and find ways through them.

I began to ask myself: when something goes right, what is the pattern that worked? What time of day works best for me to create? Have I slept well? Am I calm and focused, or energized and intense? Is it important for me to have feedback, and if so, what kind and from whom? What materials and subject matter bring joy to my process?

Through journaling, I created a framework for myself that works with my natural cycles and energy. Although I am sharing it with you here, I am not advocating you use it (although it is completely open-source, and I would be honored if it could help you). What I am advocating for is that you and your clients identify and develop your own creative process, through journaling.

Give yourself and your clients plenty of time with each stage of this process, and acknowledge each stage in meditations, journal entries, and so forth. As time passed, I found that I repeated this process over and over again, creating a spiral-like understanding going upward, growing in insights and creative output that I was happy with.

Acronym it Out

The framework for my own personal creative process is an acronym that has *evolved* over the past few years as my work has developed. It is, well, *EVOLVE*.

E—Edify

At this stage, I am "filling the well," with art, meditations at my shrine full of shells and stones from beach walks, journaling, looking at art, yoga, eating right, sleeping well, exercise, Artist's Dates, and reading.

V—Variegate

In this stage, I gather ideas, sketch, collage, play, research, experiment. During this phase, I can work in short spurts, any time of day or night, when the Muse hits. I try to gather ideas freely and without judgment.

O—Originate

Here is where I often get blocked. In this phase of my process, I choose an idea, start my plan, make a mark on a canvas and then respond to that mark, choose a place on my outline and then write about that place. This is the realm of the time clock, the work ethic. Suit up and show up. Do the work, set the timer. Act on that plan—start making the first thing, anything, just take action.

L—Luxuriate in the Zone

When I have *originated* something, the hard part is over for me. I am in the creative Zone. The process of making art takes over. This is the place where time flies, where there are no distractions, and where I am getting engaging with the right side of the brain. The challenge is to stay there. All of the things that I have set up in my process—a place to work, good health, adequate finances, a schedule, are so I can get to *this place*. The paint, the words, the characters come alive.

I love this part. For others, the difficult part may be edifying themselves, or the process of validating. Identify and develop what works and what needs attention.

V—Validate

In this phase, I engage with a Master Mind group in a formal setting, with the goal of growth, critique, and support. In this group, we are focused on reviewing each other's art and giving creative input.

This is where we need healthy boundaries. Clients can learn to ask for what they need from validation partners, and let them know in a kind way whether they are crossing the line of what is needed at this time. We need to be open to new ideas, but also protect ourselves so we can go and work again. I think this is very important. Set expectations at the beginning, and choose accountability partners that will be supportive and not break the artist down. It is important to work with people who understand intentions and not try to change, in an essential way, what the artist is doing.

E—Evolve

In this part of the process, I assess past work and process in my journal. What worked for me? What did not? What felt right? Where am I stuck? What part of the process needs attention? I capture this in my journal as I edify again, starting the evolution all over.

The *EVOLVE* framework is a way to remember that we are ever shifting, to understand where we are in the creative process and to be okay with that. When you finish one project, or get stuck and don't know what to do, you can go back to the beginning and do it all over again, where the spiral keeps turning, ever rising towards better art and a deeper understanding of ourselves as artists and human beings.

5 Tips for Helping Professionals

If you are a therapist or coach, offering your clients a chance to "create their own system" may empower them to discover what works best for them. Here's another acronym that offers tips to help you do this with your clients:

W-R-I-T-E

1.   W—Words

Ask your client to choose a positive, creative word such as WRITE, CRE-ATE, LOVE, RISE, ALIVE—and make it into an acronym just for them-selves. This is their own private "system" that can help them drive their own process, discover strengths and challenges, and move through cre-ative blocks.

2. R—Rock the Timer

Ask your client to use a kitchen timer to write for 20–25 minutes on each "letter" of their acronym. Use EVOLVE, if you wish: write for 25 minutes on Edify, for instance, listing the ways, as many as you can think of, that you would like to Edify in yourself to go deep and fill the well.

3. I—Ideate

Ask your client to choose one idea from their list, and spend 25 minutes going deep, taking notes, looking up definitions, etymologies, colors, histories, sketching, freewriting—about that idea. I call this the "Variegate" stage.

4. T—Take the Plunge

Taking into account your client's idea and the research they have done, ask them to Originate a poem, a painting, a play, or whatever genre they work in. If it helps to start this, too, in the journal before moving it to another format, do that. Then work it to a final form within a set period of time. Deadlines are essential.

5. E—Evaluate

Challenge your artist to take that piece of work, and show it to a trusted friend, get feedback from an ongoing writing or art group that understands what they are trying to do, and put it out into the world.

See what I did there? I created the *WRITE* acronym for this exercise. Creating your own acronyms to break down their process in journal work can empower you and your clients to discover and own a process that works.

---

 5 Tips for Clients and Journal Keepers

Here is another idea, building a framework within a single letter. Here are 5 "S's" for creative productivity:

1. Schedule it

Write in your journal at the same time every day. Notice what is the best time for you. Early morning with your notebook and coffee? In a café on your laptop surrounded by white noise? Or with your old typewriter at the midnight hour?

2. Set it and forget it

Consultant Francesco Cirillo developed the Pomodoro technique using a tomato-shaped kitchen timer. People in all industries now use this technique, which is to set the timer for 25 minutes, work on your project for that long, then take a five-minute break. My friend Kevin, the other member of my *CoDependables* writing group, calls each 25-minute timer session a "pomo."

3. Synergize it

After you have written or painted your work, get in a different mindset to edit and evaluate. Sometimes you need a bit of time away before diving into the assessment part of the process.

4. Share it

Create your own accountability group, even if it is just with one other person, or join a coaching group or painting group. At the moment, I actually have four groups (maybe too many, but it is working). The commitment keeps me on track with my projects and helps me to not get overwhelmed, to get new ideas, and have a place to commiserate with fellow artists.

5. Start it over

When you get to the end of a project, get it out there, and start your "S" process all over again!

 3 Journaling Prompts

The following journaling prompts are intended for both visual artists and writers alike.

1. **Positive Shapes:** Set your timer and write about a favorite shape—circle/sphere, triangle/pyramid, polygram/cube, or scutoid (look it up, it's a thing!). What things are this shape, what do these shapes remind you of? A pomo I wrote on the pyramid ended up being the

basis for a chapter in my book on the creative process, so let your mind roam shapes!

2. **Negative Spaces:** Artists often use this exercise, draw the shapes around a theme, rather than drawing the thing itself. If you are an artist, sketch the shapes *around* the thing you are wanting to draw, some everyday object in your room. If you are a writer, try to do one "pomo" focusing on the "negative space" of a subject. For instance, write about racism without mentioning the words racism, black, white, color, etc. You will be working in the land of metaphor.

3. **Re-Weaving the Net:** Using both positive shapes and negative space, shadow and light, or contrasting color sets (orange and blue, red and green, or yellow and violet), switch the "warp and weft" of your chosen subject matter. Make what is light, dark, and what is dark, light. Write the hero as a villain and the villain as a hero. See what happens.

 ## About the Author

Shannon Borg is the author of three books: *Chefs on the Farm: Recipes & Inspiration from the Quillisascut Farm School of the Domestic Arts*; *The Green Vine: A Guide to West Coast Organic, Biodynamic and Sustainable Wines*; and *Corset*, a book of poems. She writes and paints in the San Juan Islands, and is studying creativity coaching with Eric Maisel. Her next book, a memoir of food and writing, *26 Kitchens: How Neither Here nor There Became Home* is forthcoming in 2021.

Journaling With Your Inner Muse

36

5 Simple Techniques to Overcome Creative Blocks

Diane Hopkins

Our Inner Muse is the source of inspiration behind every creative endeavor we embark on—whether that be writing a book, painting a picture, or starting a business. Creative blocks happen when inspiration appears to dry up, indicated by a lack of motivation, self-sabotaging behaviors, or showing up but drawing blanks.

Being blocked is a common symptom of our Inner Muse getting drowned out by at least one of two different voices in our head—the Inner Critic who tells us what we're doing is rubbish and the Inner Censor who has plenty of reasons why we shouldn't be doing it. The Inner Muse is an archetype that can be called upon in one's journal to bring inspiration and clarity to creative projects and to understand the underlying fears and thoughts responsible for feeling blocked.

The five journaling techniques outlined in this chapter will help you guide clients through creative blocks by empowering them to cultivate a direct and ongoing relationship with the source of their own creativity.

1. Journaling on the Creative Block

When a client is creatively blocked, they must face their underlying fears and worries before they can hear the voice of their Inner Muse. They can do this by writing about the symptoms of the block they're experiencing. Encourage them to write for at least five minutes using a timer. Timed writing focuses the mind and pushing to write for at least five minutes creates the need to dig beneath surface responses.

Describe the block. . .

I can't write, I'm completely blocked. I keep telling myself I need to write. I even put it in my calendar. But I can't bring myself to do it. . . . I keep thinking writing is a waste of time, that I should be doing something more useful and there's no real point because I'm not a real writer. Who am I to think I can write a book?

Journal entries like this can reveal limiting beliefs and unhelpful thought patterns that come from our Inner Critic or Censor. Once these patterns are exposed you can address them with your client and help them construct alternative ways of thinking that will support their creative goals.

2. Writing About the Fear

Sometimes clients encounter a creative block because they are afraid of what will happen if they move ahead with their project. It's common for these fears to include perceived consequences of creative failure and success, so your client will benefit from journaling about both.

I fear failing because. . .

I worry that no one will want to buy my paintings and it'll be for nothing. What if I'm not a good painter, like I think I am?

I fear succeeding because. . .

If I do create a successful business then men will be intimidated by me, no one will want to date me and I'll never find a partner or have love in my life again.

These fears (whether realistic or not) are silently sabotaging your client's creative goals. Bringing them to the surface means you can tackle the emotional charge that is responsible for blocking them. If tears and emotions come up during this process, an important fear has been revealed. A release of emotions may clear the fear itself or the client could require further help addressing these concerns, like learning to handle criticism of their work. Identifying and working through underlying fears will create space for the Inner Muse to be heard again.

3. Dialogue With the Inner Muse

It's common to get blocked by indecision or doubt over the content of a creative project. With this journaling technique, a client initiates a direct conversation with their Inner Muse. They simply ask questions they would like answered and their Inner Muse responds.

Client:

What is the most important thing I need to share in this book?

Inner Muse:

That you've learned a lot about yourself from your divorce and how you've used those insights to live a more meaningful and joyful life.

Client:

But is that important enough? Will anyone else find it interesting?

Inner Muse:

It'll be interesting to other people going through a divorce. You'll mirror many aspects of their experience and they'll be both comforted and guided by your insights.

As you can see, the Inner Muse can be called upon to give specific creative advice and also act as a supportive coach, reassuring clients of the value of what they're doing. Used regularly, this technique helps clients trust themselves as the source of their own answers.

4. Journaling on Different Creative Choices

It's also common while working on a project to get stuck debating two or more different creative choices. Instead of staying blocked while they wait for a solution to arrive, clients can journal for five minutes on each option they are considering, writing as if they have chosen that one.

Dear Inner Muse, if. . .

My book was about my experience recovering from a chronic illness, then I would focus on the part where I created a better life for myself after I recov-

ered. I want to give hope to those still struggling that they've got so much to look forward to when they get better.

Dear Inner Muse, if. . .

My book was about creativity being part of the cure for chronic illness, then I would probably need to do some research on the relationship between illness and creativity and interview some experts. I'd also need to include some case studies of other people who'd discovered a creative outlet while they were ill.

By doing this, your client gets to take all the options for a test drive to get the clarity they need in order to make a choice. A journal is the ideal place to experiment with different ideas, safe from the need to impress an audience or respond to questions from others.

5. Intuitive Freewriting

The aim of freewriting is to escape the tyranny of the Inner Critic and Censor by learning how to access the intuitive right brain. This technique is especially beneficial when a client is overanalyzing their project or cannot access their own creativity.

This type of journaling is done by writing as fast as possible, with a notebook and pen, without stopping or thinking at all beforehand. A client can either write down their project name, its broad topic, or a specific part of it and then let their Inner Muse take over.

My business idea. . .

Something to do with coaching and helping people deal with their emotions in a more practical way because I really believe if we face our emotions head on then we'll be able to live much happier and more productive lives.

The insights might be surprising or obvious but both are useful, either highlighting overlooked aspects of the creative project or validating what has already been identified. Clients who struggle to access their feelings or intuition will benefit from incorporating freewriting into their journaling practice.

Using these five techniques within a regular journaling practice will help clients train themselves to access their Inner Muse whenever they need unblocking. Developing trust to look within for answers is fundamental to successfully completing creative projects and living a meaningful creative life.

5 Tips for Helping Professionals

1. At first, clients should establish a daily practice of journaling with their Inner Muse, done at the same time each day so it becomes a habit. Later, once confidence has been developed in the techniques, they can pick it up when needed.
2. Don't be surprised if clients alternate between creative breakthroughs and being stubbornly stuck in their Inner Critic or Censor. This is a normal part of the process and they may second-guess what their Inner Muse has to say until they've developed a regular journaling practice.
3. Unless your client specifically asks to share their journal responses with you, it's better for them to keep their journal entries private so they don't self-censor. Encourage them to share the parts they feel comfortable sharing or simply offer the key insights they received from doing the journaling.
4. Keep a sharp eye or ear out for limiting beliefs, thought patterns, and fears that are counterproductive to your clients' creative goals. These will show up as reasons or justifications for not moving forward. As these ideas may be deeply ingrained, your clients may not even realize they are sabotaging their own creative dreams.
5. Your role is to reinforce the insights your clients discover in their journaling practice and to give practical advice and support for taking action on them. These techniques should be used to build confidence in them discovering their own answers.

5 Tips for Clients and Journal Keepers

1. Getting in touch with your Inner Muse takes practice. At first, your Inner Critic or Censor may interrupt constantly. Don't give up if it feels hard or awkward. The voice of your Muse will get louder with regular journaling and you'll soon start to see meaningful results.

2. Journal every day if you can, especially when you're beginning to communicate with your Inner Muse or if you've taken a long break. Being consistent makes it easier to get in touch with those deeper feelings, thoughts, and ideas.

3. Try journaling after taking a hot bath, meditating, or anything else that relaxes you. You may find relaxation exercises also loosen up your mind so you can more easily access your Inner Muse.

4. Be aware of your Inner Critic or Censor trying to hijack your journaling. Start to recognize their voices. Accessing your Inner Muse requires the analytical part of your brain to take a backseat. You'll know you're accessing your Muse because you will be writing quickly without thinking, editing, or judging.

5. If you're going into analytical mode while you're journaling, try writing by hand in a notebook. You can even try writing with your non-dominant hand to see if that helps. Remember, there's no need to write correct or realistic answers. Your journal is a place for you to discover your deepest creative desires.

 3 Journaling Prompts

1. Dear Inner Muse, what do I really want to write/paint/create? Dear Inner Muse, what am I really afraid to write/paint/create?

2. Dear Inner Muse, what stories, beliefs, or secrets are holding me back from writing this book/starting this business/getting back into painting?

3. Dear Inner Muse, what would I do if I didn't worry about failing, hurting someone else, or being judged by others?

 ## About the Author

Diane Hopkins is a nonfiction book writing coach and editor for creatives, coaches, leaders, and entrepreneurs. She guides aspiring authors in writing memoir, self-help, and business books using personal stories to connect with their readers and inspire meaningful change. Diane also works as a speech coach and editor, helping clients turn their stories and expertise into powerful messages of transformation as invited keynote speakers at big events including business conferences and United Nations events, TEDx, and TEDWomen. You can learn more about her work at www.wordandwing.co and contact her at diane@wordandwing.co.

Altered Book Journaling

37

Re/voicing Re/finding of Self

Chris Leischner

Conservative thinking is being socialized into our academic and community cultures and pressures are being brought to bear on what and how an individual can question the world around us. With the wide swath of change being cut by neoliberal and conservative agendas across our society, social work and the helping professions seem to conform more and more to social control than to social change.

At the university level, social educators tend to develop course activities that facilitate and test intelligence or convergent thinking, the kind of thinking where there is one right answer to a question or problem. In social work, however, right and wrong is an unsuitable measure as so much of social work is about divergent thinking, where multiple responses to a question can be fashioned. There is no one right answer and expansive ideas and critical responses, ideally, should be encouraged and nurtured.

One of the most compelling arguments for divergent thinking is that as a social worker the need for a creative approach to understanding client complexities is needed. However, it can be dangerous to tell your own truth, as it can distance people from you, burn bridges, and result in a less-than-popular standing in academia or the community. These types of alienation then become a "power over" that encourages one to stay silent.

A student in one of my social work classes produced a "paper" that was a powerful example of speaking your truth through altered book journaling. Students were asked to do an altered book journal that paralleled the theory of early childhood development stages with their own lives. In altering the pages of an old book, this student found words that spoke to her being silenced as a child. She found pictures, her own art, ephemera, and pieces of articles that re-created a stage in her childhood that suddenly was awakened and understood. We help others find their own voice and speak for themselves when we give them tools that incite their creativity and curiosity, because if we accept their silence, we accept their pain as unchangeable.

Altered book journaling provides an opportunity to engage people in "knowing" of a deeper kind. It helps develop a curiosity about how we know and how we connect what we know with the world around us and the world within us. Part of who I am in the world is a Social Work Activist, so I have engaged my energy in facilitating opportunities for learning that can lead to transformational change and resistance.

As a closet artist and a biophilic bibliophile, I originally took up altered books as a creative means of exploring my talents and my world. Within days of becoming involved in this multi-medium, resurfacing of an other-wise "dead" book, I came to know that this multi-senses, multi-dimensional embodied process could provide an avenue for me to engage my clients and students in knowing of a different kind.

As an activist, it is important that every time I engage my energy to facilitate learning, I need to believe that that learning can lead to funda-mental change. I need to engage students and clients to help them become more curious about how we know and how we connect what we know with the world around us. My role is to facilitate creativity among students and clients.

Using this specific tool, the altered book journal, I explore one form of connecting the personal to the political and assist participants in their explica-tion of those internal pieces of knowing with the wider environment they exist in. My work focuses on a form of creativity that makes the connection between and among images, words, and palimpsest (a manuscript or piece of writing where the original writing has been effaced to make room for later writing but where traces of the original writing remain).

Altering or repurposing a book, making it something that it was not before, is comparable to helping a person experience themselves as something they were not before. A re/voicing, re/finding of self is a process of wiping clean the written word of the book and re/voicing self onto those pages.

On an activist level, altered books are a creative multi-medium, dialogical process of consciousness raising that utilizes personal ephemera, media mes-sages, images, and personal knowledge to engage participants in a process of imagining hope and change. This comes about through encouraging a person to connect what they think they know with what is in the world around them.

The topics are generally spontaneous and come from feelings that have been subdued or denied.

One altered book page that was created showed a picture of a 1950s woman, steaming hot dinner in hand, apron starched and high heels on, serving a goliath man in army fatigues and a weapon in his hands. On the clothesline behind him blew sheets with messages of servitude and subservience. A chain connected the woman to the man. The chain was real, and the man was an action figure cut in half to fit into the book.

The woman was a black-and-white sketch, empty of promise, while the clothesline had real small wooden clothes pegs holding up the messages written on cloth. The page was painted a foreboding gray and the text was about having stayed in a controlling relationship like many women of her age but not being able to break the chains. So, she journaled on the next page about this experience and how it was still with her, the anger and fear.

She portrayed these in black and red scrawls repeatedly, then she wrote his name and glued the pages together. We journaled a page that explored breaking the chain and she created a bright-colored page full of names of people who would support her and ways that she could take back her power through education, symbolized by a small book. She wanted independence and she represented this with birds and butterflies of rainbow colors, glued and pasted all around a picture of her as a small happy child. There were many more intricacies to these pages, and they chronicled a sense of hope, with a bird and butterfly on each page reminding her of that independence.

Altered book journals can be a continuous method of exploring self. By exploring the links between oppression in a format that by its very definition destroys to build again, we can engage in a process of consciousness-raising. It can also be a vehicle for exploring our personal connection to public issues, a method to encourage divergent and creative thinking and a way of knowing that encourages praxis and transformative change. Taking pieces that are seemingly unconnected to our lives and making them a part of a journal can provide creative connection to a greater whole.

On an environmental level, the creation of an altered book is a way to reuse and recycle books and materials that would otherwise be discarded. In repurposing a book as an altered journal, there is an opportunity to explore an idea, write your own text, and create your own personalized message with found art or your own art. You can create a place for your own family history, make a political statement, or just wander through your thoughts, finding bits of wisdom and perhaps more questions. The options are endless.

For me maybe the most important aspect of an altered book journal is that in years to come the reuse of materials otherwise discarded will be valued as good for mother earth. In our over-polluted, resources-devalued, and throw-away lives, we need to reconnect with the environment that we depend on. Shifting away from the anthropocentric bias that is firmly rooted in our North American culture requires us to become conscious of not just ourselves and the context of our lives but also of the very earth that sustains that life.

The creation of altered book journals relies on finding new meaning in throwaway objects. Ephemeral, paper, cast-off pieces of our lives find new life and meaning within the covers of altered book journals. Encouraging diver-gent thinking in our students and clients is how we will learn to think beyond the restrictive bounds set by neoliberal agendas. Breaking the bonds of silence requires creative and thoughtful contemplation of self and our world. We not only see a new purpose in re/creation of self, but we are re/connected to the reality of others and can begin to see value in everything.

5 Tips for Helping Professionals

1. Altering a book, including the painting, gluing, and drying pages, can take time. A one-hour session is not long enough for most cli-ents, so if you cannot schedule a two-hour session, break up the pro-cess by painting or gluing during a part of one session and writing in the next session. Just remember that if you have glued one side, then if you try to paint on the back side, what you have glued will come off. Try to spread the book open and use both pages as one. Glue pages together to reduce number of pages and rip out pages. Write at an angle or sideways on the page.

2. Each entry could be started with a prompt, a quote, or a statement from the last session that sparks curiosity from you or your client. "Last week you made an interesting comment about . . .".

3. Keep a box of prompts handy for clients for those days when ideas just do not seem to come easily. Things like "My world would be better if . . ." or "I can breathe easier when . . .". Or take some thin painter's tape and cover over words on the page, then paint over the entire surface revealing the words left "standing" on the page to provoke ideas.

4. Ask the client to bring in pictures, letters, and special objects (and learn how to reproduce them so that originals are not damaged) to act as a starting place. Remember when gluing into the book that if

you are putting in pages, then you must take out pages. Use a ruler to rip close to the book signature (binding). Glue your page to the piece of paper left. Put wax paper between the pages and put a weight on them overnight.

5. There is no right or wrong in compiling these pages, so help your client to explore deeper with questions, ephemera, or objects that help them remember or connect, such as an old photo or a piece of old music, a candy wrapper or jingle.

5 Tips for Clients and Journal Keepers

1. Keep a shoe box for old photos, pretty wrapping paper, Christmas cracker paper, pictures, pamphlets, labels, grocery lists, recipes, anything that catches your eye.
2. Use white or black gesso to cover the page (a process called "palimpsest"). The gesso is available at any art center.
3. I like to string together words in a free style, starting with one word and just letting the words come, not making sense or worried about what it will become.
4. Related to number 3, you can try "just being in the word."
5. Use as a prompt, "If I could tell the little girl/boy I used to be anything now, what would it be?"

3 Journal Prompts

1. I like to start my altered books with a dedication. This way I know my "audience" and if it is me then I dedicate my altered journal book to me or some version of me.
2. One of my favorite pages to do is a page titled "These things make me happy . . .". This allows the writer to collect all kinds of positive images and words, ideas and "stuff" to reflect on when down.
3. Asking a person "What was your very first memory?" can illicit some very powerful images that can be captured through color, form, and images.

About the Author

Chris Leischner is a social work activist and textile artist who makes her home in Youbou, BC. Chris has presented at National Conferences on Creativity and Altered Art as activism and she has taught altered books at University of Northern BC and Royal Roads University. She uses altered book journaling in her social work practice and in her own life to un/cover and re/cover those things hidden and forgotten. She has been a social worker for over 40 years, working to bring creative thought and divergent thinking to learning and life.

Journaling With Groups and Leaders

PART VII

Loving Is a Creative Act

38

Facilitating the Four Practices of Writing Alone Together

Ahava Shira

Prologue

In the spring of 2007, I initiated a writing group with two other women, all of us living on a small island in the Pacific Northwest. Possessing over a century of combined journal writing experience, we began to gather monthly to write in our journals together.

Each time we met, we put our pens to the page, unleashing our thoughts, feelings, memories, body sensations, hopes, fears, dreams, and whatever else emerged as we opened into the free fall of words. After ten, 15, or sometimes 20 minutes, we read our freshly penned words aloud to each other.

Accustomed to keeping our handwritten pages hidden, we discovered how liberating and cathartic it felt to give immediate voice to our unedited expressions. Inspired by these feelings, and by the desire to share the transformation we were experiencing, we went to work mapping the process.

Within the first few years of our collaboration, we named what we were doing "Writing Alone Together," and recognized four distinct practices in which we were engaging over and over. At that point, although we had each been facilitating writers' groups in various forms for years, the three of us started to test the four practices out with our respective clients and students.

In 2014, after seven years of creative labor and incubation, the three writers (Lynda Monk, Wendy Judith Cutler, and myself) published our book, *Writing Alone Together: Journalling in a Circle of Women for Creativity, Compassion and Connection.*

During the past ten years, the three of us have facilitated Writing Alone Together with a variety of groups in a variety of settings. In my role as mentor and facilitator, I have worked with students in elementary and high school classrooms; adults at a mental health drop-in center; women in a quiet room at the back of a busy café and in our public library's private meeting rooms; women with fused spines at a yoga retreat; women writing about pleasure in my tranquil garden studio; and women writing their love for the Earth on Zoom. Although I adjust my style depending on who is present, my role is always the same: to guide participants in the four practices (or creative acts) of Writing Freely, Reading Aloud, Listening Deeply, and Bearing Witness.

Act 1. Writing Freely

A Group of Writers Begin to Put Words Down, Bravely, Boldly

The act of "Writing Freely" challenges so much of our conditioning about writing and self-expression. In our logic-favored, left-brain-privileged educational system, most of us learned:
1. There is a "right" and a "wrong" way to say something.
2. We must have our thoughts clearly organized before we write them all out.
3. Without a rigorous attention to grammar, no one will understand our words.

Conversely, what most of us never learned is:
1. Writing is a process of discovery.
2. We don't need to know what we are going to say before we begin.
3. What we do need is permission to allow the unimpeded flow of our words.

Permission. It's of utmost importance. I devote a considerable amount of air time cajoling writers to let go of others' rules and expectations (including, and especially, their own) and to write however and whatever they like. I also use my powers of persuasion to encourage them to risk being imperfectly, and impeccably, human: fallible, vulnerable, strong, intelligent, awkward, lyrical, emotional, and everything in between.

As added inspiration, I use writing prompts as entry points into the writing. These can be words, phrases, quotations, song lines, questions, or sentence starters. I could call them "scene" starters, or "fire" starters, as they are meant to spark their curiosity and lead them passionately onto the blank page.

I also enthusiastically assure them that there are as many ways to respond as there are to be human!

Act 2. Reading Aloud

Then Stumble and Speak

Many writers hesitate at the first mention of "Reading Aloud," which is part of the reason I always acknowledge it as a choice. Whether they feel their material is too personal, too fresh, too raw, too vulnerable, or too anything, I honor their boundary, and their decision to pass, as an act of self-kindness and respect.

That said, over the years I have devised all kinds of creative ways to encourage students to *get in on* the act of voicing. For instance, I suggest that everyone reads aloud at the same time. That way they all get to practice speaking their words, while the pressure is off over being heard. Another way I lower the stakes of sharing is by offering a variety of possibilities: "Share a line, or a couple of lines. It could be the first one or last one. Or reflect on how you felt as you were writing, or give it to someone else in the group to read."

Those who do choose to speak their newly sprouted words have described it as exciting, frightening, nourishing, nerve-wracking, and healing. There is room for all these reactions here, for when Writing Alone Together, all the words are stages and the next time they share, like the next time they write, it will probably feel different.

Act 3. Listening Deeply

Give Their Fullest Attention

Most of us have been conditioned to judge and criticize our creations and then to compare them and come up either feeling superior or inferior. It starts at school with grades and curves. It continues with sports, cheerleading, or debating teams. We hope to win and fear losing. Not here. As with every act of Writing Alone Together, this third practice of "Listening Deeply" invites and supports a different way of valuing ourselves and each other.

We listen with our whole bodies: minds, hearts, and spirits, ears, and eyes, noses . . . all of our senses. We also listen with our subtle bodies, energy bodies, and intuitive bodies.

As the facilitator, it is my responsibility to keep reminding the group that this is what we are doing here and how we are being here. Acting here. Because we all need reminders. The habitual conditioning runs deep as does the mindless stream of thoughts we often attribute to the inner critic. It's just what we do as humans, how we often operate when we are on auto-pilot.

Hence, we focus on the creative act of listening. "We are learning to be curious and open, and to appreciate the unique contribution of each voice and its particular expression," I tell my students and clients.

Act 4. Bearing Witness

Receive All of It With Acceptance

The "closing" or fourth act of "Bearing Witness" embraces all the others. The writers have been unconsciously engaging in it throughout the first three acts. After gaining access to their own immediate and unrehearsed expression, they shared, in whatever chosen ways (including silence), their spontaneously erupted words. Then they were exposed to each other's uniquely written truths.

So, this is the meta-cognitive climax. In acknowledging how we have been witnessing our own and each other's process, we are also affirming the beneficial, and benevolent climate we have (all) created through the four practices. Allowing each writer's words to be as they are, without the need to change or improve them, we honor the full breadth of our expression, celebrating how diverse and voluminous this being human is and how wide our hearts can reach into compassion.

Final Bow

Devote Themselves Again and Again to These Act(s) of Loving

As I coach my students through the four practices of Writing Alone Together, I am acting as a catalyst for transformation, while inviting each writer to act similarly and to become creative catalysts for loving self and others. Through repeating this series of creative acts, over and over, we are all engaging in a dramatic shift in awareness, playfully redirecting our attention toward authentic expression, interconnection, and compassion.

5 Tips for Helping Professionals

1.   Freedom is a verb. Invite your clients and students to act on it through letting their words loose on the page.
2.   Let yourself be drawn toward prompts that inspire and enliven you. Chances are they will enliven and inspire your clients and students too!
3.   Let yourself discover innovative ways for your students or clients to share. For example, Sometimes I suggest the writer read their spontaneous words backwards line by line. Or start in the middle. Or repeat a line that felt especially significant. Then I invite each writer to do the same.
4.   Invite those who are listening to take note of their favorite line or phrase of the reader. After the reader is done, invite the group to share them aloud as an echo of affirmation.
5.   Help your group find a nonverbal way to acknowledge appreciation for each reader's words. In my groups, we often use fluttering fingers, which is the sign language for applause.

5 Tips for Clients and Journal Keepers

1.   You are vast, with so much of your insides, and insights, uncharted. Let your words draw your wisdom and beauty and power out. Be they vulnerable, ecstatic, miserable, or laughable, they are yours. And because they are yours, they matter.
2.   The wilder your words, the wider your heart gets to open. Letting yourself write what you are afraid of or unsure about gives you an opportunity to love yourself a little more each time. Your self is inexhaustible, fickle, and may even be prickly at times. But it is yours. Be proud and positive with it.
3.   Play at reading your words. Enunciate, articulate, pause, and let the words settle into the listeners' ears before continuing. This is your time to speak. Shine on!
4.   See how deep your listening can go. Can you hear the readers' words with your belly, elbows, soles of your feet?

5. Watch out for the critic when you are bearing witness. If you hear a voice that's pointing out the faults of the reader or their writing (or that is comparing them to your own), pause and breathe in, put your hand on your heart and reaffirm your intention to be a witness not a critic.

 3 Journaling Prompts

Respond to the following three questions in your journal:

1. What do you hold dear?
2. What or who holds you dear?
3. How else do you want to be held? By whom?

 About the Author

At 20 years of age, Ahava Shira wrote her first journal while on a three-and-a-half-month solo backpacking trip through Europe. Co-author of *Writing Alone Together: Journalling in a Circle of Women for Creativity, Compassion and Connection* (2014), Ahava Shira holds a PhD in Language & Literacy Education from the University of British Columbia, where she developed the arts-based, contemplative practice of Loving Inquiry. Ahava mentors writers and facilitates writing workshops and retreats in the Pacific Northwest and online. Author of a poetry book *Weaving of My Being* (1998), a spoken word CD *Love Is Like This* (2010), and the forthcoming memoir *Messy*, Ahava's poems and essays have appeared in *Living Artfully: Reflections from the Far West Coast*, *The Art of Poetic Inquiry*, and *A Heart of Wisdom: Life Writing as Empathetic Inquiry*). Originally from Montreal, Ahava lives on Salt Spring Island with her husband and a farm-full of naturally creative beings.

Journaling in the Virtual Space

39

Jennifer Britton

2020 has expedited confidence levels in what is possible in the digital space. The vibrant virtual and remote ecosystem provides an opportunity for expanding what journaling can look like. Whether you have started to work "remote by choice" or "remote by chance," journaling in the virtual space can be an important part of connection, collaboration, and grounding for individuals, groups and teams.

There are many different digital pathways which bring people into the realm of journaling in the virtual space. Whether it is part of a group coaching process, an online video journal for education, or as part of a virtual retreat, digital journaling opportunities and applications continue to expand.

This chapter explores the following:

- Digital or analog?
- Five examples of where journaling has been incorporated into virtual programming. From virtual retreats, to ongoing virtual group coaching and on-demand video-based programming, these examples illustrate how journaling can be used to foster connection, collaboration, clarity, and focus.
- Tips for Helping Professionals wanting to incorporate journaling into their digital and virtual practices.

 Tips for Clients and Journal Keepers Who Are "Remote by Choice" or "Remote by Chance"

With virtual work having become the new way of working for so many, screen time has taken on new meaning. A major question is,

"Do we journal digitally or remain traditional with paper-based journaling?" Keep in mind that journaling in the virtual space doesn't have to be digital.

Studies have found that digital retention is different from analog retention. A study by Mueller & Oppenheimer (2014) found that writing things out creates an opportunity to reframe things in our mind. This has implications for what is retained and remembered over time. Digital or analog, what is your choice?

Working virtually or remotely affects work and life. For some, physical distancing feels like social distancing. Many experience a sense of isolation and disconnection with others. Journaling can be a tool for connection and collaboration.

As I explore in *Effective Virtual Conversations*, the ecosystem of virtual learning is vast. The virtual learning ecosystem, including formal and informal approaches, ranges from virtual team development to meetings and formal education. In this chapter I want to share five different examples of journaling in virtual programming. Consider how you might apply each to your own work.

Virtual Journaling Application #1—Virtual Retreat Format (Focus and Grounding)

I originally started experimenting with journaling in the virtual space back in 2006, with the launch of my first virtual retreats. These included one-day virtual retreats for business owners and multi-session evening virtual retreats around work-life topics.

In those days, the notion of doing a retreat online was foreign to many. Early adopters saw the possibility and promise of what time spent *retreating* from their home or a hotel or even a cabin could hold. This helped to shape my belief in the need for more "pause points" virtually.

In the virtual retreats I run, each hour includes dedicated "alone" offline time. Journaling prompts provide anchors to reflect and pause. Prompts provide an opportunity to take note of what's working, and what plans need to be put into place. Retreatants have noted that these blocks of reflective pause are critical for creating more focus, clarity, and grounding.

Virtual Journaling Opportunity #2—Reflective Pauses in Ongoing Group Coaching Programs (Connection and Clarity)

My early experiences with incorporating journaling questions into virtual retreats then segued into bringing them into ongoing group coaching programs. In these programs, where groups meet for months or even a year, journaling provides an opportunity for connection with others.

I host two Coaching Labs throughout the year focusing on ongoing conversation and learning. One of the favorite types of calls are the reflective prompt calls. In these sessions, 15–30 minutes are earmarked for real-time journaling in the group setting, framed by prompts I share. Setting a timer for 75–150 seconds, I ask the group one question at a time, giving people the opportunity to journal and capture their responses.

For business owners planning their next steps and reflecting on what's working or not, or leaders using the pause to consider the next steps in a complex environment, this experience provides moments of grounding and clarity. It creates clarity about what's happened and what lays ahead.

A final part of these calls is to leave space for Lab members to connect with others in virtual breakout rooms, sharing their insights. This completes the learning loop of reflection and processing, leaving them with an invitation to put that learning or insight into practice before we meet again.

What could you do to incorporate journaling into ongoing group coaching?

Virtual Journaling Opportunity #3—Journaling Prompts to Inform Peer Conversations (Connection and Collaboration)

A third application for journaling in the remote space has been to include journaling and journaling prompts (often created by the group) as an opportunity to create Connection and Collaboration. In many group coaching experiences, I have members meet in between group calls to discuss the questions they have journaled about. This peer-to-peer interaction has led to new collaborations being formed, and tighter connections across these groups which meet on Zoom.

What might you do to incorporate journaling for peer connection?

Virtual Journaling Opportunity #4—Journaling Prompts as Part of an On-Demand Business Development Process (Clarity and Focus)

Journaling has been an important part of the 60-Day Coaching Business Builder Accelerator program, geared for coaches growing their businesses. Reflective pause frames the start and end of the week check-in and check-out accountability reflections. Daily assignments for the 60 days of the program also incorporate journaling opportunities. Journaling has created clarity and focus in an on-demand learning context.

What might you do to incorporate journaling into current on-demand programming to create CLARITY *and* FOCUS?

Virtual Journaling Opportunity #5—Journaling Prompts as Part of an Ongoing Blog Series (Sparking Conversation)

"What's possible?" asked my first of more than a hundred Weekly Journaling Prompts at the Teams365 blog back in 2018.

Started as a precursor to the launch of my 2018 workbook planners *Coaching Business Builder* and *PlanDoTrack*, I introduced a new weekly column at the Teams365 blog—the Weekly Journaling Prompts. It was intended to provide short questions to get individuals to think differently. It has also been one of my favorite columns.

The weekly journaling blog prompts then morphed into a quarterly digital volume, bringing together 12 weeks of prompts in an eBook.

Based on facilitator requests, the blog graphics were converted into square Conversation Sparker Journaling Cards. Available as a deck of 50 digital or physical cards, facilitators, leaders, and coaches have been bringing them into their own meetings and conversations.

What Could You Do to Scale Your Journaling Prompts Into Different Products or Services?

I hope that this chapter inspires you to explore different journaling options that are available in the digital space. The digital space provides us with a wide variety of different media to tap into. What exploration do you want to undertake?

5 Tips for Helping Professionals

1. Incorporate journaling in multiple ways into the programming you offer for individuals, groups, and teams. How can it be an add-on to your other approaches?
2. Consider the power of the pause. What can you do to create more "micro-pause" points in your conversations and programming for people to stop, focus, and explore?
3. Consider the variety of mediums through which journaling is possible: text, audio, video, photos.
4. Think how journaling virtually can help connect people. Connection in today's virtual world is something people are hungry for. How can journaling serve as a connection point?
5. Consider how journaling in the virtual space can create grounding and centering. For the decade-plus I worked globally, my journals were a space to note my daily adventures, learning as a professional, and a place to make sense of the world I was experiencing. Journaling is an important part of what Karl Weick terms "sense making."

5 Tips for Clients and Journal Keepers

Journaling virtually can provide you with multiple opportunities for connection, clarity, and collaboration. It may be part of a virtual retreat or part of a standalone virtual journaling process.

1. Leverage the power of the pause to gain new insights. If journaling is part of an online or virtual program, explore how it can be a bridge to connect with others virtually.
2. Just because it's digital doesn't mean it needs to be a digital journal. Consider analog (hard-copy) as well as digital journaling opportunities. Experiment with both and see what resonates best with you.
3. Use journaling to consider "What's beyond the screen?". I was first introduced to journaling myself as a youth working in Algonquin Park. My summer journals are still treasured resources, providing a snapshot into my early years as a leader engaging with the world. Look beyond the screen to capture "What's outside your window?" in the natural and physical world.

4. Explore digital platforms. From Trello, to Pinterest, there are many ways to digitize elements of your journaling, as well as capture or earmark ideas for the future.
5. Use your journal to connect with others.

3 Journaling Prompts

Next time you journal virtually, consider these prompts:

1. What's possible virtually is . . .
2. My mantra around virtual is . . .
3. I want to foster connection by . . .

 ## About the Author

Coach, author, and thought leader in group and team coaching, Jennifer Britton has been an early pioneer in the virtual and remote space. Since the early 1990s she has led teams and programming virtually, first in the international humanitarian sector, later through her company, Potentials Realized, an award-winning coaching skills training company.

Since 2004 her focus has been on virtual programming. Most days you'll find Jenn leading a myriad of virtual programs—from remote team development, to virtual retreats for business owners, to coaching skills training. Jennifer Britton is the author of five books including *Effective Group Coaching* (Wiley, 2010), *Effective Virtual Conversations* (2017), and *PlanDoTrack Workbook and Planner for Virtual and Remote Professionals* (2019). Jennifer is the co-host of the Remote Pathways podcast which explores the many pathways to remote work. Email Jennifer at info@potentialsrealized.com.

Reference

P A Mueller & D M Oppenheimer, The Pen Is Mightier Than the Keyboard: Advantages of Longhand over Laptop Note Taking. *Psychological Science*, 25, 2014, 1159–1168. doi:10.1177/0956797614524581

Journal Partners   **40**

Two People, Two Journals, More Benefits

Krupal Bhagat and Sarah King

"Writing with another person nurtured my relationship with writing."

—Krupal

"Having a journal partner makes me do something I enjoy and believe in but that I wouldn't necessarily do alone."

—Sarah

Have you ever resolved to keep a daily journal, written religiously for a week, and then realized you haven't picked up the journal for months? Journaling is a solitary activity, and in that lies both its strength—we can do it alone—and its weakness—it lacks the structure and social benefits built into activities we do with others. If you or your clients are looking for a strategy to help make writing a regular habit, why not consider a journal partner?

A journal partner is someone with whom you commit to share the process of writing. It's the person who sits across from you, at the table or on the screen, and writes in their journal at the same time as you write in yours. At its most basic, that's it. You can call your partner at 10 AM, start writing by 10:05, and be done by 10:30. You've done the important thing: the writing. If you choose, you can share your words, but sharing is entirely optional.

The benefits of the open-ended writing we do in journals are well known. Psychologist James Pennebaker studied "expressive writing" and found that writing for 15 minutes a day over four days leads to measurable improvements in cognitive function and physical health. Professional writers, led by Peter Elbow and Natalie Goldberg, use "freewriting" to generate ideas, and work through blocks. Educators assign "reflective writing" to promote learning. By making you write regularly, a journal partner helps you tap into these benefits of open-ended writing. In practice, journal partnerships often expand beyond just writing, which brings additional benefits.

First of all, writing builds connection. There's something about the act of reflection—and after all that's what journaling is—that slows us down and promotes taking time to chat. If you've written something intense, acknowledging it releases tension. If you've had an "aha" moment, sharing it is satisfying. And if the writing has been a little "blah," it's reassuring to hear that yes, that happens.

Second, writing moves projects forward. Writing projects are the obvious ones: novelists and dissertation writers have known for years that sitting in a room with another person helps you keep writing. A weekly writing session can also help you process a work challenge, a difficult relationship, or a design problem—whatever you need to tackle.

The beauty of journal partnering, like journaling itself, is its flexibility. Our partnership is constantly changing. When we started writing together, we had no prompts and never talked about what we'd written. When COVID-19 and the lockdown hit, we started meeting online and added prompts, mostly about how we were coping. We also added a few minutes of talking about our responses. Then, when we started working on this chapter, we used some of our writing time to brainstorm.

So, do you have a friend you never seem to get in touch with? Reach out and suggest you meet regularly to write—and catch up. Have a project you never seem to get moving on and know someone else in the same situation? Reach out and suggest you use journaling, and the accountability that comes with having a partner, to move forward step by step.

How to Choose a Journal Partner?

The most important element in a journal partner is a commitment to the writing process. You can have absolutely nothing else in common with your journal partner but if you both believe in writing and commit to doing it together, your partnership will work.

Conversely, if you have a friend who agrees to do it just to please you, it won't work. Why? Because the only guaranteed benefit of the journal partner is that it will make you write regularly. The other benefits are possible, but not guaranteed. So, if you're wondering if someone might make a good journal partner, ask questions like, "Have you ever kept a journal? What did you get out of it?". If the person acknowledges the value of journaling, there's journal partner potential. If not, move on to someone else.

How Might a Professional Use Journaling With Clients?

If you've read this far, you probably have ideas about how to incorporate journal partners into your work. Here are some of ours.

If you're an advocate of journaling and you have a client who is reluctant to write, it can be a way of introducing someone to journaling. You might say, "Let's write together and you can see how it works for you." Our partnership actually started this way. Krupal had done a project about the benefits of expressive writing, but she wasn't comfortable using it herself. Wanting to give her a gentle push, Sarah suggested writing together. Pretty soon, Krupal was hooked.

You could also guide a client, particularly if the person is enthusiastic about journaling, to reach out to someone in their life to be a journal partner. The goal could be to help them journal more regularly, or to deepen a relationship—whatever the client needs.

With groups, you could pair people up and guide each pair through the process. You might choose to create an assignment in a writing course, or create a writing group in a therapeutic setting. Depending on the setting, you could focus on the process or the product.

Finally, don't forget about yourself. What about journaling with a colleague, perhaps around a shared project, or perhaps just as a means of connecting?

What Are the Pitfalls of a Journal Partner?

Writing with someone, especially on a screen, may feel strange or intimidating at first. Unless there's something going on with your partner, that will dissipate quickly. Not sharing your writing reduces vulnerability and after all, it's no more strange to write with someone than it is to tap away on our phones at the same table.

Journal partnerships do take more time than writing on your own, even if you keep it simple. We think the accountability more than makes up for that, but it's an individual choice. If you're doing them with several clients, or managing multiple partnerships, you need to think through how to keep them efficient.

Like anything else you do with others, issues will come up. It's important to keep communication open and again, this is where the beauty of journaling comes in. Why not build in five minutes of writing about how the journal partnership is working. Yes, for this one to work you'll have to agree to share!

So, Have We Convinced You to Try It?

The best way to find out if a journal partner works for you or your clients is to try it for yourself. Let us know. And if it doesn't work, you can always write about it!

---

 5 Tips for Helping Professionals

1. Help your clients figure out the logistics of the partnership. How frequently will they meet? What will a typical session look like? Will they be using prompts to guide their writing? Ensure that clients feel prepared to write.
2. Think about your role. You are a supporter, a cheerleader, a guide. Promote creativity. Ask lots of questions. Help clients figure out what is and isn't working. Also think about your facilitation style. Should you be more directive or laid back? The answer depends on your clients' preferences, their comfort with writing, and the amount of time spent writing with a journal partner. You may want to learn more about their preferences at the beginning of a partnership and check in regularly.
3. Reflect! Reflect! Reflect! Make sure you've thought about your goals for the partnership and conveyed these goals to your clients. Are they motivated and ready?
4. You may encounter resistance from a client, especially if writing is uncomfortable or perceived not to be valuable. Explore these feelings. Talk or write about why your client feels this way. Perhaps he or she is not ready to write or may prefer other methods of creative expression.
5. Write! You may find it useful to write during this process to facilitate reflection. After all, it is easier to convey the benefits of writing if you've also experienced them yourself.

---

5 Tips for Clients and Journal Keepers

1. Set ground rules. Decide when, where, how often, and how long you will meet and write. Are you going to use prompts or freewrite? Are you going to share what you've written? There is no right "formula," but we recommend between ten to 20 minutes of writing. You may also want to leave five minutes before and after the session to check in with your partner. How is it going for your partner?
2. Play. Try a different pen, journal, or paper. Doodle. Experiment with the structure of the session. We've played around with the amount of time spent writing, the use of prompts, and sharing what we've written. You have the freedom to take this in any direction you choose.
3. Notice what comes up for you. Do you feel pressure to write? If you don't know what to write, write the same thing over and over again. Keep your pen moving. Some days, you may feel self-critical. Try to explore these feelings objectively and nonjudgmentally. You may want to share your experiences with your journal partner. Chances are your partner has experienced something similar.
4. Be accountable to yourself and your partner by showing up. At the same time, don't be too hard on yourself if you have to cancel or aren't at your best. Sarah once fell asleep during a writing session with Krupal!
5. Give it time. Trust yourself, your partner, and the writing process. Remember that the ultimate goal is to reap the known benefits of writing by having a journal partner keep you accountable. Who knows, you may discover other benefits along the way.

 ### 3 Journaling Prompts

1. For professionals: *What are your goals for the partnership? What barriers or problems do you anticipate and how might you and the partners overcome them?*
2. For journal keepers: *What are you hoping to get out of this process? What would you like your journal partner to know?*
3. For those days when you don't know what to write: *What is on your mind today?*

About the Authors

Sarah King and Krupal Bhagat have been journal partners, in person and online, since 2016. Sarah is an associate professor at the University of Toronto Scarborough, where she teaches writing courses, runs writing retreats, and works extensively one-to-one with students. Krupal is an Occupational Therapist who works in a pediatric setting. She is passionate about advocating for personal growth through creative self-expression and is currently collaborating in the design of a wellness journal.

The Women's Writing Circle   **41**

Creating a Community Space Through Writing and Sharing

Nancy Johnston and Shehna Javeed

When we started the Women's Writing Circle in 2014, we hoped we could share our passion for self-expression and share writing with a small group of supportive like-minded women working on our university campus. What makes this group unusual is the commitment of the group to carve out time at their workplace for a social gathering and for writing. After monthly meetings for six years, we know the circle fulfills a collective need to share in a community and to use writing for self-expression. At each writing circle, writers are invited to respond to two writing prompts created to help the individuals and group express diverse perspectives and stories.

One of our regular members captures the positive energy of the group: "For someone that routinely feels somewhat of a misfit at work, this was different; it made me feel like I actually belonged (with many others expressing similar sentiments to my own)." By writing in a supportive circle, writers have an opportunity to share ideas and join a recuperative and nurturing space.

Bringing women writers together to write in a safe, inclusive, and supportive space supports their self-expression, confidence as writers, and community building. The Women's Writing Circle began as a conversation between two writing teachers, Nancy Johnston and Sarah King, and our former campus Equity and Diversity officer, Toni De Mello. Shehna Javeed, one of our founding members, joined the facilitating team in 2016.

We recognized from the beginning that many women wanted to connect positively to other women outside of their regular work. From the beginning we decided to offer shared conversation and writing opportunities with a hot lunch because it would signal this was a positive event and encourage those who identify as women to attend during their busy workdays. Many of the women who participate take little time for themselves or to be creative, whether at home or work.

After socializing, the whole group settles in for a first group prompt, writing quietly for five to seven minutes, before we break and invite anyone to share. Members write to a second prompt and share in a small group or pairs to ensure more informal conversation. Our second prompt is often a lighter topic. We encourage everyone attending to write expressively without self-censoring and to keep their pens moving for five to seven minutes for each prompt. Everyone is invited, but not required, to share something about the experience of writing and to read from their writing. Everyone is welcome to share their emotions and ideas without fear of critique on style or content. The combination of these two prompts ensures that everyone has the chance to participate as a listener as well as hear their own voices.

We create our prompts to be topical, responsive, and relevant to the women who attend. We don't rely on master lists from the internet or writing books, but tailor ours from lines from poems, essays, or talks we have heard. Our writing prompts might reflect seasonal events or lean against issues related to their experience as women. One writer responded to a prompt about an important woman who was a storyteller in their life. She shared, "My aunties were story-keepers who only opened up when we worked side-by-side. They revealed secrets when doing the dishes." When ideas like these are read aloud, other participants often expand with similar or parallel stories, both acknowledging difference and solidarity in the telling.

We also encourage women to express their emotions together in writing for healing and resilience building. We invited writers to explore and expand on the sentence opening, "I am happiest in my skin when . . .". We've also adapted the familiar letter-to-oneself to explore our personal histories and strengths as adults. Another popular prompt is a letter of gratitude that is reversed to invite everyone to write about how others might express gratitude for something they have done.

Together, we also celebrate and honor important cultural and political events, like International Women's Day and Black History Month. These events have generated prompts about resilience in communities, leaders who have inspired us, and the myth of the single story. Inspired by our members, we work to create prompts that can appeal to our diverse members and their breadth of experience. One of our participants shared that she was "able to tap into [her] intersectionality, reflect and find meaning in experiences and commune with amazing women from all over the campus." We also have collaborated with campus students and leaders from our Women and Trans Centre for International Women's Day when we celebrate such with a guest writer and facilitator.

As facilitators and writers, we continued our Women's Writing Circle while our participant writers were working remotely under the pandemic. We kept our model of two prompts that allows writers to share their emotions and expressive writing. We have worked hard to ensure confidentiality and solidarity in our online events. We look forward to having future writing spaces, online and in person, with our community. By sharing our learning and experience, we hope that other equity-seeking groups can use this model to create a safe space for expression and community building through writing.

5 Tips for Helping Professionals

1. We begin with the premise that anyone can write. Writing is first and foremost about expression. Women do a lot for others but have few opportunities to express themselves. In a workplace, some work roles may further perpetuate this lack of expression and so we provide the space for such. We challenge ourselves to write freely, pen to paper (encouraging, but not demanding, no laptops), and to write without editing ourselves. To identify writing prompts, our advice would be that you tap into the day-to-day content and create simple prompts that are relevant and relatable.

2. Ensure that the space for self-expression through writing is equitable for all levels of writers. In our circle, we engage in active and empathic listening but we do not ask questions when content is being shared nor offer applause. Some expression may be happy while others may be sad. Applause increases pressure to be "good at writing" and takes the focus away from the sharing of experience that occurs in this space. We remind everyone at the start of every Circle of the ground rules including no applause. Remind everyone that expression allows for exploration rather than perfection.

3. Confidentiality of the space is respected, so that the topic of someone's expression is not discussed outside the Circle, even with that person.

4. We offer two prompts. One is co-facilitated in the larger group and women can volunteer to read or share what they wrote about. This is not required to participate. We note that that there are some who avidly attend but rarely share in the large group. The second prompt is conducted in the same way, and then we break out into small groups of two or three, where women can read or share the content of their writing. Groups of three build warm connections.

5. Food is important to the shared experience. In the hustle and bustle of busy lives and busy days at the office, we offer women the opportunity to come and write while enjoying a warm meal. Not having to pack a lunch is a small bonus that some women savor. The aroma of warm food in the space and a shared meal builds community in unspoken ways. Leftovers are also taken away for dinner or the next day's lunch.

 ## 5 Tips for Clients and Journal Keepers

1. If you want to create a small group of expressive writers for a circle, start small. You may want to have a co-facilitator to help organize an event, come up with ideas for prompts, and time keep.

2. Encourage everyone to write silently in the prompts and to write without stopping or criticizing their work. Writing silently together creates a shared space and carries its own power.

3. Be supportive by listening to each other. Some group members might not have the same comfort or confidence sharing their work. Pay attention to your own needs too. Encourage everyone to participate as writers and listeners, but avoid demanding everyone read their work, especially if it is personal and new.

4. Minimize your own negative self-talk. We all have voices that say, this isn't good enough and you're not a writer. Encourage people to share if they are willing or to talk about the process.

5. Keep a journal. Consider writing in a single journal or file that you can come back to later. Find something you enjoy in your own work, circle a sentence or ideas, and continue your writing prompt with fresh eyes. Try to observe what is happening around you and if there is something that strikes you as meaningful, jot it down and write about it. Keep your journal with you to capture such moments before they slip away.

3 Journaling Prompts

1. Morning routine: Consider your morning routine and rituals, from the moment you wake up. We go through our morning rituals on automatic pilot after we get out of bed and either get ready for work or for our day at home. Consider how you go about your morning routine, synchronized or unsynchronized with others.
2. Seasons and a new beginning: Consider your connection with nature as we begin a new season. Imagine yourself in a place where you engage with nature. It could be a walk on campus, your spot in your garden, the plants on a window sill, where you enjoy the sights of nature. Engage your senses. Describe and write about sights, sounds, experiences, or emotions.
3. Black History Month: We begin with a preamble about Canadian activist Viola Desmond for Black History Month. Your group might focus on other local Black or racialized leaders and artists. We ask participants to consider stories of struggles and triumphs and seeking equality. Write about who you know within your own diaspora or your life, who embody this struggle and write about them.

About the Authors

Nancy Johnston is a writer, teacher, writing coach, and textile artist living in Toronto. She is an associate professor who teaches writing and courses on disability studies at the University of Toronto Scarborough. Her passions are teaching writing and textile art for expressive and restorative play. From studying the poetry of Emily Dickinson, she has learned "To tell all the truth but tell it slant."

Shehna Javeed is a lifelong learner with a long career in higher education administration and student advising. She enjoys writing and public speaking, and she was a TEDxUTSC speaker in 2019 with a talk titled "Do You See People for Who They Are?", on the immigrant hustle. She lives in Toronto with her family.

Expressing Feelings in the Virtual Journaling Group

42

Mary Ann Burrows

Living from the depths of our hearts sounds like a wonderful way to live. But then life happens, we shut down, and in a fierce effort to protect ourselves, we close off. What if sharing our feelings could help us to stay open and closer to our heart? What if standing as a witness to another could also help us see hidden parts of our own story? Witnessing vulnerability can be the key to the self-encouragement that we need to be able to step forward into our unknown places.

Journals are a valuable tool. They allow people to clarify their thoughts and feelings and gain valuable self-knowledge. Journals help people experience better mental health, lower stress, and gain increased clarity and a greater sense of peace. Our journals become our personal reference guide, holding the wisdom that we have learned about ourselves through the ups and downs of our life.

We can refer back to them to see where we were, how we transformed, and what we learned. They become the vehicle that holds the stories of our truth and the place that unearths things that we may have forgotten. Our journals hold our epiphanies, our a-ha moments and our dreams, our deepest thoughts, disappointments, and revelations.

Coaches and therapists often encourage journaling as a way to help their clients tap into and process their thoughts and feelings as well as resolve the past and provide hope for the future. Journaling captures on paper the feelings and thoughts that clients have in their heads. While journaling is a wonderful tool for both coaches and clients, there are often obstacles that people must overcome before they can embrace the act of journal writing and begin to enjoy its benefits.

It can be difficult for many people to express their feelings on paper and even the thought of identifying and then writing feelings down can become a mountain of additional stress in a client's life. A journal group is a way that can help people start and stay on the path towards their higher self. Members of a group are more likely to write consistently, to stay aligned through accountability, and to develop a ritual of daily practice in their everyday lives through weekly prompts and homework.

A virtual group can be also the perfect, safe place to experience our life with the extended support of a wider community. The group becomes a sacred space where members can stumble and fall as they learn to express their feelings through their own writing, through sharing and through the witnessing of others. The group serves as a support for people who are drawn to journal but may struggle with implementation, motivation, expression, or accountability. Virtual journaling groups are also fun and become a community of like-minded people that its members look forward to connecting with online with peers from all over the world.

If you are curious about journaling but need support to get started, journaling can be made so much easier when you have the support of interesting and interested people to help you along. Working together in a group will give you daily inspiration and help you learn how to express yourself, upping your commitment to YOU, by helping you stay on track with daily prompts that encourage you to slowly dive into the deeper layers of your being.

The added benefit of sharing with others at the weekly meet-ups is that the experience gives life to our stories. As a participant, you have the opportunity to not only live the experience, but also to experience some surprising emotions that may surface when you hear your own voice sharing your words. At times, we often hear fear or anger in our voice, fear and anger that we didn't even realize we were holding onto.

Group journaling is also a way to help people meet an even deeper side of themselves with love and compassion. Listening to others within a group atmosphere allows one to witness a transformation. Active listening also helps people meet themselves as the author of their own life, when they recognize parts of themselves inside another's story.

The virtual group becomes a tribe with a safety net. It becomes the place where participants are able to see that it's okay to mess up and that it's okay to be themselves. It's like the easel to the artist, a place to play, express, have fun, learn, and grow, while among friends.

If you're a coach or a therapist, you'll agree that small shifts start to happen when clients begin to let go of self-doubt, step into their power, and share their stories. In order to help bring clients closer to the place where they are willing take the first step, they first need to feel curious enough to take the risk and have a willingness to explore and express their thoughts and emotions. A group can help your clients take that first step, becoming their safe sanctuary and a place where they can experience a soft landing.

Clients often say that they feel they have room to breathe and feel less pressure to gather their own words and express themselves through writing in a group setting. They also express that they often learn more through listening to the stories and lessons of others than they do during a one-to-one coaching session.

During the weekly private group meetings, participants are encouraged to share a sentence or two, without judgment, and quickly learn how to actively listen to one another, without jumping in to give advice or correct. They learn to help each other work towards discovering their personal answers through the writing of their own stories and experiences.

If you're a coach, using the right journal prompts can help take your journal keepers swiftly into their own light. Journal prompts offer participants a door to go through; and sharing what they find offers a further opportunity for the group to see parts of their own life inside the story, hopefully unlocking their own wisdom.

Group participants wear two hats, the writer of their own experiences and the active listener, holding space for others as they share their work. One can experience his or her own growth through the transformation of another, as a witness to a healing that happens when vulnerability is shown. Witnessing others also encourages us to reach further into ourselves, helping us to see that it's okay for us to show the world a little bit of who we are. As we learn how to hold space for others, we are able to see that we will also be met with love and support when we share.

If you're a coach or therapist, the group atmosphere also provides your clients with an extension of connection and support. They are helping one another to explore themselves in a safe place, where other members also act as role models for each other. Watching how other people process and progress is also inspiring and encouraging. To help with its success, the coach should emphasize not only the journaling content but encourage friendship and social support aspects as well. The longer a group meets, the more they journey together through life's ups and downs from illnesses and deaths and job changes to births, celebrations, successes, and the realizations of dreams. Through all this, they become more connected.

Journal groups also offer the experience of witnessing transformation, helping both coaches and participants see key connections transpire in real time, cementing these experiences in our hearts and minds and making us all feel more alive.

Setting Up a Virtual Journaling Group (for Coaches)

- Decide on your genre (writing, gratitude, feelings, success, daily journal, art, dream, spiritual, etc.)
- Set up a sharing platform with easy access and log in (search "private content sharing platforms")
- Pick your virtual platform (search virtual platforms)
- Set up your group rules and boundaries (see next)
- Write your themes
- Launch

The Year-Long Group

Consider setting out a year-long program with monthly themes and gear the prompts and homework to reflect the theme. For example,

September—Emotions

Week 1—Tension

Where do you feel tension in your body? If you didn't have to push it away, what feeling are you feeling right now? What is your feeling trying to say to you? Where is it in your body?

Week 2—Beauty

What do you feel defines beauty? Write about a beautiful moment in your life.

Week 3—Happiness

What are your thoughts about happiness? What was the happiest day of your life?

Week 4—Dreams

What are your wishes and dreams? Who are the people you want to spend more time with?

Weekly Homework Journal Prompt Ideas (Limit Answers to 500 Words)

- What is the biggest lie I tell myself?
- This is how I respect myself.
- This is how my own worry becomes my wisdom.
- This is how my body reacts when I feel afraid.
- This is what home feels like.
- What would be my ideal day?
- What area of my life do I want to change and why?

How to Choose the Right Virtual Journaling Group for Clients and Journal Keepers

1. Do your research and pick a great virtual journaling program / coach.
2. Check out the coach's coaching style. Ask for an interview or a practice session.
3. Ask your current life coach or creativity coach if he or she would consider running one.
4. Group sessions are a great way to have some professional coaching, usually at a fraction of the price.

---

5 Tips for Helping Professionals

1. Keep the class sizes small and intimate.
2. Assure your clients that their spelling and grammar don't matter.
3. Know what you want to accomplish in your group.
4. Set up rules for confidentiality but do not limit expression of self. (Journaling in itself has no rules, no boundaries, and no requirements.)
5. Establish guidelines for sharing.

Additional Tips:

- Encourage that the sharing of stories occurs in a way that will help others learn and grow as a result of the experience
- Set goals and set up weekly sessions with intention and care
- Set boundaries around giving advice and counseling others
- Prepare your journaling activities in advance with a creative structure that is both loose and that has a clear process
- Start sessions with a five- to ten-minute freewriting period to get the flow started
- Limit time on sharing to help keep the class running quickly
- Provide homework that helps people journal throughout the week and focus on something to share
- Sharing should always be optional

---

5 Tips for Clients and Journal Keepers

1. Everything you write is right.
2. You are the author of your own story.
3. Honor yourself by honoring your feelings about sharing or not sharing.
4. Listen to others with curiosity, without judgment or critique. People need to feel heard and learning to listen to another person's story is one of the greatest gifts that you can give to them. Being an active listener plays a huge part in people feeling support and connection.
5. Bearing witness to another means to be fully present, to not look away, and to listen and hold respectful space for them as they share their story.

 3 Journaling Prompts

Prompts can be simple. They don't need to be complicated.

1. The best day of my life was . . .
2. My first memory was . . .
3. My wildest dream is . . .

 About the Author

Mary Ann Burrows is an artist, a life/creativity coach, and the author of two children's books, *Oh, Monkey* and *Gator on My Back*. She is also a contributing author to the book *The Creativity Workbook for Coaches and Creatives*. Find out more about Mary Ann on her website: www.maryannburrows.com.

Positive Vision Days for Busy Leaders **43**

How a Longing Created a Vision

Fiona Parashar

First, I had the longing and then I had the vision. My deep longing, after 20 years in a big city, was to return to the green countryside of my childhood. What is the difference between a longing and a vision? For me, a vision has an ephemeral, positive, fizzy feeling and sits outside of my body. A longing is painful. A yearning in my heart and a dampening ache in my body and soul. I could feel my spirit being crushed by the lack of green beauty. My bare feet longed to walk on fresh grass and to ease into a slower pace of life where I could breathe in smells of fields that fed sheep and cows. I had a profound desire to watch my children blossom in nature's playground of gentle rolling hills, generous oak trees, and fresh, dappled-lit rivers. I had green blood and it needed to be fed. I recall writing a poem in my journal which started,

How could you know if you've never known/the feel of green in your blood?

My longing was finally satiated by our family move from London to Bath. A Georgian, golden, symmetrical, shimmering gem of a city that nestles into seven green hills. Gold and green, that's the daily view. My soul settled. Instead of a fish wildly flapping for its life on a pavement, I was a salmon returning home in deep, enriching, healing waters.

The vision came next. What if I created something? What? I saw a one day, one-on-one retreat in Bath to connect stressed executives to their vision. A modern-day version of "taking the waters" to revive their jaded spirits. The vision took shape. I grounded it, honed it, and tested it. It worked, better than I dreamt.

So we find ourselves a decade on . . .

Imagine you are like Mark, a senior stressed-out leader in a big city, time-starved and longing to carve out time to think about what is important and what's next. He feels he is at a crossroads, but he cannot find time to reflect. In fact, he hardly has time to finish his thoughts. The clamor of his open plan office, the surge of traffic noise on the streets and the demands from clients, staff, and expectations from his family all contribute to a lurking, recurring fear . . . he has lost himself and can't even recall where or when.

This is our typical client.

Mark arrives at a beautiful setting and his coach leads him through a stimulating mix of writing and creative exercises with some time out in nature walking. Mark feels so beautifully heard and so inspired by the natural beauty of the green hills rolling out ahead of him that within the first hour he weeps. The sense of release is intense. The healing begins, the magic starts to occur, and he returns to the office energized and clear.

> *I felt turbo charged. It is like a metaphoric colonic irrigation and a rigorous work out for the brain.*

So what happens in between? How can you create a Positive Vision Day for your clients or for yourself?

I created this mix of exercises that comprise the day while I was finishing my thesis in my Positive Psychology master's exploring the role of "meaningful goal setting in creating a flourishing life"—a psychological exploration of visioning.

What Is the Positive Vision Day?

A rich, coaching-intensive day with a mix of journaling pre-work, walking in nature, and semi-structured exercises to encourage writing, drawing, and visualizing throughout the day, building on the executive's strengths and values. All the exercises are underpinned by psychological theories.

The writing is an essential part of the process which is constantly grounding and capturing the client's insights as we travel through six hours of varied and creative exercises. There is significant and regular breakthrough thinking in these sessions and the role of freestyle writing and journaling prompts helps this thinking become weightier and more actionable.

Before the Day

Mark receives journaling exercises: stimulus questions (see the following journaling prompts) and an online strengths questionnaire (www.via.org).

The journaling questions "set the tone" for the Vision Day. Mark reports spending many days on these, treating them in an iterative fashion as his thinking deepens. *"I knew that I wanted to be totally honest when I saw the questions"* and *"as I started to write, I realized I had so much more I wanted to say so I kept going deeper and deeper."*

The day consists of seven different exercises outlined next, and there is a dynamic interchange between verbal and written exercises throughout the day.

The Download

Mark is invited to talk uninterrupted for 45 minutes in a stream-of-consciousness manner, bringing everything that needs to be considered for his future life and career into the room.

The coach does not interrupt and listens deeply.

Mark is startled that he can talk this long. This is a clearing, presencing exercise, and Mark finds himself with tears in his eyes as he starts to reconnect with himself. *"I'm so sorry I didn't mean to cry; I don't know why I am crying."*

The coach writes down his past, present, and future narrative, divided into hopes and fears in each of these time spans. The coach shares this as positive feedback.

"Mark, this is how I experience your presence, your story, your vision."

The coach highlights the *positive* presence and qualities they see in Mark; the *resourcefulness* and *achievements* from his narrative of his past; and articulates Mark's *positive vision* that is emerging.

This is a powerful moment for Mark, more tears and some laughter. Mark has not considered his story through this positive lens, so hardwired is his brain for the negativity bias. Mark feels affirmed and listened to, and now can see his positive vision starting to take shape. Together Mark and the coach have given positive words to a swirling mass of thoughts. The coach invites Mark to capture this through writing in his own words.

The next three exercises are set up to stimulate different parts of the brain and are conducted in swift succession, building energy and creativity.

Drawing, Power Questions, and a Visualization

Picture 1000

Mark is asked to draw three pictures with no words. The pictures sum up:

- How he is now
- How he was six months ago
- How he would like to be in his ideal future

Mark feels surprised that his rudimentary drawing holds so much emotion and detail as the coach elects a description about what he has drawn.

Power Questions

Mark and the coach co-create this next exercise. Mark is asked to distil his issues/challenges/hopes/dreams into three power questions.

Working within the Power Questions parameters the questions must be:

- An exciting and energizing question stated in the positive and in the future
- Ownable and sustainable by themselves
- Created in language that energizes and excites them

80th Birthday Visualization

Mark closes his eyes and listens to a guided visualization led by the coach, where he envisions celebrating his 80th birthday, in a place he feels happy and safe with loved ones. He is asked to imagine the whole celebration and reflect back across the decades of his adult life, accessing wisdom from his wiser future self. He finds himself profoundly moved by this and will recall it for many years. He writes down what he experienced.

Values Walk

Heading outside for a walk amidst nature, Mark is asked to share three peaks and three troughs from his life as he walks side by side the coach. This deepens the intimacy of their relationship and simultaneously energizes them both. Together, the coach and Mark explore the values that have been honored or violated during these peaks and troughs. He is struck by his resilience.

Strengths-Based Actions

Mark describes his signature strengths (identified from the VIA strengths test found online at www.via.org) and then uses these as stimulus to brainstorm possible actions for each of the Power Questions from the morning.

He makes a commitment to the most resonant of these actions and confirms them in writing. The coach and Mark crystallize the essence of the session.

Mark is invited to capture his insights after each of these exercises with written prompts to ensure that moments of clarity and mini peak experience moments are landed throughout the day in his own handwriting and choice of words.

The Ending

Mark enjoys an upbeat coaching call to celebrate his progress after six weeks. He is delighted with his energy, clarity, and renewed sense of purpose.

When I had this vision, I had no idea that it would be so impactful for clients and my business. And the hidden surprise is how fulfilling it feels for coaches too.

Clients report feeling renewed by the mix of writing, walking, and talking in nature. This intensive coaching experience delivers clarity and energy and connects them to a compelling positive vision.

Coaches report that it becomes their favorite experience with their clients; a deep immersive day of intimate and powerful dialogue in a beautiful setting close to home.

It has become my most fulfilling work. A longing that became a vision that I hope might someday become a legacy.

 5 Tips for Helping Professionals

1. Most leaders are familiar with an "away day" concept for a team but not for an individual and the Vision Day provides an opportunity

for clients to physically and metaphorically step away from the day-to-day. The Vision Day is a tried and tested formula that keeps a client's energy and focus sustained over an intensive six-hour period of coaching. Starting with the pre-work, the Vision Day combines discussion with a blend of powerful journaling prompts. This format helps clients to synthesize the information and the semi-structured approach allows for the pace to be kept up. Ensure you allow time for the writing and encourage the inward reflection with journaling guidance in order to capture insights.

2. Walking in nature with your client is essential even if it rains! We have incorporated this element even if we deliver the Vision Day in a virtual environment. (We do this by talking on a mobile phone through earphones as we both walk.) Allow time to capture the conversation through writing—as the intimacy and creativity will have deepened.

3. During the Download, clients report a feeling of being heard and held and a chance to bring their complete self into this space. Leaders often feel lonely or unsupported and this is a moment they realize they can unfurl. It is important to allow this emotionality to flow in the Download uninterrupted, as it clears space for the positive vision to emerge.

4. The 80th birthday visualization is often a highly emotional experience for clients and few have ever gone as far ahead on their inner timeline. It is also often the most impactful and memorable exercise of the day being recalled years later. Be ready to hold the emotion.

5. During strength-based action planning, the writing of the actions is linked to accountability. By having this written in freehand rather than the coach sending an email helps with ownership and increases the likelihood of the actions happening.

 5 Tips for Clients and Journal Keepers

1. Give yourself the gift. Take a day out or with a coach or friend or your journal in a beautiful setting. Work through the exercises to keep your energy up and access different ideas.

2. If you are doing the Vision Day just with yourself and your journal, you can write uninterrupted for 30 minutes for the Download or speak into your phone "voice memo" then listen back and notice the positive aspects of your story.

3. Draw three pictures very quickly of past, present, and future. Do not worry if you can't draw, just move the pen on the paper. Take time to journal and explore what the pictures mean and what feelings and emotions they contain within them. There is usually unconscious feelings and desires to explore here.

4. For the 80th Birthday, take some time to close your eyes and imagine your future self, celebrating your 80th birthday in full health and happiness, then capture what you saw, heard, and felt. Offer yourself a piece of wisdom from your 80-year-old self about the challenges and choices you are currently exploring.

5. Thinking about three peaks and three troughs in your life, journal about the values that you feel were honored during the peaks, and the values that have been trampled on in the troughs. You will notice a pattern which helps inform a good blueprint for life going forward.

3 Journaling Prompts

These journaling prompts serve as stimulus questions to help your client start visioning forward towards change:

1. In what ways would you like your life/work to be more fulfilling?
2. What ideas do you have about the next chapter of your career/life?
3. What would you do if you knew you couldn't fail?

About the Author

Fiona Parashar is founder and CEO of Leadership Coaching—a coaching company on a mission to inspire and develop positive leaders and improve their well-being. A passionate journaler all her life, Fiona is a positive psychologist and certified meditation teacher. Positive Vision Days received an award for excellence and innovation in coaching from the Association of Business Coaching and we certify coaches in the methodology, as well as deliver to hundreds of leaders.

Journaling in Leadership Workshops

44

Juhua Wu

Journaling is generally considered a private, personal activity that rarely gets talked about in leadership development. Yet as soft skills such as active listening, effective communications, and empathy become essential leadership skills, the ability to observe, notice, and reflect has become more important than ever. I have been journaling for decades, but it was when I became a coach that I started to use journaling for my own leadership development. More recently I began to use journaling in leadership development workshops, both as a participant and faculty, and I have found it to be immensely valuable as an experiential learning tool.

Coaches know that at the center of every coaching engagement lies the critical inquiry of our clients on the questions of *Who am I? What do I want?* The concept of using self as an instrument for growth and change is foundational in leadership coaching. This is true for both the coach and the client.

As the coach, you trust that everything you receive from the client—what she says and expresses, the words, the metaphors, the tones, the sighs, the pauses, the body shifts, and the energy changes—is significant reflection of how she thinks and feels. You mirror these back to the client so she can touch a deeper level of awareness about herself—her identity (who am I) and vulnerability (how does this affect how I perceive who I am). Often, shifts in thinking happen in these moments of clarity, and the choice forward becomes easy. The client gets unstuck, becoming more conscious of the assumptions, judgments, or interpretations she brings to the situation.

Journaling in leadership workshops can provide the kind of experience that allows for honest and intimate inquiry and reflection on self. As a leader, your ability to observe and discern what's going on in a situation or in a room, and the impact for you and others, is deeply rooted in how aware you are of yourself and your environment. Journaling provides opportunities for tracing your thoughts and feelings individually, and for sharing insights with the group after these reflections. It is a wonderful training tool to enhance a leader's self-knowledge, and how this in turn impacts and is impacted by the self-awareness of others.

A private self-reflection through journaling can be accomplished in public within a group so long as you create an opportunity for it right from the beginning. My experience of journaling in leadership workshops has largely been with programs that meet more than once, which is typical of leadership development workshops—participants attend modules over several months to develop various aspects of their leadership. Each participant and faculty member gets a journal book from Day 1 and uses it throughout the program. At the end of the program and thereafter, the journal serves as a journey of growth that these leaders can review as they continue to reflect and grow. For leadership workshops that occur in one sitting (e.g., over a weekend), journaling can still be introduced as a valuable way to explore the self as leader and encourage leaders to continue journaling after the workshop as a reflective practice.

In either type of workshop, participating leaders are encouraged to cultivate their noticing—of not only what's observable outside of them but also what arises within themselves. The latter is particularly novel for many people, and even more so for busy leaders who are often on the go, jumping from one meeting or encounter to another to meet relentless external demands. The intentional act of noticing what's inside oneself, and tracing the thoughts, reactions, and emotions through the written words can bring forth valuable insights. The act of journaling goes beyond mindfulness and records the awareness as well as response and impact, which can be reviewed and reflected upon again later.

During the leadership workshops that I have been involved in, participants are encouraged to write down their reflections in their journals. Sometimes, reflection times are built into the agenda; other times, they are impromptu based on what is occurring in the room. Most of the time, the journaling time is brief—a few minutes to ten to 15 minutes. Sometimes prompts are given; other times, other creative ways of reflection are asked. For example, participants may be asked to express their takeaways in a haiku or poem.

Typical training workshops often incorporate breakout discussion groups to have active dialogues. Participants are expected to jump right into a conversation to express their thoughts, reactions, or even strategies to tackle a problem. Yet people process information differently. Many of us cannot arrive at deep reflections from dialogues without first processing and reflecting on the information received. Journaling helps to equalize the different styles of contemplation and expression. We sometimes ask the group to journal on their own for a few minutes before switching to group dialogue. In my experience, this deepens group engagement, as well as stimulation of different parts of the brain for the individual workshop participants.

Some of the journal prompts we use are seemingly ordinary questions. However, like coaching inquiries, the key is not whether the question is simple or complicated, but whether it leads the client to touch the crux of what is happening in the moment—which may reveal a lifetime of thinking and behavioral patterns. For example,

- *What's happening with me now?*
- *What does all this mean for me?*
- *How am I showing up?*
- *What I need is. . .*
- *If I explore rather than endure. . .*

In today's volatile and changing environment, our clients in leadership positions face tremendous pressure to make decisions in often uncertain times and circumstances. Leaders and managers must "show up" for others when they themselves are struggling amid uncertainties and changes. They must balance what they know, what they want, and the expectations of others, including families, superiors, and the people they lead. It is easy to overthink, overanalyze, and become overwhelmed. Then they focus on completing the tasks on hand, and might find themselves just surviving and trying to cope through hurried, busy schedules.

As a leader myself, when I occasionally struggle with these issues, I rely heavily on journaling and coaching to help me stay aligned with what truly matters in how I show up and respond in various situations. When you don't have a well-cultivated relationship with yourself to allow for a deep exploration and discovery of your inner world, you are operating from an incomplete self. The most effective leaders must function through the whole self, not only with intellectual intelligence and grit, but also with emotional intelligence, integrity, and compassion. A few minutes of journaling to contemplate the impact of the learning in an inward-looking way can be meaningful investment that pays dividends in growth, leadership development, and change. The shift may not happen right at the workshop, but the act of reflective writing plants a seed for transformation both in the moment and well into the future.

5 Tips for Helping Professionals

1. **Journaling is a meaning making process.** Help leaders make sense of themselves, their actions and reactions, and the impacts they experience from others or have on others, by incorporating journaling in your leadership training workshops.

2. **Don't overcommit to a planned agenda.** You can encourage participants to continue journaling more during lunch or session breaks. Giving one or two reflection questions or prompts as homework between workshop days is a wonderful way to encourage reviews and reflections of the day's learning; and sharing of insights the next day can help to inform any necessary shift in focus for the following day's content.

3. **Try to come up with prompts that can touch the heart** so that the reflection through journaling is not limited to analysis, goal setting, or actions, but reaches the motivating energy and what is truly meaningful at the heart of the matter.

4. **Use a well-bound journal book** (not an 8x11 print-out program workbook) with your workshop so that participating leaders will want to continue journaling in the same book after the workshop.

5. **Have the faculty members or co-facilitators keep journals** as participants do. This can normalize the act of journaling for those who are not accustomed to it, or to using it in leadership training. You might also want to cultivate a culture of reflection through journaling throughout the program or training.

5 Tips for Clients and Journal Keepers

1. **Journaling can take various forms.** There is no one way to journal, except to write down whatever comes to mind. Especially during workshops when the journaling time can be limited, you may write down just a few words that come up, or you may write a flowy description with lots of details. And yes, you can even compose a poem or doodle, as long as you are genuinely exploring, learning, and making meaning of what's going on.

2. **The key to journaling is to keep the pen moving.** You want to capture as many of your thoughts and feelings as you can *in the*

moment, before your rationalizing mind has a chance to catch up, and when your survival instincts haven't yet bottled up your raw emotions and insights.

3. **Try to keep a habit of intentional reflection through journaling,** not just during a leadership workshop, but on a regular basis. Use prompts like these to help you be the leader you would like to be: *who am I as a leader? What I need is. . . . If I cannot fail, I will. . . . Self-care means for me. . . .*

4. **Journaling doesn't need to take a lot of time.** Even (or especially) when you think you don't have time to journal regularly, as little as 15 minutes each day can help you feel centered and energized in unexpected ways.

5. Journaling is a great way to reflect on your growth in the specific leadership areas you choose to focus on, progress toward your goals, and align yourself with how you want to show up on a daily basis. **Writing truthfully and from the heart** will get you back on track if you find yourself feeling undecided, lost, or behind.

3 Journaling Prompts

1. I believe I have more than enough of. . .
2. If I had no fear, I would. . .
3. What my heart really wants is. . .

About the Author

Juhua Wu is a leadership coach credentialed through the ICF, and Director at the Center for Community Practice, University of Rochester Medical Center. She works with leaders and change agents to facilitate transformation of systems and individuals through her work at the University and her own coaching practice. With 20 years of working in various leadership roles strategizing, managing, and advising within diverse organizations and industries, Juhua now helps leaders uncover their purpose, clarify goals, master their selves, strengthen skills, prioritize actions, and maximize impact. Her work at the Center focuses on strengthening public health workforce and system capacity for healthy community and individual well-being.

Techniques and Applications

PART VIII

Journaling as a Transformational Coaching Tool

45

5 Powerful Journaling Exercises for Coaches and Clients

Emma-Louise Elsey

More than ever, people are turning to coaches to get help for their careers, businesses, and lives. But there's always more to discuss in a coaching session than there's time available in the session, and there's always more going on in someone's life than what they share with us. So, I use journaling with my clients as a powerful complement to coaching.

In this electronic age where we're all busier than ever, journaling provides a sacred space to leave our devices behind, slow down, and connect to ourselves. It's also a great way to create additional time between coaching sessions for clients to reflect, increasing their self-awareness. Most crucially, journaling is an act of befriending ourselves, of getting to know ourselves *deeply*—and this is what makes journaling transformational.

Exercise 1. Have a Conversation With Your Inner Critic

The goal of the inner critic is to keep us safe. This usually means staying with what we know—and not taking risks. Yet, our clients specifically come to coaching to make changes in their lives. So, when our clients connect with their goals and dreams, that's when we see their inner critics come out in full force.

This journaling exercise is a powerful way to learn to identify when our critic is on the rampage and what it's upset about. In this simple conversation technique, we offer kindness, deep listening, and openness.

The client needs to find a strong, nurturing adult within for this conversation. To begin, clients must feel grounded, calm, and connected to themselves. This enables them to listen compassionately to the critic, but *not* allow themselves to be bullied or railroaded.

Step 1. Start by helping your client decide on a starting question to ask their critic. This could be something like, "Hi, inner critic, what is it that you want me to know?" If you've been working towards a specific goal with your client, you might start with, "Hi inner critic, what do you think of me doing _____?" or "What concerns do you have for me around _____?"

Step 2. The client writes out the ensuing conversation, swapping back and forth between their critic and nurturing adult self, giving the critic or judge full voice for all its concerns, whatever they may be. The goal of the nurturing adult self is simply to *listen* and *acknowledge/validate* their critic's concerns. The client should continue the conversation until the critic has run out of steam.

Step 3. To end the conversation, the nurturing adult should calmly summarize the critic's concerns, and check that the critic feels heard.

Over time, with this process, the client will befriend and validate their critic, ultimately calming and reassuring it, so that the client can take the bold steps needed to create the life they want.

Envision the Future

Often clients come to coaching with "should" goals: things they think they should be doing but that aren't who they truly are. For example, some clients desperately seek academic, career, or financial success at the expense of more personal, creative, or fulfilling goals and ideas. And sometimes clients struggle to actualize their goals because what they want is fuzzy and not clearly expressed.

It's no wonder that achieving these goals is a hard slog. When this happens, it's helpful to go "big picture" by asking clients to start with the end in mind: what is the future they want to create?

The following journaling exercises are a great way to get people past doubts, "shoulds," and obstacles to clearly envision the life they desire—and connect to deeper level outcomes like community and personal qualities rather than status symbols and milestones.

Exercise 2. The Rocking Chair

Ask your client to imagine they're blissfully happy and healthy and 90 years old. They're sitting in their rocking chair, looking back over their *ideal* life. What have they achieved and are proud of? Who is with them or around them? What do they see, feel, and hear? And lastly, as they look back over their long life, what added the most meaning to their life?

Simply ask them to write about this experience, leaving nothing out.

Exercise 3. The Retirement Party

Ask your client to imagine they're at a party where someone has written a speech celebrating them. What do people value about them? Who is at the party? What have they achieved in their family, career, business, community, or in the world? What would they be disappointed not to hear about themselves? What do they value most in their life? What are their priorities and goals as they look ahead?

Now ask your client to write out that speech, remembering to wrap up with where they're headed next in life.

Exercise 4. Magazine Feature

This is a good exercise for a business owner, senior executive, or someone who wants to make a difference. First ask your client to imagine they've achieved a great milestone in their life or career. This could be an award received, a book written, something they've established or created, a fundraising or financial goal reached, a travel accomplishment, a charitable activity, or something else.

Now ask your client to write a feature article as if for a magazine about the recent milestone and success they've achieved and, equally importantly, who they are as a person.

Exercise 5. Get to Sleep "Monkey Mind" Journaling Exercise

There seems to be an insomnia epidemic, often due to what Buddhists call "monkey mind," where our brain roams out of control swinging from one thought to the next. This powerful journaling exercise will help you get the sleep you deserve, so you have the energy you need to succeed!

Step 1. On a fresh page in your journal, write down literally everything that's on your mind. Whatever pops up, write it down. This could be a great idea, what to have for breakfast, a feeling, memory, grievance, or worry, that you need a haircut, that you need to see the dentist, or something else. Keep writing until you can't think of anything else. And no judgment please! Anything goes here.

Step 2. Ask, "If there was something or some things I missed, what would they be?" Now write these down. When you're done, review the items on your "monkey mind" list.

Step 3. Let go of your "cheeky monkeys," those items you have no control over. Do this by putting a big X through each item.

Step 4. Identify your "gorillas." These are items that are really bothering you, that your mind keeps going back to, however big, small, silly, boring, or illogical they are. Circle these items.

Step 5. Now, for each "gorilla" item you've circled, pick an action you'll take ideally as soon as tomorrow, like phone the dentist or the hairdresser, buy milk, research holiday ideas or personal trainers, call mom, set up a meeting with school, etc. This will calm your brain. The action doesn't have to be big—it can be the smallest possible step—but get specific and do it as soon as you can. (Tip: letting go is also a valid "action.")

Step 7. Ask yourself, "How busy is my mind now on a scale of 1 to 10?" If your mind busyness score is 2 or less out of 10, that's wonderful. Then acknowledge and thank your brain for all these great thoughts and ideas. However, if your mind busyness score is 3 or above, ask yourself, "What haven't I mentioned yet that needs to be seen, felt, or heard?" Then keep writing until you're done, following the process for any new items.

Once your score is 2 or less out of 10, it's time for sleep!

---

5 Tips for Helping Professionals

1. If you're not already journaling, get journaling yourself! Buy some (more) books on journaling, try different journaling approaches and exercises, and learn what works—and when. Then you'll be in a much better place to help your clients.

2. Let the client lead. We may have a coach's agenda to help the client grow in a "big picture" way, but it isn't our role to force the situation. Instead, let the client's needs and journey inspire the journaling exercises you agree on together.

3. Ask for permission. Remember that the client always has the right to refuse a journaling exercise or change the focus/wording of an inquiry.

4. Play! Ask clients to make a list, describe something in detail, complete a sentence stem, freewrite, etc. They can keep a gratitude or needs journal or have conversations with their critic, best friend, or future self. And you can also ask people to draw, paint, or write a haiku. The possibilities are endless, so have fun.

5. There is something special about getting off our devices and using pen and paper to reconnect with ourselves. Encourage clients to get a beautiful notebook and pen they like to write with, keeping the two together. But if a client is determined or excited about writing online, remember what matters most is that they start journaling!

 ## 5 Tips for Clients and Journal Keepers

1. Always take a few moments to slow down and connect with *you* before you start journaling. This can be as simple as taking three to five deep breaths.

2. Choose your environment. Do you feel relaxed? Are you free from interruption? Is this somewhere you can connect with yourself?

3. Be honest and truthful—always. Think of your journal as your ultimate best friend and allow whatever wants to come out to *come out*. Carl Jung said, "The gold is in the dark." So too will be your greatest personal revelations.

4. No judgment or criticism, *unless* you specifically invite it in, as in the critic conversation exercise. Unless it's a managed conversation, your critic does not have a place at the journaling table.

5. Privacy is vital. If you're worried someone will find or read your journal you may end up censoring yourself or avoiding writing altogether. Consider how and where you'll keep your journal safe and who you might need to talk to, to express your wishes for privacy.

3 Journaling Prompts

1. What matters most to me? Write down what matters most 1) right now; 2) this week; 3) this month; 4) this year; and 5) in my whole life.
2. Think about a challenge you're having. Now ask, "What could be getting in the way?" and list at least ten things.
3. Describe your ideal day. Imagine waking up. Now write out how you would feel, what you would do (or not do!), who's around you—and every little thing that would make up your ideal day.

About the Author

Emma-Louise Elsey began her coaching journey in 2003. Originally a project and relationship manager for Fortune 500 companies, she combines her passion for coaching, creativity and love of systems to create coaching resources for coach and client alike. A professional life coach and NLP practitioner, she's the founder of the Coaching Tools Company and recently Fierce Kindness. com. She began journaling in 2006 to manage anxiety and a vicious inner critic, and although it was an awkward start she continues to journal today.

Spontaneous Writing for Reluctant Clients

46

Liz Crocker

I am a perfect example of someone who has always been reluctant to write in a journal. Of course, as a teenager, I had the requisite "locked diary." Its tiny key was so flimsy that anyone with a safety pin could have read my so-called "deepest, darkest secrets." But, in truth, my entries were mostly adolescent drivel that were neither thoughtful nor revealing.

Interestingly, I never wrote in my diary about the daily details or the cumulative impact of my mother's alcoholism or her sudden death when I was 15. I didn't put words on paper about any of this for 30 years and, even then, I did not write in a journal.

Even though I've been writing for my whole life, I've never kept a journal. I've shared matters of the mind and the heart through letters of friendship, of thanks, or of memories (especially on the occasion of someone's death). For example, I wrote longhand letters to every American I knew in 1963 to express my profound sadness about the assassination of President Kennedy and I wrote to every American friend again, in 2016, this time via email, to share my thoughts and feelings after the United States election.

I've also written weekly newspaper articles, political speeches and policy papers, travel diaries, business plans and marketing materials, and even books. And I've saved some of these non-journal writings as touchstones of particular chapters of my life: a resignation letter from a Board when I felt my principles were being challenged, my nomination speech when I ran for political office, my travel diary when I journeyed through Africa 50 years ago, and some old letters and cards to my husband. During COVID-19 days of self-isolation, I revisited some of these materials. As someone's journal writings might do, reading these words from other times often sparked related and poignant memories.

Friends have extolled the virtues of keeping traditional journals, dream journals, and gratitude journals. Out of respect for their urgings, I've made a couple of halting attempts but have always ended up concluding "That's not for me."

Why have I been so reluctant to keep a journal?

1. I'm not very disciplined when it comes to things I am "supposed" to do every day. Keeping a journal is in good company along with exercises that might help my joints and other regular activities that might benefit me that I don't seem to have the discipline for.
2. I own an array of beautiful (albeit empty) journals just waiting for me but I don't want to despoil them in the event that I don't keep up with daily or even weekly entries.
3. Even when I've been truly troubled or full of angst about something, I haven't wanted to commit my internal truths to a journal because I'm afraid that 1) writing them down will make them more real and "more real" feels uncomfortable; and 2) if I were hit by a bus, someone else might find and read what I've written and be either hurt, bewildered, or shocked and possibly think less of me.

But even though I've not had the practice of keeping a journal, I do understand and appreciate the transformational power of writing. In the early 1980s, I was invited to join three women who had a weekly writing group. We called ourselves the "Word Exchange" because we often wrote single words on little pieces of paper and then pulled them out of a bag as "prompt" words to stimulate writing for no more than ten minutes. When the ten minutes were up, we took turns reading what we had written and marveled at the phrases, thoughts, images, and emotions that had emerged from just a single word.

Sometimes we howled with laughter at some brilliant magical nonsense and sometimes we sat with tears streaming down our faces, surprised that a single word had unearthed buried and poignant memories. We thought that we had invented this provocative technique of writing quickly for ten minutes, without forethought or a predetermined plan or an internal editor. We called it "spontaneous writing" and came to learn this technique is also known as "expressive writing" or "therapeutic writing."

Our mantra was "just write." For example, one day I pulled out the word "carry" and ten minutes later I had written this:

> *I have carried children before they were born and carried them again*
> *as babies, crooning them to sleep;*
> *as toddlers, whispering away the pain of scraped knees;*

as teenagers, giggling hysterically, trying to piggyback them across the room.
I have carried small puppies new to our family,
and then carried them again to their graves.
I have carried cut-up food to my mother,
hoping it could nourish her intoxicated soul.
I have carried disappointment and resentments for years
unaware of the magnitude of the burden.

Meeting weekly with this small group not only introduced me to the richness of spontaneous writing but also taught me about the importance of needing to feel safe when digging into and writing about old memories. The "Word Exchange" served as my preparatory launch pad to a different group of women who also used spontaneous writing to develop a book.

Three of us, all friends, learned that each of us had grown up with at least one alcoholic parent and we decided to write a book to share our experiences and what we had learned over the years. We developed a list of 66 "loaded" words which all instantly sparked memories for us and then chose 14 of those words as our prompts for spontaneous writing. This creative process allowed us to "lose our minds and come to our senses." Spontaneous writing enabled us to discover how we *felt* about our pasts, not just what we *thought* about our childhoods.

As we wrote, we came to better understand how events from decades earlier had affected us. We also explored the research about the transformational power and benefits of writing about trauma and learned that such writing has been shown to enhance both psychological and bio-physical health. Some of the benefits of spontaneous writing include improving immune system functioning, reducing blood pressure, enhancing lung and liver function, improving memory, promoting healing of wounds, and reducing stress hormones.

And so, after many decades of not keeping a journal and still not having a practice of daily writing, at least I now appreciate both my reluctance to do so *and* my deep appreciation of the transformational power of writing. I believe it is possible to hold two seemingly opposite perspectives at one time and so I legitimately present the provocative question:

If someone does not want to keep a journal, how can one embrace the potential of writing?

In the interests of your overall health, honor your story. Write what you see, write what you feel, write what troubles you, write what gives you joy.

The technique of spontaneous writing only takes ten minutes, it's a technique that is effective, and it is perfectly designed for reluctant journal keepers.

5 Tips for Helping Professionals

1. Become familiar with the literature about the healing benefits of writing about trauma. Sharing this research about improving one's health may inspire clients to give spontaneous writing a try.
2. Understand and honor resistance to journaling. Suggest spontaneous writing as an alternative way to explore people, places, words, and memories.
3. Read! Collect books about people's stories and struggles. Have memoirs and poems available to recommend and share. A reluctant writer may be inspired by someone else's story or poem and want to try telling his or her own.
4. Do what you ask clients to do. If you ask a woman to list five things or people that she is grateful for, do that yourself. Both of your lists become fodder for further exploration. Pick a word (anything from "giraffe" to "fear") and, with your client, do an exercise in spontaneous writing.
5. A favorite expression of mine is "We nourish from overflow, not from emptiness." Acknowledge that your work can drain you. It is "hard work because it is heart work." Know what nourishes you. Fill yourself up. Guard against getting to empty because then you won't be able to nourish others.

5 Tips for Reluctant Clients and Journal Keepers

1. Get a journal with pre-printed quotes or a children's coloring book with prompts on each page. Imagine you are having a conversation with the words/prompts. What do they suggest or evoke? What's your response or reaction, even if it's only a single word? Write or draw to capture how you feel.
2. What's getting in your way of writing? Are there metaphorical weeds in your garden? Name them and write them down as a symbolic

act of pulling them out to make room for new seeds or transplants. What's your vision for your land?

3. Rilke said that we should not always seek to know answers but, rather, "live into the questions." What questions are confounding you? Can you embrace them or at least place them atop a gentle hill so you can roll with them and let gravity show the way?

4. If you have an inner critic, what would you like to say to that critic? Can you soften your inner voice using compassion? Can you debate with it? Consider inviting that inner judge to only show up for a specific preset amount of time, say 30 minutes a day.

5. Write down four key questions: what do you want? What are you doing to get that? How's that working? What are you willing to change? Take any problem or wish and write down the answers to these questions. What becomes clear?

3 Journaling Prompts

1. Identify a worry, a problem, or a joy and write a haiku poem which is a Japanese form with three lines of five syllables, then seven syllables, and then five syllables again. Here's an example: the bank statement came/the image of debt is clear/I don't know what's next.

2. Make a list of the places you've lived. Pick one and describe it in as much detail as possible. For example, where is it? What's the street name? How many rooms does it have? What age were you when you lived there? Recall smells, friends, events, and emotions. The more you write, the more you will remember.

3. Draw a large heart shape and fill it with words to indicate what you hold in your heart.

About the Author

Liz Crocker is the co-author of *Privileged Presence: Personal Stories of Connections in Health Care* and *Transforming Memories: Sharing Spontaneous*

Writing Using Loaded Words. In addition to being a writer and an editor, Liz has been a teacher, entrepreneur, health consultant, and policy adviser. She founded and still proudly owns Canada's oldest Children's Bookstore (Woozles) and openly admits to being obsessively passionate about reading and sharing books.

Journaling With Poetry   **47**

Embracing Change Through Poetic Process

Cynthia Holloway Kelvin

Let's begin with an overview of this three-part process. Part One explores a poem through a multi-sensory experience. Part Two invites the client to discuss aspects of change and engage in journaling, in order to deepen reflection. In Part Three, facilitators witness clients as they share their reflections, offering them validation, feedback, and support.

To begin with, professionals demonstrate how poetry is used globally, as an agent for change. They support clients in recognizing their reactions to change, while strengthening their ability to accept change and create new opportunities for growth. This three-part process provides a way for professionals to deepen reflection, while helping their clients develop a mindful, solution-focused perspective.

We use the following poem to illustrate how a professional might work with their client.

Home

Terhi K. Cherry

> I am fearful in my place of quiet,
> like in the arms of a stranger.
> I have four walls, three windows,

I can see the sky from many directions.
This country said *come in, rest your head*,
then closed the borders around me.
Today, sunlight enters the room.
I can examine my scars from different angles.
Run my hand across the wallpaper.
Look for my fears in dusty corners,
the homes I've left, the shores, the cities.
Seclusion moves in.
I push the window open, breathe.

*Poem included with permission of the author. For educational and therapeutic purposes only.

Part One: The Experience

The facilitator invites the client to explore the poem. The facilitator creates a relaxed environment, adopting a playful and casual style, while creating an interactive atmosphere.

The facilitator and client each receive a copy of the poem. The facilitator prompts the client to read the poem aloud or silently (whichever feels comfortable). Next, the client is invited to listen, as the facilitator reads the poem aloud. The client is then asked if they would be willing to read the poem together—each reading certain lines or alternating stanzas. The facilitator may guide the client toward verbalizing specific parts of the poem, for example, *the homes I've left, the shores, the cities.*

The facilitator might invite the client to recall memories of previous "homes"—transporting them back to places of residence, but also of a vacation home or places they may have visited. The facilitator encourages them to recall "beyond the mind's eye," imagining sounds invoked by the seashore or the pungent aroma of the city. It's important to associate the poem's imagery with the client's memories. As the reading begins to conclude, the facilitator initiates a pause . . . and then leads the client to connect with their breath. The client is then invited to share reactions or responses.

Next, the facilitator encourages the client to move beyond the literal poem, noticing the sounds and movements that the words invoke. If the client focuses on a rhythm, ask them to tap or hum it, as the facilitator joins in. Perhaps the poem inspires a piece of music. Ask the client to describe it. If you sense that the client is receptive, invite the client to retrieve the musical selection on a device and listen to it together.

The client may become aware of movement, inspired by the poem's sounds, content, or structure. Ask your client to describe this movement—listening carefully to what the client says and asking clarifying questions. Imitate this movement from your chair, or stand, if the client appears willing to stand. If the client stands but is slow to engage, invite the client to share their movement with you, by having them direct you in making their movement. Once you are moving, you may invite them to mirror you, if they are comfortable.

In "Home," we might consider movement in the whole poem or in a specific physical section:

Look for my fears in dusty corners
then closed the borders around me.

Both the client and the facilitator might assume a constricted physicality and then move into a searching stance—by looking for fear in dusty corners—and then completing the movement by transitioning into a wide-open stance for the line, *I push the window open, breathe.* The series of movements may be repeated a few times with the client. As this naturally concludes, invite the client to sit and connect to their breath, drawing awareness to their body sensations—the feel of the clothes on their skin, their feet on the ground, etc.

In the next sensory experience, help the client imagine tactile sensations present in the poem, such as *Run my hand across the wallpaper . . .* or, *like in the arms of a stranger.* Invite clients to reflect on how they relate to each sensation and identify what memories are associated with those sensations. If any tension arises, invite clients to explore their reactions. When this naturally concludes, bring their awareness back to the room. Encourage the client to reconnect with their breath.

Part Two: The Invitation

Prepare the client for journaling by inviting them to reread the poem aloud. As they finish, ask them to focus solely on the part or parts in the poem where they feel that change occurs, however slight. From "Home," consider the line, *I can examine my scars from different angles.* Invite the client to share a moment that changed for them—between experiencing pain to healing—and then examine their real or metaphorical scars.

If the client verbalizes that there is no significant change in the poem, or remarks that there is an undesired change that has occurred, ask them to consider the change they wanted or hoped to see, and what would be necessary, in order to change direction.

Encourage them to explore via journaling *both* the poem and the *experience of processing* the poem. Was anything uncomfortable, and if so, why were they able to do it, anyway? This discussion is intended to validate the client's journaling, while encouraging them to let all of this go, as they choose a prompt to focus on, for instance a prompt like the following:

1. Journal about any change that is present—was it necessary or desired? What is your reaction to the change?
2. Explore via journaling any undesired change or the absence of change. What would you have preferred to happen, instead?

Part Three: Reflection

Invite the client to share all or part of what they have written. Remain present and stay alert for expressions of avoidance, fear, acceptance, willingness, creativity, and whatever else stands out as impressions of how the client deals with change.

Invite clients to reflect on how feelings can change in many directions. Remind them that, as we recognize change and work through struggle, we embrace, accept, and evolve. We become better able to meet life's challenges with courage and resilience.

Closing the Session

As the session concludes, acknowledge and celebrate the client's willingness to engage with this process. Remind clients that the purpose of this exercise is to increase their capacity to successfully deal with life's transitions, losses, and opportunities. Reinforce the idea that the purpose of this exercise is *to increase their capacity to successfully deal with change, no matter the context*. A poem, like life, may have several changes—some subtle, some severe, some expected, and some unexpected.

There may also be stagnation and refusal to change; encourage clients to entertain it all. Helping professionals can reinforce the idea that, with practice, we can increase our confidence in ourselves to meet life's challenges with resilience and courage.

5 Tips for Helping Professionals

1. Remind the client that the focus should be on their reflection of the poem in relation to their own life. The poem is a vehicle to explore the client's own thoughts, feelings, and behaviors associated with their relationship to change.
2. Mirror the level of client's engagement by displaying flexibility and openness. Match the client's level of expression while also remaining open to when and where you can encourage the client to stretch and open more to the experience and to their own self-expression.
3. Invite the client to journal freely without having to identify, describe, or analyze exact parts. Applaud the client when they identify a word or a phrase (or several) when a moment of change is observed. Guide the client in noticing opportunities for change within the poem that they otherwise may have missed.
4. Encourage the client to modify this practice, in order to readily engage in this process. Clients should be encouraged to shorten this process into a daily or weekly practice. They might also lengthen the process by engaging in deeper contemplation. They may modify the length of time in which they work with a particular poem, exploring one change at a time or focusing on the poem as a whole.
5. Encourage the client to view every poem as an opportunity for learning. If clients struggle with a particular poem, encourage them to journal about their struggle—allowing their frustration or indifference to serve as teachers.

5 Tips for Clients and Journal Keepers

1. Let go of any expectations around your ability to perfectly interpret the meaning of any given poem. Notice any feelings of perfectionism and explore that in relationship to change.
2. Remember that the value of this exercise is *in the process of choosing out of context*. Each poem will be different, and many poems may frustrate you as you search in vain for change through directness or even rich subtlety. Let all that go. Rather, be open and mindful in approaching the material and whatever emerges.

3. Experiment with different forms of poetry, lengths, etc. Search for poems through bookstores, online searches, etc. Discover poems that you relate to and poems that you are irritated with and indifferent to. Notice if your reactions change, as you change.
4. Experiment with different forms of journaling. Write a response poem or a stream of consciousness. Write a song. Describe a particular image in detail. Let the words come forward without judgment, only noticing. Where do you avoid, embrace, or justify a change?
5. Experiment with creating a ritual around this process. Identify ways to use poetry as an affirmation in managing anxiety or bringing about the changes in life that you desire.

 3 Journaling Prompts

1. What memories, thoughts, and feelings does the word "home" conjure up in you?
2. Pick another word of your own choosing and see what memories, thoughts, and feelings are evoked.
3. Choose a poem to journal about using the previous three-step process as a guide.

 About the Author

Cynthia Holloway Kelvin is a clinical psychologist, creative therapist, and performance consultant working with individuals using creative therapies for anxiety management, healing, and personal growth. In addition, Cynthia facilitates groups and workshops utilizing writing and performance for personal growth and evolution. You can find Cynthia though her creative writing and performance workshops at evolvingstage.com.

Refreshing Experience With the Most Powerful of Writing Craft Tools

48

Sheila Bender

When asked to keep a journal, many prospective journal keepers don't know what to write. They believe that to write, they must have something important to say and, moreover, must know what that is before setting their words on the page. Actually, it is the opposite. Rendering images that come through our senses—through sight, hearing (and that includes dialogue), smell, taste, and touch—allows journal keepers to find what it is they have to say.

The German poet Rainer Maria Rilke wrote in *Letters to a Young Poet*: "Describe the things in your environment, the images from your dreams, and the objects of your memory. If your daily life seems poor, do not blame it. . ., there is no poverty and no poor indifferent place." By using observations of the sort Rilke suggests, the writer finds much where others have not found much at all.

It is a powerful exercise to describe a place one might have judged worthless but for writing about it—a patch of weeds at the side of the road, an unfinished bridge that goes nowhere, a board game with missing pieces, a stocking with a hole in it, a broken table. Describe a junk drawer or a child's broken toy or a necklace not worn in years and a world opens up. What Rilke told his correspondent to do was to show in writing, rather than judge, summarize, or generalize.

Another author, John Gardner, asks writers in his book *The Art of Fiction* to describe a lake from the point of view of a man who has just fallen in love and then to describe the same lake from the point of view of a man who has just committed a murder. For journal keepers, writing from close, sensory observations of one's environment most often conveys a reliable projection of honest feelings and desires.

Rilke's advice includes permission to come to writing in a state of not-knowing and then experience the deep power language bestows when observation rather than knowing is employed. The remembered smell of burnt toast, the sound of a train whistle as one lies in bed about to fall asleep, words others taught us, the smell of the janitor's floor cleaning supplies where we went to school, the taste of berries plucked from a vine on a sunny day, the unfamiliar feel of silk sheets at a friend's house, how a dandelion looks close up, all have the potential to open the world to us.

Images bring up much for us to *experience* again as we write. The journal keeper might ask, "What does the sound of a train's whistle I hear now bring to mind—worn interiors, tired strangers, the outside seeming to retreat as if running away, raindrops blurring windows, a conductor punching holes, one-self as a child digging in the mud as a far-off train whistled into an unknown landscape?"

Experiencing events as a consequence of using our senses and our own words allows our words to illustrate feelings we hadn't realized: awe at how we handled a situation, for example. When we trust our senses, descriptions offer evocation and with it the power of knowing. Coming at truth slant means not having to shy away from or override what the words have allowed us to experience—the sadness of loss, fear of the unexpected, the pleasure of joyful times. It means finding a new perspective delivered by the observations, details that arrived because our unconscious chose them.

Windows Are Good for Inspiration

- Look out a window and list what you see that you have seen before (five items minimum).
- Look out the same window and list what you have not seen before (five items minimum).
- Do this exercise many times over a week.
- Then look at the accumulated lists and ask yourself what each item causes you to remember, whether from that day or from long ago or from a time in between.
- Write paragraphs for some that interest you.
- Start each paragraph with a timestamp: today, five o'clock; 1957 summer; around my birthday, 1960; right now.

What Has Someone Said?

- Write down a line of dialogue you've heard.
- What ambient sounds from outside or of your own making filled the moment or memory?
- What smell was in the air?
- What did the weather feel like?
- Describe the air in the room and the settings and props—what you remember of items big and small, obvious and hidden.
- Describe their shape and color, their height and placement.
- Within four or five minutes at the most, you will be rolling along, totally interested in what you are writing.

Practice Describing by Comparing (Using Simile)

The trick here is to make an unexpected comparison, something perhaps only you would say because of what you associate with the sound, taste, look, feel, or smell. Here are some questions to use as models and following the questions are my associations expressed as similes (the use of like or as to make a comparison):

- What is the sound of a clothes dryer like?
- What is the sound of leaves crunching underfoot?
- What is the taste of asparagus?
- What is the taste of lemon juice without any sugar?
- What does a seagull look like when it swoops to steal another seagull's meal?
- What does your bookcase look like?
- What do bedsheets feel like?
- What does a bee sting feel like?
- What does sour milk smell like?
- What does the ground smell like after rain?

  My answers:

- The sound of clothes in the dryer is like the sound of roller skates across the wooden floor of an indoor rink.
- The sound of leaves crunching underfoot is like the sound of my father's newspaper snapping as he straightened the pages.
- The taste of asparagus is like the taste of grass blades we chewed in the field where we lay watching the clouds.

- The taste of lemon juice without any sugar is like the taste of the onions that have rotted.
- A seagull swooping to steal another seagull's meal looks like my first-grade teacher ripping my paper out of my hands.
- My bookshelf looks like a deck of cards someone forgot to knock against the table to square them.
- When I hang my bedsheets outside to dry, they feel stiff as cardboard when I unpin them.
- A bee sting feels like the edge of broken glass on the floor.
- Soured milk smells like the smoke from the paper mill in my town.
- The ground after it rains smells like a book I open for the first time.

Almost any observation using simile can become the first line of a journal entry. By paying attention to what you hear, see, taste, smell, and touch, first sentences will come to you:

- The sound of ice dropping from the ice-maker is like the sound of a stone thrown by my young grandsons into the bay where I live.
- The sound of wind through the trees is like the slide of one nyloned leg against the other as I rush to my office.

As journal keepers, we rely mainly on our sense of sight and our sense of touch when we write. But new associations to write about come up when we also observe the sounds, tastes, and smells that are part of our memory sensations.

Once you stretch into observation mode, you will find more and more to say: "The sound of running my fingers through my hair is like the sound of a belt pulled from its loops." And if the sound brings back a memory—undressing in the girls' locker room, being unable to decide what to wear for a special occasion, unloading your belongings in the airport security line bins—you are launched into writing an entry in your journal. This technique brings immediate engagement with your writing, a most important part of journaling.

5 Tips for Helping Professionals

1. Brainstorm with clients until they have an "aha moment" and know what they want to describe.
2. Clients don't have to know why a particular object urges them to write. When they write, surprises will come.

3. When a client slips into abstraction (i.e., beautiful, wonderful, hideous, angry, awestruck), ask questions that bring specifics back into play: what did you see that made you describe this as beautiful? Where in your body did you feel awestruck? Were there tingles in your fingertips or did everything seem to go silent in a crowded room?
4. Encourage clients to be unique. The comparison doesn't have to be accurate to anyone but the writer, but it needs specifics on both sides of the like or as and should compare things usually considered dissimilar.
5. For instance, if I said a bee sting was like being poked with a needle, there wouldn't be much energy in that comparison because they both are needles piercing the skin. More useful is to write, "The bee sting felt like the times my teacher said I'd never learn to read."

5 Tips for Clients and Journal Keepers

1. Don't think too hard about what to describe. If it pops into your mind unbidden, it is usually a good choice.
2. Stick to your senses. If you would not have tasted something you are describing—say an iris blooming in the yard—imagine what it would have tasted like: "The purple iris in the yard could, I imagine, taste a little tart, like a blackberry picked before it fully ripened."
3. After you write, look at your journal entry for words that aren't sensory words, words like beautiful, ugly, horrible, or delightful.
4. Find sense imagery to use in place of those words. Instead of an ugly insect, you might write, "All the legs on the centipede seemed to holler towards me."
5. It is important to remember that there is nothing too small for a writer to observe. In writing, you have the opportunity to make a mountain out of molehill and the opportunity to surprise yourself with the way you register the world around you.

3 Journaling Prompts

1. Think of a place no one usually notices. Write the details of what you observe there using your five senses—perhaps one detail for each

of the senses—sight, hearing, tasting, smelling, and touching. Even the air can have a taste and even quiet has some sounds in it.

2. What do you see outside your window that you haven't noticed on another day? Use as many of the five senses to describe it as you can. Add in memories evoked by the senses.

3. Describe what you observe in terms of something else to bring experience to the page: the ground after it rains smells like. . . . The sound of ice dropping from the ice-maker is like. . . . The sound of wind through the trees is like. . . .

 ## About the Author

In 2002, Sheila Bender founded Writing It Real, an online community for those who write from personal experience. Her instructional books include *A Year in the Life: Journaling for Self-Discovery, Creative Writing DeMystified, The Writer's Journal: 40 Writers and Their Journals*, and *Keeping a Journal You Love*, among others. Her newest volume of poetry is *Behind Us the Way Grows Wider*. Her memoir, *A New Theology: Turning to Poetry in a Time of Grief*, has comforted many. She is a frequent speaker and instructor for writers' conferences and learning centers around the West and Southwest.

Writing and Not Writing

49

Liz Verna

Not writing at all, especially when there is intention and plans in place, can be attributed to a lot of things. Laziness, procrastination, or forgetting something that's not normally in your daily routine are the obvious guesses for why the pen remains untouched. But not writing can also be an opportunity to see areas of creative energetic depletion or defenses acting as blocks. Sometimes what seems like a day packed with activity, leaving no time for creative introspection, is really a day of defensive avoidance, the same way "I forgot" can be code for "I'm afraid to tread this unfamiliar soil."

If what your client or you as a journal keeper wants to do is write on a regular basis, whether for self-exploration or as part of a creative project, then attention must be turned to finding the defenses sabotaging this desire. It can be simple habit to sink into self-judgment, to say "I can't" or "I'm not good enough" or "I don't have any ideas" in the face of not writing. To do this is to gloss over potential clues that point to a larger system of defense mechanisms. So, this becomes an excellent starting point, to examine the feelings that come up about not-writing. Are feelings of self-chastisement and self-deprecation familiar? What are the origins of these feelings and what other parts of your client's life do they touch? There is also great safety in inactivity: what are some hypothetical dangers of writing and, perhaps, of revealing?

This writing *about* not writing is an interesting way to illuminate fears hidden from sight and blocking creative flow. It is also a way to alleviate the building pressure of *should*. I *should* be able to write every day, it *should* come easier, I *should* have endless ideas and inspiration. In my own history with journaling, I struggled with the idea that writing wasn't "real" writing unless there was a definite endgame. I felt pressure to write books or skits or screenplays or anything legitimate enough to prove to myself I was actually a writer, and became frustrated when I couldn't.

Times when I didn't write or didn't write *well enough* filled me with doubt and depression. Was I creative or not? Why did I have this impulse and then choke on it? Judgment weighed heavily and became the overriding voice in my head, shutting out any creative ideas. It was the beliefs I had about myself and my writing that crushed my creativity under the 500-pound bag of judgment, not the writing itself.

Often you will hear a client or journal writer devolve into judgment and self-recrimination in the face of a dry spell and search for the answers within, but I have found it just as helpful to look without, at the world built around the journal keeper. Toxic, uneven or unsupportive relationships or endeavors are an energy drain and can have more to do with losing the impetus to write than disinterest. Unhealthy situations will leave even the most energetic writer emotionally exhausted, with nothing to bring to creative work.

It's important to note that writers keeping a journal who have struggled in the past with depression or codependency may find that their chosen comrades reflect a dysfunctional version of themselves. As they heal and rise it may become apparent that the previous choices no longer fit and can indeed slow progress. A careful look around at the company we keep is an important way to track the efficacy and placement of our energy.

Even with clients who write regularly, there may be certain topics or feelings consistently embellished or ignored. Avoidance or misrepresentation is very telling in writing and can illuminate what is unresolved in the subconscious mind. This particular version of "not writing" is often tied to subconscious internalized messages or blocks that make it hard to work on other projects, writing or otherwise. As a helping professional, you can offer clients a safe way to explore frightening or uncharted material with your guidance. The very act of drawing attention to areas of avoidance is an opportunity for a writing prompt or the space to talk about the elements *around* something, maybe a trauma still too raw to explore.

I noticed an unsettling pattern in my own journaling only when I gained the wisdom of going back to reread it. Painful events or trauma in my life was woefully absent in my writing, and the suppression of these feelings was so complete that even after much time had passed it was still difficult to access the memories when I finally felt ready to examine them. This reflected how I was handling my life, which is to say, I wasn't. I was ignoring and avoiding, and for me, the aha moment was in the gaps, the connections I didn't make. Only through rereading old passages did I begin to see the patterns of glossed-over history that coincided with periods of emotional shut down. What I didn't write became more revealing than the actual words on the page.

Not-writing is an opportunity to use writing as a two-way mirror. The surface rationalizations for not writing are merely the gateway to begin writing *about* and *around* the beliefs and defenses held by the journal keeper. Delving into the elaborate systems of protections beneath the surface of consciousness can take away some of their size and power, and perhaps wrest them free, energizing and reigniting a creative flow that touches every aspect of the journal keeper's life.

5 Tips for Helping Professionals

1. Writing about not writing helps your clients reconnect with what they enjoy about the endeavor and takes the pressure off the way it's supposed to be, so that they can immerse themselves in what it actually can be.

2. As little as ten minutes dedicated to writing in-session can provide a routine, structure, and safe space for your clients to build the habit of writing while getting guidance around defenses and fears disguised as lack of motivation or intention.

3. Reframing a block as a defense creates the space for exploring its validity and origins while forging a pathway around it. It is empowering to name the defense as just that, simply a mechanism, something that can be ignored, debunked, or circumvented.

4. Connecting real-world realities with the muse of writing is important because often the blocks preventing creative flow are reflected in the real-world coping mechanisms happening in your client's day-to-day life. Where else are you not following through on your intentions? Career? Relationships? Parenting? The work of getting writing on track provides exponential payoff in that it pulls on all the other areas of your client's life.

5. If you use a client's writing in-session, discuss what's evident in the words. As a helping professional, your observations may speak to *the writing* as evasive or angry or traumatized, which then doesn't reflect on the client. This provides a safe viewing distance for discussion of potentially triggering material in a neutral zone.

5 Tips for Clients and Journal Keepers

1. Creating a writing practice is an everyday endeavor. It is more important *that* you write than *what* you write. Begin with just five minutes a day.
2. Rereading and reflecting provides another perspective. As you read, ask yourself, what do I see in this writing? What do I notice or realize? What can I learn?
3. Post-journaling reflection is rich with opportunities for writing prompts. Write any questions or especially mind-blowing observations down as future topics to write about.
4. When in doubt, write a list of gratitudes. It will lift your mood, attract more things into your world to be grateful for, and make your journal a warm, wonderful oasis you'll want to visit often.
5. Inauthentic writing is also a form of not-writing. As you journal, pay attention to how some of the content "lands." Are you writing about true, honest emotion or do your words miss the mark? Flag false writing and use it as a writing prompt to examine what's going on. Are you detached from the feelings and therefore can't find the right words? Is honesty scary for you? The answers speak to your coping mechanisms in all aspects of your life: where else are you inauthentic? The journey toward true articulation of feeling or memory requires a quieting and magnification not common in everyday consciousness. Only the writer knows how true the words are, only you, the writer, decides how real things get.

3 Journaling Prompts

1. List the feelings that pop up when you plan, think about, or sit to write. These are the voices of defense mechanisms shouting into the wind. Capture them, examine them. Challenge their validity. Are they true?
2. Identify a reason why you aren't writing and list other abandoned goals that have fallen prey to the same reason. Illuminate how this defense disguises itself to apply to any potentially threatening change. Its loyalties do not belong to writing alone.

3. Scan the past week, jotting down a list of things you attended to. How much attention is going towards things that don't feed you back? Negative people or situations suck more than their share of your time, making creativity lethargic.

 ## About the Author

Liz Verna is a Licensed Creative Arts Therapist and Writing Guide who uses writing to channel creative energy and harness it to clear the path to artistic flow and productivity. She has written for over 40 years and during that time she has come to depend on her writing to clarify her own subconscious impulses and transform them into conscious intentions and goals. She has worked in broadcast media, education, customer service, and mental health using creativity and communication as her foundation for connection, which she now helps clients to wield in their own lives. Contact Liz Verna at www. GuidingWrite.com.

More Journals, Fewer Lesson Plans   **50**

Using Reflective Journaling to Create School Culture

Jude Walsh

The School

Fourteen creative dreamers, a principal, a teacher coach, and 12 teachers, planned for two years before opening the school in question. Foundational beliefs included collaboration (every child is everyone's child), integrated learning and curriculum (each day included a two-hour literacy block for reading, writing, speaking, and listening), and reflection (know the why and how as well as the what of teaching and learning). All students, teachers, and families committed to continuous learning and improvement.

We felt we were building the plane as we flew it. One of our most precious mantras was: do what's best for the kids. A large part of that was creating a positive school environment where it was okay to make mistakes, okay to think outside the box, okay to try new things, and to deliberately reflect on how this was working. Journals were a perfect place to document our reflections and dreams, our growth and inspirations.

Why Journal? And What About Lesson Plans?

In most schools, lesson plans must be submitted to the office weekly. There are two reasons for this. First, so that the principal could verify that the teachers were focused on the curriculum (that is, preparing students for the standardized tests). In reality, few principals have the time or the expertise to evaluate lesson plans. Second, it was done in order for teachers to document they were on track and covering what was required to be taught that day.

Lesson plans are often tied closely to textbooks and curriculum objectives. For example, *Teach the lesson on page 17, How to write a complete sentence, Do Exercises 1–10 as a group, Assign exercises 11–20 for homework.* In reality, it is difficult to plow lockstep through goals and objectives, teaching to a curriculum guide as opposed to the students in front of you. Rarely can a teacher complete everything from that day's plan. Rarely do students learn in lockstep. In addition, writing and submitting these plans took a great deal of teacher time.

In our school, lesson plans were not reviewed. Teachers were expected to have plans but no one was going to check them. This reflected our trust that our teachers knew what needed to be covered and would find ways to do that. It was understood that tomorrow's lesson might change based on what happened with the students today.

Structure

Our model was to constantly assess student skills and regroup children every five weeks, placing them in multi-grade classes with other children working on the same level. These groups cut down the frustration some students experienced when the class moved on before they understood the material *and* allowed students whose skills were ahead of the content to move to a group where they could be challenged. All of our teachers knew the curriculum requirements; they worked as a team to move all children forward. Every teacher was responsible for every child, not just the children in his or her classroom.

Staff agreed to keep daily journals and in them to reflect on our practice and our culture. What went well? How could it be better? What was the emotional temperature of the group? Were they excited about learning? Confident? Confused? What did I notice today? These were points of discussion included in weekly staff meetings. Teachers made notes about children and these observations, along with academic evaluations, were used for guidance when regrouping.

Lesson plans focus on content; *what* has to be covered? Journals are reflective, examining the process of learning, learning styles, creating culture, and how to connect and collaborate. They focus on the big picture, the *why* and *how* and *where next.* Are the students succeeding, growing both in knowledge and as learners? How are we doing as a staff, as a learning community?

Making Journaling a Visible and Celebrated Practice

In the classroom, students observe their teachers writing ideas, thoughts, etc. into their journals. Teachers deliberately model this. "Oh, I just had a great idea for a class project. Give me one second to jot that in my journal." Or, "James! That is an outstanding insight. I want to write it into my journal because I have an idea for something more to do with that." Or, "Let me share something with you all that I wrote after school yesterday when thinking about our lesson and planning for today."

Teachers are public about their journaling. Students see journaling as purposeful, part of the teacher's daily work and processing. They see teachers taking their journals with them to their weekly professional development where teachers meet for one hour in the middle of the day. This professional development focuses on a text read by all stakeholders. Each week one of the staff shares how that information was implemented into classroom life, demonstrating how theory is put into practice.

Teachers might share videos or slides, work samples, sample lessons, and of course journal excerpts. Everyone had read the chapter and was familiar with the content, so this was a sharing time to bring that content to life. We made a building-wide announcement as the sessions started. Students knew their teachers were learners too.

Student Journaling

Journaling begins with our youngest students. Kindergarteners keep a group journal. The teacher solicits a sentence or two from the group that she writes on the chalk or white board. She copies it and students place the sheet into their journal notebook. They read these sentences as a group. By the end of the school year, students copy the sentence into their own books and add a sentence of their own.

From first grade on students are encouraged to write reflective pieces, first about books they have read and later about whatever projects they are doing. By fourth grade students are keeping daily literacy journals, "books read" journals, and of course their writing notebooks. Eventually students transition into reflective journals, looking at their work in all subjects and in all group interactions from a meta viewpoint. This includes interactive journals between group project members.

Our teachers are very busy throughout the day, often having little time to interact with other staff. Two teachers solved that problem by sharing a journal between them. One wrote about that day's subject matter, classroom interaction, discipline, unit ideas or plans, etc. and passed it to the other teacher who would repeat the process the next day from her end. This kept them current on curriculum progress as well as keeping them inspired by the activities going on in the classroom across the hall.

Journaling provides opportunity to write and reflect. We all are process aware, conscious of what we are doing, how we are doing it, and why. The journals are a great source of documentation. We see where we were and where we are. They remind us how consciously we teach and how aware we are of all the individuals involved. Journaling is an integral part of who we are and how we teach and learn; it is part of our identity and culture.

5 Tips for Helping Professionals

1. Provide plentiful materials: a variety of journals, markers, pens, pencils; an overhead projector or a whiteboard where writing can be shared with the whole group at one time; computer station and printer, paper, etc.
2. Talk about journaling every day and make a place for journaling in the daily schedule.
3. Promote and celebrate journaling via all public information channels (school newsletter, parent meetings, parent conferences, media events).
4. Provide time and support for professional development that incorporates journaling across the curriculum and community.
5. Provide opportunities for families to learn about and try journaling themselves (invitations to classrooms, family nights, guest speakers).

5 Tips for Clients and Journal Keepers

1. Model! Model! Model! Have the children see you writing. Talk about your writing. Share your writing.
2. Create a conducive physical classroom environment. Have a variety of materials available as well as comfortable places to journal.

3. Incorporate journaling opportunities across the curriculum: math, science, art, and music.
4. Reinforce journaling practice and reward taking risks. Tell kids they're doing a great job. Note the growth reflected in their writing. Journals aren't right or wrong. Journals are a place to take chances, think outside the box, and be wildly creative.
5. Allow ample time to journal.

3 Journaling Prompts

1. What was the best thing that happened today? What was the most difficult thing? What do I want to happen tomorrow? (Students)
2. When today did I successfully incorporate journaling into the curriculum? How can I do more of that tomorrow? (Staff)
3. What is my superpower? Am I using it or am I ignoring it? Why? (Everyone)

 ## About the Author

Jude Walsh, EdD is a writer and creativity and mindset coach. In addition to being a co-founder, she was the teacher coach at this school for five glorious years. For more information, visit www.secondbloomcoaching.com and www.judewalshwrites.com.

Journaling as a Tool in Coaching Clients

51

Joyce Chapman

In the profession of coaching, personal coaches serve in the capacity of catalysts to aid a client in achieving personal goals. In addition, the client can be moved toward the discovery of their true self, their life goals, and to the realization of their life purpose. As coaches, we act as the inspirational and motivational agent, and the client is successful through his or her own effort.

I have found that one of the very best methods which allows a client to "self-discover" is through journal keeping. This tool not only draws out what the client already knows, it also gives a coach quick access to understanding a client and aligning with a client's wishes, hopes, and dreams. In encouraging a client to write down what he or she wants, both the client and coach gain insight and clarity as the real truths are uncovered, discovered, and rediscovered. Journaling is a tool which empowers the client, allowing them to control their growth through self-discovery. This is an important aspect of the method and one which many clients find both reassuring and refreshing.

Clients can journal about any area of their life to create a future of their choosing. Often the articulated goal may be a gateway for deeper exploration. They can also journal about the past to provide needed closure and reconciliation so that they can move forward to achieve their future goals and dreams.

As a pioneer in the journaling and dream coaching world, I have thoroughly researched, and continue to research, the journaling field. I have found that some clients tend to be timid when it comes to journal writing, so I begin with questions that gently lead them into the magic of interviewing themselves. I begin by explaining that writings never have to be read or seen by anyone else, but that sharing insights with me (as their coach) is a definite help in our work together. Some of the questions I often suggest clients work on first, include:

- What would I like journaling to do for me?
- Where am I in my life right now?
- Where would I like to be five years from now?

These are powerful questions to position the client as the observer into an empowered place of choice and potential increased clarity.

Questions are powerful tools for realizing the available options one might have. After the client gets adjusted to using pen and paper, and the coach and client become more comfortable with each other, additional questions to suggest as journaling prompts can include:

- Who am I today?
- Who was I yesterday?
- Who do I want to be tomorrow?
- How do I know I am on the right track?
- How do I get where I want to go?
- What part of me do I want to express?
- What do I want out of today?
- What part of my life is working?
- What makes my heart sing?
- What is my dream?
- What is the greatest strength I have that can be applied toward realizing my dream?

Out of the myriad of journaling techniques available, here are just a few which I have found to be extremely valuable in my work with clients: recording and logging for greater awareness, list-making to empty the mind and clear away continued clutter and confusion, fantasy writing to initiate change and access the inner wisdom of the subconscious mind, dialogue writing (a technique I call "creative conversations") to get questions answered, and story writing to identify problems and create solutions.

There are an unending number of journaling techniques, which can assist clients in many ways. I recommend a three-ring notebook for client writings because this allows flexibility for inserting and moving pages around. However, in today's technology, many clients may feel more comfortable journaling on their computer. There are a variety of journaling devices available—what is important is the journaling itself, the actual writing, not the mechanism attached to it. The dating of each journal entry provides an evolution of thoughts and feelings, providing tangible evidence of progress and growth. A summary, which I call a "feedback statement" is written at the end of each session. A feedback statement not only serves to acknowledge learning but is an aid toward clarity and integration. The feedback statement may be instigated with questions such as

• What have I learned from this?
• What do I need to do to change this?
• What is brought to mind when I read what I have written?

When a client and coach begin to discuss journal entries together, the coach can aid in clarifying those thoughts and feelings that may have been left unsaid. This can help the client pinpoint patterns of thoughts, feelings, and behaviors that might otherwise never be revealed. The sharing of the insights derived from journaling thus become the impetus for growth. Together, the main messages of the work can be discovered and important points can be marked for further reference, thought, and discussion. A coach can draw out patterns that might be noted and guide clients toward a higher level of integration, as well as suggest further writing and different perspectives to pursue. Together they become the definitive "dream team," always growing and learning.

The world of journal keeping is vast and there are an infinite number of journaling methods. Research done within the journaling field (as in any other field) constantly formulates new theories, techniques, tools, and skills that enhance the techniques of the past. Many of these will be discovered and used by those in the coaching profession as well as those in other professions.

Journaling in coaching provides both client and coach with a roadmap for action so that dreams of today can become realities of tomorrow!

To arm yourself with this valuable tool, I recommend you become a journaler yourself. There are numerous books, in addition to my books, *Journaling For Joy* and *Journaling For Joy: The Workbook*, that can assist you in discovering the value of journaling for self-understanding.

5 Tips for Helping Professionals

1. Provide your client with a relevant quotation and have the client imagine a conversation between him or her and the author of the quote. Invite the client to see if this conversation leads to any new insights or new journaling prompts.

2. If journaling is a new concept for you perhaps begin by surfing the internet, reading books, articles, and journal writing resources to become knowledgeable about this transformational tool yourself. Always be open to create a plan to learn more, follow that plan, and try new personal writing techniques for yourself and with your clients.

3. Write a letter to one of the authors of journaling books that you admire and ask his/her advice. Reread this letter, then prepare to contact him/her with your questions. Be sure to take notes of this conversation and have fun getting more tips in the future.

4. Write an email to each one of your clients to explain why journaling is a practice that is a powerful and useful tool. Of course, be open to have many more exchanges and welcome all questions!

5. If you are already well informed, and feel confident to begin coaching others, prepare a method for monitoring or capturing their journaling insights. Remember it is always very beneficial to keep notes as you listen to your client's journaling, to record the session and prepare for future work with new journaling assignments.

5 Tips for Clients and Journal Keepers

1. Write your answer to the following in your journal: *My coach wants me to journal.* Is this something I want to do? If yes, why. If no, why not?

2. Write a letter to your coach to tell him/her what results you want from your coaching.

3. Write a list of questions that you currently want answers to. Your list can include any questions you might have about journal keeping.

4. Write your dream novel. Write the story that pictures you living the dream you want to claim in your life. Take from 30 minutes to an hour and write in your dream journal. Include a descriptive setting that portrays you, your feelings, your environment, and other involved characters. Allow your words to draw the pictures for you. Incorporate your values, motivators, wishes, hopes, and dreams into your plot, and write a story climax that shows how all the dream work you've done has paid off in wonderful ways.

5. Make a list of every life experience you've had that you believe has impacted you so far. Title this writing "My Personal Road to Higher Consciousness." (You may want to buy a separate journal for this assignment because you will want to add to it often.)

3 Journaling Prompts

1. Write a letter to your coach to explain why you'd like to become a person who keeps a journal for personal and professional growth.
2. Write a list of questions for your coach so he/she can be aware of your wishes, hopes, and dreams.
3. Make two lists to give to your coach including the following:

    - What I want to let go of and why
    - What I now want to add into my life and why

About the Author

Joyce Chapman is a best-selling author, speaker, teacher, professional and personal coach. As a pioneer in the field of journal keeping, she provides step-by-step journaling techniques for actualizing dreams to individuals, groups, and companies through her books, newsletters, workshops, training programs, and coaching sessions. She is known for her landmark books, and their companion workbooks: *Journaling for Joy: Writing Your Way to Personal Growth and Freedom*; *Live Your Dream: Discover and Achieve Your Life Purpose*; *Celebrate Your Dream: Fulfill Your Destiny One Wish at a Time*; *Notice & Journal: The Workbook*; *Notice! The Art of Observation*; and *Raising A Dreamer: How to Inspire and Guide Young Dreamers to Live a Dream-Centered Life*. To contact Joyce visit her website: www.joycechapman.com.

Conclusion

As the authors of these pages have demonstrated, journaling is an effective tool for personal growth, learning, and transformation. They've shared many client examples, as well as many journaling tips, tools, methods, and prompts to help expand and enrich your understanding of how to use journaling, both personally and professionally. We invite you to take a leap, even if it means going outside of your comfort zone, and to trust in the transformational power of journaling!

We offer you some final musings and journaling prompts to bring this rich resource you are holding to a close.

> Journal writing is a way of finding narrative, constructing story, and of depicting experience and relationships in our lives.
>
> —Christina Baldwin

Our stories are captured in the pages of our journals. Our thoughts, feelings, and dreams all rise up and out through the stories we tell ourselves, and through the stories we choose to write down and focus on. Our life narratives matter because they offer us a way to make sense of our experiences and to deepen our self-understanding. They hold the thread of our values and desires, while also weaving us into connection with others and the world we live in.

Journaling is ultimately a storytelling act and a meaning-making practice. As you have discovered in this book, journaling can be done in many different ways and can help with many distinct areas of health and personal growth—for coaches and therapists and also for our clients. Journaling can be done alone and in groups with others. One can write with pen and notebook, or on a computer, although we strongly advocate for journaling with pen in hand, in part because the neuroscience suggests that different language and emotional centers of the brain are accessed when writing by hand versus employing a keyboard.

Why Does This Simple and Profound Act of Taking Pen to Paper Offer so Much Opportunity for Personal Growth, New Insights, Healing, and Renewal?

Perhaps, in part, this is due to the affirmation inherent in taking time for oneself to pause and reflect. Every time we take time to journal, we are saying to ourselves—*Taking time for myself matters. This life I am living matters. I want to capture it, explore it, understand it and fully engage with the richness of being alive. I want to write it down. I want to digest my life.* Journaling is an essential tool and practice for living a more conscious and awakened life.

By its very nature, journaling is a reflective practice. This means that we take time to examine our lives in ways that help us seek new understandings while also keeping us tethered to what matters most in our lives. It is a way of being and living and learning that helps us continually discover our creative self-expression and our values. All at once it supports us, helpers and clients alike, to be deeply nourished by what we do in our lives and work. As our contributors demonstrate, a reflective journaling practice helps us discover new possibilities, aha moments and also live more mindfully in the here and now.

Individuals Can Make Journaling Their Own Unique Life-Enriching Practice

We have seen that journaling can be done any way a person wishes to do it. It is a creative and healing art filled with possibilities. As I and others have said, "whatever you write, is right." We are always the experts of our own lived experiences, and because of this, journaling is a practice that can support our self-actualization and feelings of empowerment.

What Is Therapeutic Journaling?

When we use journaling in transformational work with others, we encourage a more therapeutic approach to journaling. Together, we have discovered and learned many ways to do this from the wide range of chapters shared in this book.

In summary, I offer you Kate Thompson's thoughtful description of therapeutic journaling:

> *Therapeutic journal writing takes particular writing techniques and uses them to support the tasks of therapy. It implies the conscious intent and deliberate attempt to write in ways which will produce change, healing and growth. It is reflective (thinking about, pondering, exploring) and a reflexive (integrating and using the awareness gained from reflecting) practice which can help with greater understanding of the self and the world and the self-in-the world, offering a way of looking at the self, relationships and context in writing.*

There are many good reasons to use journaling in our own lives and in our transformational work with clients. Transformational journaling is a creative, accessible, and enjoyable practice. It can be hard, too, as when it brings us into the deeper truth of our lives and longings. Then it can feel unsettling. Writing for ourselves is a courageous act!

Journaling is the perfect self-expressive tool to integrate into coaching and therapy because it helps our clients to. . .

- Deepen their learning
- Take inspired action
- Feel more empowered
- Gain perspective
- Increase clarity with life decisions
- Tap into inner ways of knowing
- Nurture overall health and mental well-being
- Heal trauma
- Reduce stress and burnout
- Resolve conflicts
- Grow as leaders
- Define and achieve goals
- Experience better outcomes
- Improve communication
- Enrich relationships
- Notice and clear limiting beliefs and patterns
- Access inner strength
- Connect with nature in nourishing ways
- Spark creativity
- Write the story they want for their lives!

Final Journaling Prompts

How do you want to use journaling in your own life and work as a coach,
   therapist, helper, healer, or change agent?
In what ways do you want to bring transformational journaling into your
   work with clients?
What are some key learnings that you have gained from reading this book?
How will you apply this learning in your life and work?
What resonated most with you in this book?
What is the next chapter in your own life story?

Bonus Gift From the Editors

Do you ever get to the end of a book and want more?
   We wanted to share some additional resources with you through the following free gift:

> *Transformational Journaling Kit for Coaches, Helpers and Healers* from
> Lynda Monk. Access this free gift here: https://iajw.org/transforma-
> tional-journaling-kit/

Thank you for reading this book. May you live well with journaling as your
trusted companion for self-discovery, self-care, and creative self-expression.
Journal writing makes a difference. *You* make a difference.

Index

Note: *Italic* page references indicate boxed text.

Printed in the United States
by Baker & Taylor Publisher Services